Applied Research
in Aging

Little, Brown Series on Gerontology

Series Editors — Jon Hendricks
and
Robert Kastenbaum

Published

W. Andrew Achenbaum
Shades of Gray:
Old Age,
American Values,
and Federal Policies
Since 1920

Donald E. Gelfand
Aging: The Ethnic
Factor

Jennie Keith
Old People
As People: Social
and Cultural
Influences on
Aging and Old Age

Theodore H. Koff
Long-Term Care:
An Approach to
Serving the Frail
Elderly

Jan D. Sinnott,
Charles S. Harris,
Marilyn R. Block,
Stephen Collesano,
and Solomon G. Jacobson
Applied Research
in Aging: A Guide to
Methods and Resources

Martha Storandt
Counseling and
Therapy with
Older Adults

Forthcoming
Titles

Linda M. Breytspraak
The Development
of Self in Later Life

Paul Costa and
Robert R. McCrae
Emerging Lives,
Enduring Dispositions:
The Stability of
Personality in Adulthood

Carroll L. Estes
Political Economy,
Health, and Aging

C. Davis Hendricks
Law and Aging

John L. Horn
Aging and Adult
Development of
Cognitive Functions

Noel D. List
The Alliance
of Health Services
and the Elderly

John F. Myles
Old Age in
the Welfare State:
The Political Economy
of Public Pensions

Albert J.E. Wilson III
Social Services
for Older Persons

Library of Congress Cataloging in Publication Data

Main entry under title:

Applied research in aging.

  (Little, Brown series on gerontology)
  1. Aging—Research. 2. Gerontology—Research.
I. Sinnott, Jan D. II. Series.
HQ1061.A623 1983   305.2'6'072   82-20908
ISBN 0-316-79282-9
ISBN 0-316-79283-7 (pbk.)

Library of Congress Catalog Card Number 82-20908

ISBN 0-316-79282-9

ISBN 0-316-79283-7 {pbk.}

9 8 7 6 5 4 3 2 1

ALP

Published simultaneously in Canada
by Little, Brown & Company (Canada) Limited

Printed in the United States of America

Acknowledgments
Discussion on pages 65–67 adapted from Jack Botwinick, *Aging and Behavior,* 2nd Edition, pages 370–371. Copyright © 1978 by Springer Publishing Company, Inc. Used by permission.

List of Archives Cooperating with the Laboratory for Political Research, The University of Iowa, from *S S Data,* Newsletter of Social Science Archival Acquisitions (Spring 1981), Vol. 10, no. 3. Used by permission.

Applied Research in Aging

A Guide to Methods and Resources

Jan D. Sinnott
Professor of Psychology, Towson State University, Baltimore
Guest Scientist, National Institute on Aging

Charles S. Harris
Research Associate, Bureau of Social Science Research

Marilyn R. Block
Director, National Policy Center on Women and Aging,
University of Maryland

Stephen Collesano
Survey Research Program Director,
American Council of Life Insurance

Solomon G. Jacobson
Human Services Development Consultant, Washington, D.C.

Little, Brown and Company
Boston   Toronto

Foreword

Where is it? In each of the billions of cells in our bodies? Or in our minds? Then, again, perhaps it is something that happens *between* people. Ought we not also take a look at the marketplace as well? And at the values expressed through our cultural institutions? Undoubtedly, the answer lies in all these factors—and more. The phenomenon of aging takes place within our bodies, in our minds, between ourselves and others, and in culturally defined patterns.

The study and analysis of aging—a burgeoning field—is deserving of an integrated spectrum approach. Now, Little, Brown and Company offers such a perspective, one designed to respond to the diversity and complexity of the subject matter and to individualized instructional needs. The Little, Brown Series on Gerontology provides a series of succinct and readable books that encompass a wide variety of topics and concerns. Each volume, written by a highly qualified gerontologist, will provide a degree of precision and specificity not available in a general text whose coverage, expertise, and interest level cannot help but be uneven. While the scope of the gerontology series is indeed broad, individual volumes provide accurate, up-to-date presentations unmatched in the literature of gerontology.

The Little, Brown Series on Gerontology:

—provides a comprehensive overview
—explores emerging challenges and extends the frontiers of knowledge
—is organically interrelated via cross-cutting themes
—consists of individual volumes prepared by the most qualified experts

v

—offers maximum flexibility as teaching material
—ensures manageable length without sacrificing concepts, facts, methods, or issues

With the Little, Brown Series on Gerontology now becoming available, instructors can select the texts most desirable for their individual courses. Practitioners and other professionals will also find the foundations necessary to remain abreast of their own particular areas. No doubt, students too will respond to the knowledge and enthusiasm of gerontologists writing about only those topics they know and care most about.

Little, Brown and Company and the editors are pleased to provide a series that not only looks at conceptual and theoretical questions but squarely addresses the most critical and applied concerns of the 1980s. Knowledge without action is unacceptable. The reverse is no better.

As the list of volumes makes clear, some books focus primarily on research and theoretical concerns, others on the applied; by this two-sided approach they draw upon the most significant and dependable thinking available. It is hoped that they will serve as a wellspring for developments in years to come.

Preface

When Charles Harris first convened a group of "researchers on aging" to discuss issues specific to our field, the intent was to discuss and solve some problems, not to write a book. But as we discussed the issues and problems in doing research with older adults, it became clear that a book was needed. Many of our colleagues did not have certain information or project design skills that they would need in doing their applied research. Some were trying to use textbook methods in settings to which they did not apply. Few of us were equipped to deal with the various demands of funding sources, fellow scientists, and users of research; we all wanted to be more creative in making the most of every project we did in an applied setting. Some of us had no text to use in our college classes designed for future applied researchers in aging. So we decided to prepare this book to serve all those needs.

In the course of producing this book each of us was supported by many individuals and institutions. We are grateful to Towson State University and its Psychology Department; to the National Institute on Aging and the Gerontology Research Center for its Fellowship, which partially supported this work; to the University of Maryland National Policy Center on Women and Aging; to the Bureau of Social Science Research; and to the American Council of Life Insurance. Little, Brown and Company and series editors Jon Hendricks and Robert Kastenbaum offered help and useful criticism that improved the book considerably. The emotional support of our families and friends helped carry us through this difficult task. The authors extend their appreciation to Mary F. Power, Coordinator of Reference Services, American Association of Retired Persons, National

Gerontology Resource Center, for her tireless efforts in compiling the initial resource list in the Appendix and keeping it up-to-date through the period of revisions. The professional services of indexer William Pitt, proofreader Judy Friz, and typists Pat Honey, Nancy Stinchcomb, and Rita Wolferman are much appreciated.

Finally, I want to thank all those whose stimulating comments and provocative ideas led to more creative thinking on my part and therefore indirectly improved this book. Included are James Youniss, David Arenberg, Leonard Giambra, Joan Rabin, and Nathan Shock. I (and, in turn, this book) am a product of the influences of all the persons and events that have been a part of my life, just as every other individual is a product of his or her unique environment. It is this simple fact that makes aging research such a fascinating and complex challenge. I hope that aging research becomes more rewarding for readers of this book who accept the challenge.

Jan D. Sinnott

Contents

Applied Research
in Aging

Introduction

Why Was This Book Written?

This book will guide the reader to techniques and resources needed to do research on the aging. The range of methods and techniques available for use in research is often bewildering to the practitioner. Yet it is important that more research be done on the aging, and much of it will have to be done by practitioners. This book will help make the process as straightforward and practical as possible.

Who Will Use the Book?

Those working directly with the aged will find the book useful. It is assumed that the reader is motivated to solve some practical problem through research applications. It is also assumed that the reader has some prior knowledge of research techniques.

After reading this book, the reader will be able to identify the steps necessary to undertake a research project. In those areas that may be unfamiliar to the reader, the book will provide a guide to resources.

There are special problems facing the applied researcher in aging, and the ways these problems may be overcome are discussed throughout the book. For example, many data sources lump everyone over age 65 into a single group. In the section on secondary analysis, this problem is addressed. In a similar manner, older persons tend to drop out of long-term (longitudinal) studies due to ill-health. How this affects research is discussed in the section on sampling. There are also unique problems involved in interviewing older persons by telephone—especially those with limited English-speaking ability. Such problems, including those related to designing appropriate questionnaires for older persons, are dealt with in the section on measurement tools.

It is beyond the scope of this book to resolve some problems, such as the fact that many large-scale surveys of the elderly leave out those living in institutions. Another problem is the mistrust many older people have about research—a feeling that may be shared by many serving the elderly. That obstacle will have to be overcome by the applied researcher. We hope this book provides information that helps produce research findings which improve the well-being of older people.

What Is Applied Research?

Applied research is a systematic effort to use research methods to solve a particular problem in an organizational, clinical, or community setting. Applied research

- attempts to solve a current and practical social problem
- aims to obtain usable results
- adds to previous research
- provides clear and understandable answers
- states its limits and assumptions

The applied researcher in aging may be on the staff of a university or a consulting firm. More frequently, however, applied research is done by staff persons working in organizations serving the aging. Following are some examples of settings in which researchers often work:

neighborhood service organizations
multipurpose senior centers
nutrition sites
information and referral services
older worker employment programs
recreational, arts, and humanities programs
legal aid programs
self-help support groups
home health care programs
home aide programs
retirement housing
foster and group homes

day hospitals and outpatient clinics
mental health clinics
nursing care facilities
acute care hospitals
county and state health departments
county and state social service departments
area and state units on aging
training and technical assistance programs

The applied researcher in these settings is almost always pressed for time and limited in resources. Sometimes other staff members will object to research, believing it is a costly intrusion on their other duties. As a result, the applied researcher may be viewed with suspicion by his or her colleagues in the work setting. When research is undertaken, there may be only minimal assistance available for routine research and clerical tasks. In fact, the researcher may have many other program responsibilities and may be expected to squeeze research into his or her schedule.

Although isolated from other researchers and sometimes alienated from fellow workers, the applied researcher in aging will not be working alone. There will be many persons interested in the results of the research. At least three categories of individuals participate in the research process:

- the research sponsor, who pays for the work and expects that the research will solve a certain problem
- the research users, who apply the findings to the solution of a pressing problem and expect the research results to be clear, accurate, and usable
- the researcher, who does the work and maintains quality control, but involves the sponsor and users in the design and execution of the research project

The work takes place in a dynamic system in which all three parties—sponsor, users, and researcher—work together. In a cooperative exchange, they share ideas, agree on project objectives, set timetables, select methods, review data, and prepare findings.

A couple of examples will illustrate this point. A research sponsor calls for a study on the role of neighborhood organizations in serving the elderly. The sponsor wants to find out which "best practices" may be transferred from one community to another. Among the users of the research are community organizers, who want a great deal more detail about organizing techniques than does the research sponsor. The researcher meets with the sponsor and several representative research users. They agree that the research should focus on discovering the prerequisites for setting up successful projects in a variety of settings. Throughout the research process, the researcher, sponsor, and users meet to discuss and agree on the specific objectives, methods, and data collection and analysis procedures for the research project. The final product, based on tested and proven methods, is a report which is used by organizers and planners to decide which type of neighborhood organization is most likely to provide particular services to a specific type of elderly person in a specific community.

Another example of the cooperative development of an applied research project: A head nurse in a nursing home finds that children of patients do not know how best to serve their aged parent after release from the nursing home. The head nurse sets up a training program and wants to evaluate its effectiveness. As the applied researcher, she secures a grant from a community foundation, which becomes the research sponsor. The nurse involves several ultimate users—trainers, nursing home personnel, and the adult children—in discussions on the objectives and methods of the study. The trainers, for example, are interested in evaluating different types of training techniques, while the nursing home administrator wants data on costs and effectiveness, and the intended participants want to know specifically how the program will help them. The nurse, as the applied researcher, designs an evaluation that answers these questions. The evaluation, which compares the group taking the training with an equivalent group receiving no training, shows that the program is effective in improving the quality of care given to the released nursing home patient. The findings also provide data on techniques, costs, and user benefits. The report serves many users.

Although conducted under numerous constraints and under the scrutiny of many interested parties, applied research has the potential to improve the quality of life for older persons—the ultimate beneficiaries of applied research efforts.

Steps in the Research Process

Elements of research are contained in *any* systematic approach in which data are collected and interpreted in line with a set of rules. In general, the stricter the rules, the more likely it is that the research will explain events and predict future behavior under given conditions.

Research is an analytical step-by-step process. As research proceeds, discoveries in the later stages will clarify or refute assumptions held earlier. Research is neither inflexibly linear nor rigidly sequential. Nearly all techniques used by applied researchers involve some variation of the following steps:

Establishing the Framework

1. Identify and define the research problem and prepare a list of unanswered questions.
2. Search for related work in the research and practice literature.
3. State the objectives of the study in clear, specific terms and justify why the study is being done.
4. Formulate testable research hypotheses which show relationships between variables or state the issues to be resolved during the study.
5. Define the basic terms, concepts, assumptions, and variables relevant to the research project.
6. Develop the research design best suited to provide valid answers to the research questions.

Collecting and Analyzing the Data

7. Prepare a research protocol covering the following, as appropriate:
   a. selection of subjects and gaining entry to the study site.
   b. determination of sample size.
   c. specification of data collection procedures.
   d. administrative procedures for conducting the study.
   e. setting up the situation to be studied, if not a natural setting.
8. Design and pretest the data collection forms or instruments.
9. Identify and deal with limitations in the research, such as:
   a. procedural bias due to maturing of the subjects, historical events, or the effects of repeated testing.
   b. limits to generalization due to sample size.
   c. control and manipulation of relevant variables.
   d. reliability and validity limits of the research instruments.
   e. speculative interpretations of the findings.
10. Select and apply the methods needed to analyze the descriptive and numerical data collected during the project.
11. Implement the research plan.

Developing a Useful Final Product

12. Prepare the research report covering the following:
    a. methodology used in conducting the project.
    b. limits to the research project.
    c. report of results.
    d. analysis of qualitative, or narrative, findings.
    e. analysis of quantitative, or statistical, findings.
    f. interpretation of results.
    g. conclusions and recommendations based on the findings.
13. Disseminate the report to interested users.
14. Apply findings to solve the examined problem.

Guide to Applied Research Decision-Making
―――

Ten types of decisions are made in planning, implementing, and completing an applied research project. The chart below will help you make those decisions. The decision factors are listed in sequence. Answer all the questions before you start a project—this will save time and headaches later. The chart directs you to the chapter in this book that is relevant to each decision. At the start of each chapter, another decision chart will guide you to sections within the chapter. Although the book is intended to be read in its entirety, both the index and these decision-making guides will direct you quickly to information you need.

Decision factor	Read	In order to find
1. What is possible in my research setting?	Chapter 1	General problems, benefits, and limits of research techniques
	Chapter 7	Issues in applied research
2. What is the goal of my research project?	Chapter 1	Goals of research techniques
	Chapter 2	Research questions and how they are answered
		How the goal fits into existing knowledge

These steps will be followed, with some variation, for nearly all types of applied research on aging. In all cases, it is the intuition and insights of the investigators that turn observations and numbers into meaningful statements. Research may range from exploratory studies to detailed explanations that predict behavior. Most important, in the applied sense, research may range from brief probes to longer precise investigations. The choice of method and level of precision should be based on need and capability. The applied researcher should select the most efficient method to get the answer to important problems. This book is designed to assist in that process.

How Is the Book Organized?

The book is organized around the decision-making process. Most researchers must make decisions about how to start, what questions

3. Should I review existing information?	Chapter 1	State-of-the-art reviews
	Chapter 6	Resources available for a literature search
4. Should I gather data myself? If YES, see next five questions. If NO, go to question number 9.		
5. What level of research should I pursue: description of events, relationships between variables, or analysis of causes?	Chapter 2	Designs
	Chapter 5	Types of analysis
6. What type of measuring device should I use?	Chapter 4	Instrument choice
7. If sampling is needed, how many cases should I sample?	Chapter 3	Sampling
	Chapters 2 and 5	Constraints of design and analysis
8. What type of analysis is needed?	Chapter 5	Analysis
9. Can I use data already collected by others?	Chapter 5	Analysis
	Chapter 6	Techniques and resources for secondary analysis

to ask, what techniques to use, what data to collect, and so on. This book suggests answers to those questions in an appropriate order. The attached chart directs the reader to the sections in this book that are relevant to each step in the decision-making process. Reading guidelines on how to proceed in answering each question should enable the researcher to make the decision that is most appropriate to his or her specific circumstances.

Chapter

1

Improving Choices of Research Methods in Practical Settings

The choices involved in designing any applied research on the aging and carrying it through to completion are numerous. The reader is certainly aware of some design, method, and statistical considerations, since introductory texts outline these very well. Few introductory texts, however, address the practical and political decisions that shape the choice of design, method, and statistics; yet practical considerations are as important as technical ones to the applied researcher studying the aging in a field setting. None of the texts on methodology address the habits or mental sets that seem to limit an applied researcher's options—but need not do so!

This chapter provides a general discussion of practical constraints and possibilities affecting the applied researcher of the aging, and of habits of thought that might limit his or her choices. We will start in

---

Choosing Research Methods in a Field Setting

1. How far has this area of study advanced in building its knowledge base? The project should advance the state of knowledge in this field.   Page 13 *ff.*
2. What are the constraints of various designs?   Table 1.1
3. What is the purpose of various research designs?   Table 1.1
4. How can the type of research question I have in mind be answered?   Table 1.2
5. Can more than one question be answered?   Table 1.3

---

the real-life setting, the point at which most texts end, and then outline simple additional steps on the part of the researcher which can make all aging projects more fruitful. The following issues are especially pertinent to applied research on aging and will be discussed in this chapter:

- personal and political exigencies which can intrude on research on the aging
- the drawbacks of common research approaches as applied to aging
- the appropriateness of research methods to objectives
- the formulation of research questions
- the multidisciplinary nature of projects about the aging
- the development of more complex information about aging from a given set of applied data

Five Rules for Realistic Project Choices in Applied Research on the Aging

The path that runs from initial idea to completed project usually contains obstacles, some of which appear (tongue-in-cheek) in Figure 1.1. The first obstacle for many researchers is their own inexperience and lack of desire to do a research project. Despite their disinterest, they may be pulled into research by the organization's need for the income that accompanies a grant. For example, Jane Hastings, a social worker, was busy solving the problems of frail elder clients and their families when her agency director strongly suggested that since there was research money in gerontology, she should apply for a grant. Her first reaction was anguish—she had worked *for* grants, but had never developed a project. Her second response was anger; why should a research project steal the precious time she had reserved for frail elders? How could she conduct a "real" study with such a small population of frail elders? Where should she begin? The forms sat on her desk as time passed and the deadline came closer.

One week before the grant application was due, Jane's director noticed that nothing was being done. Another social worker, equally inexperienced, was told that *her* primary task now was to write the proposal. The result resembled a "Dagwood Sandwich" and, seen in all its imperfection by cooler heads, was not funded.

The moral to this story:

- Any employee working with the elderly may be called upon to do research because unanswered research questions and the need for evaluation are common problems.

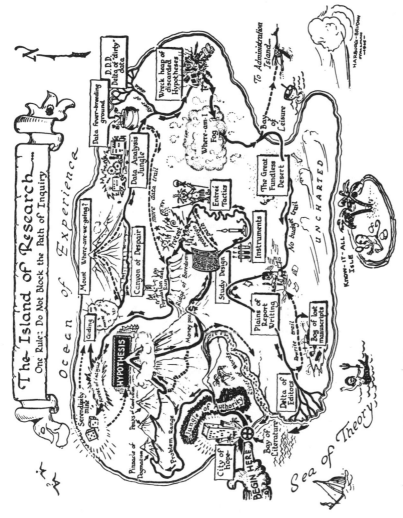

Figure 1.1 The Island of Research. (Source: Ernest Harburg and William Brudon in *American Scientist,* Journal of Sigma Xi; 54:470, December 1966. Reprinted by permission.)

The second obstacle to completion of research on the aging is the constraints imposed by policy demands on the design of a research plan. The characteristics of such a plan are simple: (1) it must meet the needs of supervisors or funding agencies; (2) it must be scientifically rigorous and methodologically appropriate; and (3) it must be achievable by the date promised using only the available resources. All three demands must be satisfied if the research project is to be a success. This book will help you satisfy the practical and scientific demands, but remember:

- Excellent projects that do not meet political priorities seldom are completed.
- Politically expedient projects that are scientifically unsound or impractical to manage may get "points" for their authors but don't significantly answer research questions.

A third major obstacle to meaningful research on the aged is unexpected problems encountered in the course of the project. For example, George Hunt began a carefully thought out project which had been approved by his supervisors and which interested him. George interviewed directors of senior centers to determine the administrative structure of each center; then he talked with elders at each center to assess whether they were satisfied with the activities of the center and its direction. However, unexpected problems developed. Two months after George mailed his interview forms to center directors and they returned them, there was a series of confrontations in the newly reorganized Office of Aging which led to the resignation of 75 percent of the center directors. While puzzling over the data from the former directors, George realized that only 10 percent of the seniors, who had been selected very carefully, had returned their questionnaires. When he began sampling and interviewing again, one of his key staff members announced she was leaving to take a better-paying job, so the work was delayed further. George eventually recovered and completed a worthwhile project.

To avoid George's experience:

- Always have several alternative plans in mind for less-than-optimal situations.
- Know how to get information from imperfect data under less-than-optimal conditions (see Chapter 5).

With these considerations in mind, we examine the issues and constraints of common research approaches used in a geriatric setting.

Common Research Approaches: Uses and Constraints

Common question: Which research strategy is best?

Better question: Which strategy is best under this particular set of circumstances?

Research questions are sometimes generated by previous studies or theories, but in gerontology they more often result from a need for information about an immediate, specific, applied problem for which no information has been previously gathered. Questions needing exploratory work cannot, of course, be handled like those within a well-researched area with well-developed theories. Yet researchers sometimes expect to produce experimental studies or complex surveys in these situations because, in planning their research, they have limited their choices or have ignored the problems frequently encountered in gathering data in institutional settings.

Research in any specific area of gerontology, as it proceeds from the most preliminary to the most rigorous and thorough approach, develops as follows:

1. Explorations and case studies—to get a feel for an area
2. Measure building—to devise better data collection techniques
3. Correlational studies—to find factors that are related to a new phenomenon
4. Theory building—to relate findings from several correlational studies and field studies
5. Experimental studies—to *prove* that selected factors really are at work in producing the phenomenon
6. Theory refinement—to let the theory keep pace with the better quality information from the experiments

Research on the aged, especially in applied settings, is usually targeted to the first three.

Without knowing where to start in designing a project, some investigators have a bias toward selection of survey methods while feeling guilty for not using experimental methods. Bias also may cause rejection of exploratory methods. Bias is a poor reason for method choice. Without knowledge of an area of inquiry and/or control of important factors, one cannot conduct a worthwhile experiment in any setting, applied or basic; one should not feel "unscientific" for avoiding the experiment. The odds are good that the experimenter will select the wrong factors and results will not be helpful. On the other hand, if a well-tested theory is available, a survey study would waste time since factors in the phenomenon have already been identified. An exception to this rule occurs when the researcher thinks that a theory already in existence omits certain important aspects of the event. We believe that none of the steps in knowledge gathering is intrinsically "better" than others, just different. Controlled experimentation may be a powerful tool, but only if it is used at the right time during a scientific inquiry.

Any one of the general steps from exploration to experimentation can be accomplished using various research approaches. Some approaches naturally go best with particular steps. For example, the experimental stage is best accomplished using the experimental method. For other steps, such as theory building, any of the methods may apply at some point.

Efficiency is sacrificed if an approach is used at the wrong time, but the "wrong" approach can still be useful. For example, an *experiment* performed in a situation where an *exploration* would have been better might yield information about a new variable. In an actual experiment on the effects of training on elders' timely reports of serious symptoms, seniors were randomly divided into those to receive training and those to receive no training. It was later discovered that simply *spending time with the friendly trainer* had an effect on the outcome of the experiment. This was a new factor to consider in future studies. So while the original experiment failed, the exploratory study it became succeeded. The applied researcher of the aging needs to be attuned to the opportunity to benefit from such possibilities.

Conversely, an exploration might be done with a population whose situation is coincidentally quasi-experimental. Such opportunities arise frequently in studies on aging, but they are usually ignored. One such instance occurs where older workers in one office may be enrolled in a group medical plan, while in another office of the same company they are enrolled in a traditional medical plan. Both sets of older workers do similar tasks and are alike in many ways, and the buildings sit side by side. Since the two sets of workers accidentally form experimental and control groups, the exploration can be analyzed as an experiment if the researcher is alert to all options.

Finding out exactly where a project belongs along the six-step progression on the previous page is a prerequisite for choosing the most efficient approach. How does a researcher determine where a project should be located on the six steps? There are two possibilities: experience and the literature (background) review. While in an ideal world only an expert designs a project and that expert knows from experience what work has already been done, in the real world of gerontological research a nonexpert is often called upon to research an area and to become an "instant expert." Reviewing the literature (or determining the state-of-the-art) helps the project planner make the decision about his or her most efficient research strategy intelligently.

Complications may arise if the most efficient strategy is, for some reason, not the strategy demanded of the investigator by reviewers of the project proposal. For example, the state-of-the-art on elders' use of over-the-counter drugs might suggest that further *explorations* on the determinants of drug use are needed. However, a call for a proposal might demand that respondents *experiment* with the effects of advertising on drug use by elders. Two options are open to the proposal writer under these circumstances: (1) design an experiment, as requested, and hope you guess right on the factors to test; or (2) design an experiment, as requested, but build in an earlier, exploratory phase of study. The second approach is strongly recommended because it yields more information than the first and makes further research possible. Such creative use of possibilities is always appropriate within the bounds of an applied study.

Fitting Approaches
to State-of-the-Art and Constraints

In Table 1.1 various common research approaches are ordered according to the six steps in knowledge gathering. In the first column, the approach is described; in the second, a possible study question is listed for each approach; and in the third, and most important, some critical limitations of the approach are mentioned. To begin using Table 1.1, ask yourself what the current state-of-the-art is in your area of interest (column one). Then check if any of the constraints in your situation will cause problems so severe that a design should be eliminated from consideration.

For example, suppose an investigator proposes to study ways in which medications should be packaged to avoid problems for elder users. The results of the research will be needed in a year to affect legislation on this matter. A literature review suggests that a great deal is known about some packaging effects and almost nothing about others. The investigator might begin by rejecting research methods 1, 2, and 6 because of their lack of generalizability and methods 9 and 10 due to time problems. Method 4 cannot be used if only a few subjects are available. Given the state-of-the-art, the investigator might propose using method 3 (exploration) followed by method 5 (correlational analyses) to explore little-known factors. Eventually, method 7 (an experimental test), in a cross-sectional method 8 framework, can pinpoint elements in better known packaging problems which might profitably be changed to avoid difficulties for elder users.

Table 1.1
Examples of Common Aging Research Approaches

Approach	Possible study question	Critical constraints
I. *Explorations and* II. *Measure Building*		
1. Case study—observe one or two cases over time.	What happens to an old woman who reports sleeplessness to her general practitioner?	Results should not be generalized to any large population until more cases are studied.
2. Clinical case study—observe one or two cases over time to systematically probe the causes of the case's behavior based on some hypotheses.	Besides what is evident to the casual observer, what would agency staff and elder service users say is related to problems in elders' taking the medicines correctly?	Results should not be generalized to any large population until more cases are studied.
3. Exploration—a probing to develop hypotheses to be tested; there is no hypothesis now.	How do elders cope with gradually debilitating health conditions?	Not useful in a limited-time, problem-solving project. Should be guided by some general expectations.
4. Survey—naturalistic exploration of the extent of a phenomenon in the general population.	What percentage of their income do American elders spend on medical services?	Group should be as large as possible and representative of (or able to be compared with) the population from which it was drawn. Expensive if a large, randomly chosen population is canvassed, sampled, and surveyed.

Approach	Possible study question	Critical constraints
III. *Correlational Studies and* IV. *Theory Building*		
5. Correlational design—obtain responses from elders who have been exposed to either situation A or situation B in the normal course of events. Relate situation to response. Control for intervening variables by use of statistics.	Which medical service systems are associated with greater use of services—those which use nurse practitioners or those which use doctors? (Medical services are chosen by patients, not randomly assigned by experimenters.)	No cause–effect relationship can be deduced from this type of design, only that two events occur together.
V. *Experimental Studies and* VI. *Theory Refinement*		
6. One-case experimental design—randomly timed intervention with situation A or situation B in a case. Relate type of situation to effect on behavior.	Is the compliance of elders better when they see the same doctor each clinic visit (situation A) or when they see several different doctors over the same period (situation B)?	Results should not be generalized to any large population until more cases are studied.
7. Experimental design—choosing elders randomly, expose them to situation A or situation B. Record their response and relate to situation. Control for intervening variables through choice of subjects (random choice).	Do elders follow their drug regimens better if (A) the packages on those prescriptions are brightly colored and the print is large, or (B) the packages use subtle shades of color and the print is small? (Packaging assigned randomly by experimenters.)	Groups need a minimal number (N) of 10. Random placement in groups recommended. Situations that can be structured this way are often not realistic or valid for everyday behavior.

Table 1.1
(*continued*)

Approach	Possible study question	Critical constraints
VII. *Approaches with Respect to Time*		
8. Cross-sectional—a test of persons who fall into different age groups at the time of testing.	What do elders of different ages expect from a nursing home environment? Test young–old group and old–old group (60- to 65-year-olds versus 75- to 80-year-olds).	Each cross-sectional group must have a rather large N. For some analyses, group members must be randomly chosen. Age effects can be confounded with generation effects.
9. Longitudinal— repeated tests of one group over time. Relate passage of time to response.	Do elders have new problems in using medication correctly as they get older?	Initial group must be so large that "dropouts" will not cause the study to end prematurely. High cost in terms of time and money committed to project. Dropouts may change nature of results.
10. Time lag—repeated tests of several groups over time, with new groups added at intervals. Relate cohort or generation membership to response, controlling for group and time passage effects.	Does every new generation of 60-year-olds expect the same medical services as every new generation of 30-year-olds? Does any difference remain constant as groups grow older?	Constraints in 8 and 9 apply.

Of course the investigator's preference may have to take a secondary role if the agency requesting this proposal demands another approach. The investigator's strategy is then (1) to propose what the agency wants done, and (2) to propose the additional approaches that *should* be taken.

> *Rule of thumb 1.1:* Before choosing a research approach, examine the state-of-the-art and the practical demands and constraints of the situation.

Rule of thumb 1.2: Consider every approach and combination of approaches before making a final choice.

Attaining Your Research Goals

Common question: How can I describe the *purpose* of what I know I *have* to do to complete this aging project?

Better question: Why do I want to do this? Why does the sponsor want it done? Will my method let me reach my broadest objectives?

Researchers, especially basic researchers, are sometimes accused of having no specific objectives or goals. Research for its own sake does produce results, but frequently takes more openmindedness and patience than some sponsors can exercise. Specific objectives are desirable; listing both applied and basic objectives before starting a research project is recommended. Extensive listing of objectives also helps the researcher take advantage of research opportunities which might otherwise be missed.

Of course, design and method choice will be influenced by stated research objectives. One set of goals for any project must relate to the main focus of investigation. For example, is the project *most* concerned with projecting trends, or with developing measures, or with assessing needs? A good applied project will have secondary and tertiary objectives as well; it may be both basic and applied, general and very specific.

Table 1.2 outlines several types of research objectives, gives an example of the questions that one might consider while pursuing those objectives, and presents some methods useful for reaching those goals. As in the medication use example discussed along with Table 1.1, a given study might have several types of research objectives. For example, if the applied objective is to reduce isolation among frail elders, both elders' social functioning *and* their choice of activities in a senior center should be studied. To use Table 1.2, examine the first column for the research objective category most like the major specific objective of your study. Expect various goals to lead to several different rows on the table and plan on creating a complex project. Remember that an agency's stated objectives not only must be mentioned and structured into the design of a project, but must be emphasized.

Rule of thumb 1.3: Make a list of objectives for a given project, and select an approach capable of providing that type of information.

Table 1.2
Finding a Method to Suit Your Research Objectives

Types of research objectives	Example	Most suitable approaches and techniques
1. Discover previously unknown processes underlying a phenomenon; knowledge for its own sake.	Understanding the genesis of depression in older adults.	Basic research. (Any of the designs or methods in Table 1.1.)
2. Understand processes underlying a phenomenon with the goal of solving a particular, real-life, identified problem.	Understanding the reasons older adults do not take advantage of free medical screening services.	Applied research. (Potentially, any of the designs in Table 1.1.)
3. Determine the adequacy of a program or policy or intervention.	How successful is an alternative center-based health care delivery system?	Evaluative research program.
4. Lay groundwork for formulation of policy.	What needs and problems of frail elders are affected by public policy decisions?	Policy analysis.
5. Determine whether a program is needed or decide on program direction.	Rank according to which strategies are best for delivering health services to minority elders.	Needs assessment research.
6. Find out what is currently known about a problem so that further research strategies might be formulated.	What is currently known about the extent and dynamics of elder abuse?	State-of-the-art review.
7. Draw further conclusions from others' data.	Can census data tell us anything about health needs of rural elderly?	Secondary analysis.
8. Predict long-term future behavior.	What will older adults who turn 60 in the year 2000 expect in the way of medical service delivery settings?	Future projections.

Forming a Usable Study Question
on Several Levels of Complexity

Common questions: What's interesting to study? What sort of question does the sponsor want answered?

Better question: What are all the researchable questions within the limits of my interests and expertise and the sponsor's interests?

Developing research questions often makes the applied researcher aware of his or her limitations. One investigator knows in general what he or she wants to study, but doesn't want to be confined by the limitations suggested by specific research questions. Another investigator is not sure how the project should proceed and therefore cannot write any question. A third investigator has a specific question in mind, but wonders how to go about answering it. In applied studies on the aging, research questions are frequently ignored in favor of a focus on "problems," since "problems" have many interrelated variables in real-life settings. But the applied project without a specific question to answer deteriorates into a general, descriptive summary from which no analytic conclusions can be drawn. Framing one or more specific questions forces the problem-solving researcher to think analytically and address causes.

All three investigators above sense the difficulties in articulating a research question. To write a good one, one must be aware of specific issues, be able to address many types of issues, and be willing to narrow one's interests, at least for the purposes of the study. Consider the most basic difficulty first: the researcher who is not knowledgeable enough to know exactly what to ask. The only solution for this investigator is to become enough of an "instant expert" through a literature review that questions come to mind more easily. The random choice of a question is not workable because, in the end, the same person who knew too little to form a specific question has to know enough to interpret the outcome. Simple acceptance of a consultant's ideas about the research question is dangerous for the same reason—the consultant goes home and the researcher is left with the problems of running a project.

What if, on the other hand, the project planner has plenty of ideas, but doesn't want to select among them? Again, examine the consequences of having no specific research question. First, reviewers will be hard pressed to judge the investigator's capability to satisfactorily complete a job that is not well defined. Second, the researcher will have difficulty claiming to accomplish a job that has no specific goal. Third, since no one can investigate *every* question appropriate to a particular area of study, the possibilities will have to be narrowed at some point. Doing so early in the planning helps simplify design and sampling choices. The expert must remember that the basic research question need not limit the investigation. It is simply a promise that *at least* one question will certainly be addressed. Most consumers of applied research in aging feel more comfortable with that assurance.

The third situation is one in which the investigator has a question in mind but is unsure about the best method for answering it, and therefore hesitant to put the question into writing. Consider the possible study questions in Table 1.1. Most are very broad questions which permit many different definitions of variables. In the first question ("What happens to an old woman who reports sleeplessness to her general practitioner?"), "What happens" may be defined as "Which medications are given?", as "What verbal response is made by the doctor?", as "How many minutes of office time are given?", or as "How satisfied is the woman after the visit?". "Reports" might be defined as summaries of patient records or as ex post facto statements by patients now in nursing homes. "What happens when . . ." might indicate an experimental manipulation or a correlation. This particular research question permits many measurement strategies; a narrower question limits the choices. It is important to state a question that permits a measurement strategy which the investigator is comfortable carrying out. When all options are explored, the investigator can usually make a match between comfortable strategies and task demands and finally delineate a question.

Notice that the question in Table 1.1, column 2, row 7 is comparatively specific in terms of measures demanded, in contrast with the question just examined. Often very specific questions are written by investigators who have a specific measure at hand that is reliable and valid for the elderly and who plan to work with that measure. Of course, this suggests that the state-of-the-art in that area of study is advanced and presupposes that the measure is pertinent. Writing hypotheses (testable assumptions) requires the researcher to be specific about the expected results of the selected measures, the research question, and the planned design. This is especially useful for applied projects on the aging because it forces the sometimes-reluctant investigator to analyze variables not yet directly examined and to restate the question using measures appropriate for the elderly. While the question from Table 1.1, column 2, row 1 might be general, the hypothesis associated with it will reflect what can be done within practical limits and what is expected based on prior research. "What happens to a woman who reports sleeplessness to her general practitioner?" is now "operationalized," and results are predicted to be the following: "Women whose records indicate a complaint of insomnia, difficulty falling asleep, or difficulty remaining asleep are more likely to be given mood altering drugs and less likely to be given a physical exam than men with the same complaints."

> *Rule of thumb 1.4:* Write a research question that reflects current knowledge about a topic, that is testable with measures suitable for a study on aging, and that reflects issues which the investigator is certain to address in the course of the project.

Asking Additional Questions in Each Study: Creativity in Studies on Aging

> *Common question:* How can I make this project answer aging-related questions pertinent to my discipline?
>
> *Better question:* How can I expand this study on aging to answer questions from several disciplines?

The researcher in aging can make a pedestrian study more interesting by asking additional, multidisciplinary questions, whatever the primary objective may be. The questions all must be related to the main goal of the study. Given the funding restrictions under which most applied studies on aging operate, the additional questions must also be such that the overall cost of the project is not greatly increased.

Why would a researcher want to make life more complicated by investigating additional questions? For one thing, the resulting study may more accurately reflect the aging experience, since it is seldom simply "medical" or "social." Furthermore, a multidisciplinary approach allows the researcher to learn new skills and to meet experts in other disciplines. On the pragmatic side, the results of ambitious projects are more likely to be published and to produce information that can lead to real-life improvements.

Table 1.3 contains an example of this type of creative, interdisciplinary question building. The additional questions are generally inexpensive to pursue, but make the study more usable, pertinent, and publishable. The study results also better reflect the real-life complexity that surrounds every applied research question about the aging.

> *Rule of thumb 1.5:* Within reason, answer as many interdisciplinary questions about the topic as possible without making the project too expensive or forgetting the main purpose of the inquiry.

Table 1.3
Creativity in Applied Gerontological Research:
Asking Additional Questions

Project: Exploratory Study of Elders' Over-the-Counter (OTC) Medicine Use
Primary Research Question (Public Health Question): Describe elders' OTC
medication use—which drugs, how often?

	Questions	Methods
With minor changes, study might also ask:		
Psychological:	Do elders who are high in self-esteem treat themselves with these drugs?	Add valid scale of self-esteem; analyze for group differences, controlling for covariation of self-esteem.
Sociological:	Do women or low-income elders buy disproportionate amounts of OTC drugs?	Analyze (subgrouped by sex and income) for group differences.
Medical:	Are these elders in danger of suffering a drug reaction caused by mixing OTC and prescription (Rx) drugs?	Ask which Rx drugs they use. Analyze for lethal combinations.
Economic (or marketing):	What proportion of elders' income is spent on OTCs?	Price OTCs they list and compare with income figures.
Methodological:	Does asking an elder about OTCs used provide similar information as observing the OTC buys of elders in supermarket checkouts? Can a composite "drug use pattern" scale be developed which gives a picture of amount and type of use?	Pilot a checkout counter observation instrument.
Legal:	Should OTC sales be regulated by law?	Analyze for excessive use of OTCs.

	Questions	Methods
Policy:	Money is available to train someone to help elders avoid drug problems. Who should be trained?	Ask where elders got drug and whose advice they sought (train those people who give advice to elders and who got results).
Other:	What is the best predictor of OTC use among elders?	Subject responses to multivariate analysis.
	What is the interaction among people's health, their acceptance of drug use, the drug use accepted in their society, and the cohort they come from?	Test another subculture; add question on attitude toward drug use; analyze, controlling for health.

Summary

These rules-of-thumb should be hanging over every researcher's desk, available for quick review at the start of each project:

Rule 1.1: Before choosing a research approach, examine the state-of-the-art and the practical demands and constraints of the situation.

Rule 1.2: Consider every approach and combination of approaches before making a final choice.

Rule 1.3: Make a list of objectives for a given project, and select an approach capable of providing that type of information.

Rule 1.4: Write a research question that reflects current knowledge about a topic, that is testable with measures suitable for a study on aging, and that reflects issues which the investigator is certain to address in the course of the project.

Rule 1.5: Within reason, answer as many interdisciplinary questions about the topic as possible without making the project too expensive or forgetting the main purpose of the inquiry.

References

Babbie, Earl R. *Survey Research Methods.* Belmont, Ca.: Wadsworth, 1973.

Blalock, Hubert M., Jr. *An Introduction to Social Research.* Englewood Cliffs, N.J.: Prentice-Hall, 1970.

Davis, James A. *Elementary Survey Analysis.* Englewood Cliffs, N.J.: Prentice-Hall, 1971.

Dubin, Robert. *Theory Building: A Practical Guide to the Construction and Testing of Theoretical Models.* New York: The Free Press, 1969.

Leedy, Paul D. *Practical Research: Planning and Design.* New York: Macmillan, 1974.

Patton, Michael Quinn. *Utilization-Focused Evaluation.* Beverly Hills: Sage Publication, 1978.

Pelto, Pertti J., and Pelto, Gretel H. *Anthropological Psychology.* New York: Cambridge University Press, 1978.

Chapter
2

Useful Approaches
to Gerontological Research

This chapter describes in greater detail some approaches and methods that have proved useful in past studies on the aging. The chapter is not intended to limit your choice of approaches.

Although all research techniques can be applied to research on the aging, some techniques are more common in applied studies on the aging than in other fields because of either practical demands or the current state of the art. This chapter outlines those techniques and the special problems that might be encountered in studies of aging.

We will go into some detail on the nature, advantages, and disadvantages of the following:

- state-of-the-art review
- secondary analysis
- case studies
- evaluation
- survey research
- policy analysis
- future projection

The description of each type of study is followed by an example of its use. Table 2.1 contains a summary of research activities which should be a part of these and related approaches.

Table 2.1
Research Activities Appropriate for Fourteen Applied Research Techniques Used in Studies on the Aging

Research activities	Applied Research Techniques													
	State-of-the-art reviews	Secondary analysis	Case studies	Clinical case studies	Demonstration projects	Evaluations	Field research	Program monitoring	Content analysis	Survey research	Policy analysis	Implementation analysis	Future projections	Needs assessment
Problem definition	X	X	X	X	X	X	X	X	X	X	X	X	X	X
Literature search	X	X	X	X	X	X	X		X	X	X	X	X	X
Data source search	X	X	X	X	X	X	X	X	X	X	X	X	X	X
Project objectives	X	X	X	X	X	X	X		X	X	X	X	X	X
Research design	X	X	X	X	X	X	X	X	X	X	X	X	X	X
Hypotheses formulation		X		X	X	X	X	X	X	X	X			X
Instrument development			X	X	X	X	X	X	X	X				X
Sampling				X	X	X	X	X	X	X				X
Subject selection			X	X	X	X	X	X		X				X
Site entry			X	X	X	X	X	X	X	X	X	X	X	X
Data collection			X	X	X	X	X	X	X	X				
Intervention				X	X		X	X						
Postintervention data				X	X		X	X	X	X				
Descriptive analysis	X	X	X	X	X	X	X	X	X	X	X	X	X	X
Statistical analysis	X	X	X	X	X	X	X	X	X	X	X	X	X	X
Interpretation	X	X	X	X	X	X	X	X	X	X	X	X	X	X
Conclusions	X			X	X	X	X	X	X	X	X	X	X	X
Reiteration	X					X	X	X	X	X			X	X

State-of-the-Art Review

A state-of-the-art review is an intensive review of literature, the purpose of which is to provide a thorough understanding of the advances in and limitations of a particular area of interest. The researcher does not collect primary data for analysis nor are new analyses of data performed. Rather, published information is carefully examined in an attempt to draw new relationships and summarize existing information.

State-of-the-art reviews are undertaken for several reasons:

1. the researcher is faced with a new question or problem to which a solution is sought.
2. the researcher wishes to develop a study or project that adds to existing research and so seeks to discover what others have done.
3. the researcher has theories about a particular issue and attempts to confirm these by seeking supportive documentation.

If the review is to be meaningful, selection of a time frame and an appropriate set of key words (or descriptors) is critical. Five years is usually a broad enough time frame to cover most aspects of interest. Rarely do state-of-the-art reviews exceed ten years, since changing social values and practices render older material on aging less useful. Key words are the terms used to gain access to the literature of interest, either through a library card catalogue, indices which abstract journal articles, or a computer search. In order for key words to be effective tools, the researcher's interests must be clearly specified.

Once material has been identified, good organizational skills are essential if the review is to yield useful information. Too often, researchers abstract each article encountered in the review. The resultant data do not always provide the overview that was initially desired. A better approach involves critically annotating information according to subtopic. Suppose, for example, you want to do a state-of-the-art review about older women as widows. Develop a series of subtopics. You might look at (1) economic security after widowhood; (2) interrelationships with surviving family members; (3) emotional adjustment to widowhood; (4) life as a single woman; (5) attitudes about remarriage. Instead of independently abstracting every article on widowhood, you would pull selected information from many articles concerning a subtopic to compare differing viewpoints in the same area.

A good abstract is a summary and will contain the following information: (1) purpose of article (usually the same as purpose of the study); (2) methodology employed (subjects, instruments, administration, and scoring); (3) results obtained; and (4) authors' conclusions and implications for future research (pages 32–33).

If the researcher has assistants to help with the review, he or she may want to provide a standard form for compiling information from each source. A sample form is provided in Figure 2.1.

Following the review, the researcher summarizes and critiques the literature. The purpose of the summary is to outline major trends; the purpose of the critique is to point out where further work is needed.

Secondary Analysis

Secondary analysis is the reanalysis, for a new purpose, of data originally gathered by another researcher. Social and behavioral scientists have been collecting data for generations, especially since the onset of the quantitative age in the 1940s. Much of the information has barely been touched since the original questions were answered, although in many areas secondary analysis has provided us with new, rich insights.

The underutilization of this information is most probably the result of two important factors. First, many researchers are not skilled in the principles and procedures of secondary analysis of survey data and therefore do not know how to begin. Second, locating and obtaining data is often difficult. In the past, poor record keeping and little coordination between research methods and data maintenance rendered access to primary data time-consuming and expensive for the researcher trying to locate and process specific information.

With respect to the latter problem, great strides have been made in recent years. The growth of archives or data dissemination centers makes it possible not only to obtain but to process data quickly and inexpensively. As archives continue to grow in sophistication, locating and obtaining data will no longer be an impediment to doing secondary analysis. Of course, archives are not essential for doing secondary analysis; there are numerous other strategies available, including the primary researcher's reanalysis of his or her own data. The key point is that archives have dramatically improved the potential for secondary analysis. (This subject is treated separately in Chapter 6.)

Since the problems of locating, obtaining, and processing data are being reduced, all that blocks greater utilization of secondary sources is uncertainty on the part of many researchers about how to proceed. As with any kind of research, the specifics of secondary

analysis depend, in large part, on the goals of the researcher. Someone interested in broad theoretical issues will probably proceed very
differently from the researcher who is trying to analyze homes for
battered elderly persons. In Chapter 6, the common features and
considerations of secondary analysis are briefly discussed, as well as
the general advantages, disadvantages, and common applications of
this technique. The limitations of secondary analysis include the
limitations of the original data, the problems of transforming the data
in preparation for a new use, and, sometimes, researchers' unwilling-
ness to share data.

Some special concerns are involved in secondary analysis of data
from aging populations. Relatively few data sets categorize data on
the elderly into discrete age categories. Most data sets will merely list
the aged as "65 years or older" and let it go at that. When the data are
displayed by five-year or one-year intervals, you face the additional
problem of inaccuracies in reporting on the very old; since there are
fewer very old, the number of subjects at that age (such as 95-year-
old males) may be so small as to be invalid from a data-use perspective. As the population of the very old increases, this problem will be
reduced. Use only valid data and cut off or truncate the secondary
data at any point at which they might be invalid. For now, one might
use data from persons up to age 75 years if the data for persons
beyond that age are not trustworthy. (See the Appendix for lists of
existing data sources.)

Case Study

The case study provides both a description and an analysis of an
individual case's behavior over a predetermined time span. A case
may be a person, a particular program, a group, or any single dynamic
event over time. The examples here focus on case studies of individuals. The researcher in aging frequently focuses on the dynamics of
one case over time in an effort to obtain depth of understanding in an
area where little is known. Because the interpretation and understanding of a case study depends upon the amount and variety of
information that can be collected about the subject in question, a
variety of sources of information should be utilized:

Direct observation. Generally the case study involves the researcher's own observation and description of the subject. A case
record contains a great many descriptions, or anecdotes, about the
person's behavior and interactions. Within ethical limits of informed
consent procedures, neither the observed person nor others involved should be informed that the individual is under observation if
such information may inhibit natural and spontaneous behavior.

Figure 2.1 Standard Form for State-of-the-Art Citations

Sort fields 1: ___ 2: ___ 3: ___ 4: ___ 5: ___ 6: ___ 7: ___ 8: ___

Check trials: _____

_____

Received: ___ Processed: ___ Revised: ___ Equivalences: ___

———————— PLEASE DO NOT WRITE ABOVE THIS LINE ————————

Source of Citation: Original Item in Hand: ___ Photocopy of Por-

tion of Item: ___ Cited in Another Item: ___ Please specify:

_____

Location of Item: Personal Copy: ___ Library: ___ Please specify:

_____

Other: ___ Please specify: _____

Form: Monograph: ___ Part (chapter, etc.) of Book: ___ Journal

or Newspaper Article: ___ Bill: ___ Law or Statute: ___

Court Decision: ___ Unpublished Document: ___

Audiovisual Aid: ___ Other: ___

Please describe: _____

Author(s) (individual: ___ or corporate: ___): _____

_____

_____

(Please list the complete names of all authors as available to

you.)

Title (include all subtitles):

No. of Pages: _____

Article, Chapter, etc., inclusive pp.: _____

Chapter No.: _____ Sec. No.: _____

Author Same as Above: ___ Editor(s): _____

Place(s) of Publication: _____

Publisher(s): _____

Edition(s) and Date(s) of Publication: _____

Document Number(s) (if any): _____

     Vol.: _____ Issue No.: _____

     Page Number(s) (inclusive): _____

     Date: Year(s): _____ Month(s): _____

     Day(s): _____

     Other: _____

(If a Proceedings) Title of This Conference: _____

_____

     Conference Series Name: _____

     Sponsor(s): _____

Series Title (if any): _____

     Vol.: _____ No.: _____ Other: _____

     Editor(s): _____

Descriptive Note: _____

_____

_____

Number of References: _____ Number of Footnotes: _____

Language(s): _____

ADDITIONAL SPACE OR COMMENTS: _____

_____

_____

_____

_____

_____

Author's Last Name: _____

The researcher may be purposefully selective in terms of the events that are recorded. The goal always is to describe behavior and events objectively and completely; the researcher does not interpret situations. For example:

This	*Not This*
Mr. X spent two hours watching television (from 1 to 3 p.m.).	Mr. X is restless in retirement.
The demonstration project cost $1,000,000 for one year's operation.	The demonstration project was overly expensive.

There is no one correct way of recording information obtained through direct observations. However, Perkins (1969) characterizes good anecdotal recording in terms of human "cases" according to the following criteria:

1. The description begins with the date, time, and place and includes a statement or explanation of the background situation or setting in which the event occurred.
2. The action—what happened, who did what or said what, and how it was done—is described as objectively and completely as possible.
3. The interactions of the person observed with others are described, together with everyone's reactions during each phase of the episode.
4. Verbal interaction is reported as much as possible in direct quotes.
5. Posture, facial expressions, gestures, and voice qualities are described without interpretation ("he frowned and clenched his fist," not "he became angry").
6. The anecdote continues until all aspects, interactions, and reactions of the episode have been fully described.

Official records on health and work history. Data from records should be recorded verbatim. No attempt should be made to interpret them until all information has been collected.

Information from other people. Facts and anecdotes are often obtainable from a case's family, friends, co-workers, and from other professionals who work with the person. This information may contain feelings and opinions rather than facts. Such material should be verified with other data and cautiously interpreted.

Environment. The environment in which the person observed lives is an important source of information because it reveals the kinds and qualities of experiences that have an impact on that individual.

The researcher may gain insights from observing and from compiling a case record, but formal analysis of the record should be delayed until as large a body of information as possible has been recorded. This limits the probability of incorrect interpretations because of insufficient information. Analysis generally involves identification of recurring patterns. The researcher then attempts to discover the cause of those patterns.

The collected data are usually displayed initially in chronological order. This allows comparison of information provided from a variety of sources. The analysis occurs as the case study is being written; it consists of placing the evidence for the event in chronological order and looking for details which illuminate the event. While some case studies conclude with a summary of findings and an attempt at interpretation, most case studies stand on their own or are included in a larger study.

The disadvantage of a case study is that it provides too much detail. Cases take time to read and cannot be easily scanned, and there are points in the data gathering process at which bias is possible, in spite of safeguards. This is especially true if the writer has been a former participant in the event being studied. Finally, however strong the integrity of the researcher, one or two subjects or events cannot represent adequately the entire universe of older persons and aging-related events.

The main benefit of a case study is that it provides rich descriptive information about an event. Since there are so many elements which interact to cause something to happen, a case study can provide a slow-motion analysis of the action. As an exploratory device, the case study is the first step in a series of research modes which lead from exploration to explanation. At the completion of a case study the way is clear for more controlled studies of those factors contributing to the outcome of an event.

Example 1: A case study
An older family member has become impaired, and the family will be observed to see the impact of the impairment on them. The case study ends with the elder's return home. The focus is a detailed description of what happens to an elderly person and his or her family during an event in their lives that starts with the onset of an infirmity.

A surprising observation during the study is that *general stress on family members* seems to be more important than anything else in affecting the readjustment of the impaired elder. This new research question (i.e., How does general stress affect family and elder adjustment?) can now be explored in a controlled study with a larger sample.

Intervention Case Study

The basic purpose of intervention case studies is to test the effectiveness of an intervention for changing an older subject's status in a measurable way. Sociologists, administrators, and economists often intervene in *events* to improve outcomes in positive ways. An administrator, for example, might try rearranging a meeting room to facilitate conversation during a meeting. The selection of both intervention and clients or events is based on the purpose of the study and the limits of the practical situation. If you are studying the effect of recreation therapy on the older woman, you have already selected both the intervention and client.

The following steps are typical in an experimental intervention case study (which attempts to explain *causes*):

1. measure base rate of performance before intervention.
2. intervene; measure rate of outcome event.
3. stop intervention; measure rate of outcome event.
4. resume intervention; measure rate of performance again.

If intervention is successful, the rate will rise and fall with the experimental manipulation; changes can be attributed to intervention. In either the experimental or observational case study, observational and measurement techniques are used to determine the progress of the subject. In the intervention experimental case study the results are analyzed to determine whether they were affected by the intervention.

The intervention case study is essentially an exploratory study that tests new approaches to serving the aged. After an intervention has been replicated and thoroughly tested, the results may be disseminated to practitioners or used as the basis for large-scale studies.

Example 2: An experimental intervention case study

Intervention studies with elders often take the form of training studies or manipulations of group dynamics in one group. An example of the latter took place in a nursing home (the case) where caregivers hoped elders would be more sociable with one another if conditions were manipulated properly. The intervention consisted of providing beer and wine to ambulatory patients who were not on special diets in a common room from 5:00 p.m. to 6:00 p.m. daily.

1. Base rate was established for patient-to-patient pleasant contact (hereinafter "contacts") by controlled observation.
2. Intervention began; rate of contacts increased (this is the experimental phase).
3. Intervention stopped; rate of contacts dropped (this is a control condition).
4. Intervention began again; rate of contacts increased again.

The in-depth intervention experimental case study of this one nursing home led to a result that seems reliable. The next steps are to retest with other cases and to analyze the reasons why the intervention worked.

Field Research—A Special Case

A field is anyplace where actions occur: a living room, an office, a senior center, or a public park. What distinguishes the field study is its natural setting. Instead of asking people to come to a clinic or lab, the field researcher goes to people wherever they are. Knowing the special language of the people involved renders this technique more useful.

Sometimes getting access to the field setting is the most difficult aspect of field research in aging. Major limitations to this approach are its cost and the time needed to get information from even a few cases. When it is done correctly, field research provides a tremendous amount of information on the lives and actions of average people and can provide unexpected insights into factors that influence those actions. Occasionally, a field report will be so lively and informative that it will become widely read. In many ways our natural curiosity about how others live increases the audience for field reports. The findings may be additive if reports carefully describe the various activities used by observers in each study.

Evaluation

Evaluation research measures the progress and outcome of a program in order to determine how effectively the program meets its stated goals. The history of program evaluation is brief. There were occasional program reviews as early as the 1920s, but the real growth occurred in the 1960s when Congress began to set aside a fixed amount of program funds, usually one-half of one percent, for evaluations. Growth in the quality and quantity of evaluations coincided with improvements in computers and advances in survey research techniques. Increasingly complex models of evaluation were attempted, and there are now dozens of texts and journals dedicated to the art and science of evaluation.

Evaluation encourages program modifications that increase the likelihood of achieving both short-term and long-range objectives. Evaluation requires time, money, creativity, and skill as well as agreement about what the program is attempting to achieve. Evaluation is tied to program planning and implementation; planning establishes minimal standards for evaluation, while implementation provides something specific to evaluate.

Three Types of Evaluation

Input evaluation should be part of the planning process that leads to development of a program for the aging. Input evaluations are of two types: (1) needs assessment, which consists of documentation and articulation of the problems addressed by the program; and (2) effort evaluation, which assesses the number of clients receiving services, staff time expenditures, financial expenditures, and other measures of the extent and type of program services.

Implementation is accompanied by *process evaluation.* There are three types of process evaluation, all geared to assessing what occurs within the program: (1) program monitoring describing what services are offered; (2) client tracking monitoring the progress of clients through the program; and (3) goal monitoring assessing whether or not the program is actively pursuing stated goals and objectives.

Outcome evaluation is the most important type of evaluation and what most people mean when they use the term *evaluation.* Outcome evaluations assess the results of a program for the aging by determining if and in what ways clients have benefited as a result of program participation. Approaches to outcome evaluation include follow-up surveys, measurements of client satisfaction, goal-attainment measurements, measurements of indirect services, and cost-effectiveness analyses. Since there are many factors that can intervene in various ways to account for a change in status, the evaluator must be able to demonstrate, through analysis, that the program's intervention is the critical factor. There is a tendency among evaluators to use only data which may be quantified and statistically manipulated. Actually a combination of both quantitative and qualitative or descriptive data is probably more appropriate for a well-rounded evaluation and may help to reduce the bias that results from too little information. Program administrators should be party to the planning of the evaluation.

Steps in Evaluation

The evaluator begins with an understanding of the program's purpose and objectives, gained by reviewing the legislation, charter, reports, and other documents which provide background on the program. The data sources may include program records, secondary data, and interviews with clients and staff. Specifying program goals can be a complex task because they may be little more than platitudes; ambiguity makes specification of intent difficult. This ambiguity also means many different types of evaluation may be considered. Finally, program goals are dynamic and change over time. The evaluator must determine which goals best characterize the program at the time of assessment in order to develop evaluation criteria.

Once program goals have been specified, the evaluator must develop a measure to determine whether or not the goals have been achieved. Since developing new outcome measures is a demanding task involving definition, pretesting, and revision, the evaluator should attempt to locate standardized measures that have been used in previous studies on the aging. Multiple measures are preferable to a single measure. Measures make the greatest impact when they focus primarily on behavior rather than on attitudes or opinions.

After carefully specifying objectives, identifying the most effective measures, collecting and analyzing data, and producing a report, the evaluator often discovers that no real-world changes occur. The evaluation does not by itself produce change; rather, evaluation exposes the strengths and weaknesses of a program and thus identifies the *need* for change. The evaluator can only encourage program improvement by offering alternatives for accomplishing program goals.

Evaluations are becoming increasingly frequent in programs for the aging because of societal concerns with cost effectiveness; researchers need to become more familiar with the full range of techniques.

The utility of evaluations may be improved by involving users, including older adult clients, in the decision-making, data collection, and analytical stages of the evaluation process. Such a user-oriented approach makes partners of those who are most vitally affected by the findings and thereby increases the value of the information from the evaluation. This is especially critical in dealing with clients who are mature adults; expand the evaluation process to answer questions the older clients themselves may have about the program.

Example 3: A process evaluation of a demonstration project
   A training project is organized to prepare adult children to care for their impaired parents in the parents' own home. To analyze process adequately, anticipated results must be defined; for example, are adult children expected to provide only emotional support or will they learn nursing skills as a result of this program? After discussion with the sponsors, users, and managers of the demonstration project, researchers set up a monitoring system which collects data on operational activities and costs during the life of the demonstration. These data will

Table 2.2
Evaluation Steps and Program Progress Applicable to Programs for
the Aging

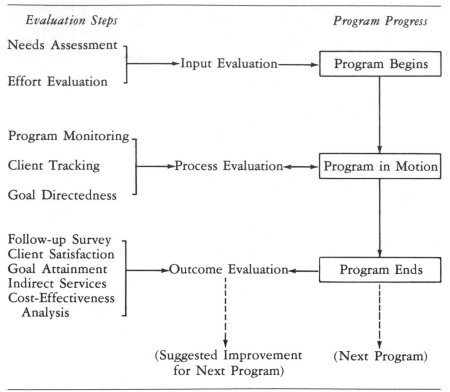

be used to relate project activities to project goals in a systematic
manner. Questions such as "What is the daily operation costing? Is
training running on schedule? Is the project on target in attracting
enough participants?" are included. The narrative will include enough
detail that another person can reconstruct this project.

Example 4: An outcome evaluation
       The program to educate adult children in giving care to their
impaired parents, described in Example 3, has been running for two
years and is now being evaluated. The first task is to find some measurable criterion of success, such as reducing the incidence of bedsores.
The evaluators and the users design questionnaires and data gathering
instruments to get information on the type of training given, the actual
care provided, the incidence of bedsores, and other items.
       The analytical task follows the data collection activities. Using
statistical techniques such as correlation analysis, the evaluators attempt
to discover if the type of training given the adult children is directly
linked to a reduction in the incidence of bedsores among the parents

they care for in their home. If this association can be demonstrated, the program may be evaluated as a success.

The assessment will be more comprehensive if the evaluator can incorporate qualitative findings produced by in-depth interviews with both children and parents.

Survey Research

A survey polls a representative sample of the population concerning opinions, attitudes, or facts in order to tell how common these are. There are few subjects unsuitable for survey research, but there are some strict limits about procedures. The first concern is careful sample selection. (Sampling techniques are outlined in Chapter 3.) Questions asked must be free of bias and must yield valid responses; that is, the responses must measure what they are intended to measure. There are two ways to collect survey data: by mail and by interview (Chapter 4).

Survey research has several limitations. It is almost totally dependent on question wording. Structured or closed-ended responses used in many surveys may miss nuances of meaning which could be gained by further probing. In surveying older persons, one must take care that terms and phrases used are understandable to the older person and that print is large enough for the respondent to read easily. The person to whom a question refers should be clear. This will avoid answers such as the one received by an interviewer who was surveying nursing home residents. The interviewer read one question to a woman who was slightly hard of hearing, instructing her to either agree or disagree: "Sometimes I worry so much I can't sleep." "Oh, you poor dear!" was the sympathetic but inappropriate response. The final caution is that conversation, not structured responses, was preferred by the elderly when they were younger, and is still preferred. If time and resources permit, some open-ended questions may elicit surprisingly useful information from older conversationalists.

The needs assessment is a special type of survey. Further description of surveys will be made in that context.

Needs Assessment

Needs assessments involve information gathering; the general purpose is to use the information generated to improve decision-making and thus improve service delivery. A need implies an urgency to supply or replace something that is basic to well-being. A needs assessment is concerned primarily with determining what conditions encountered by the elderly require remediation.

Various information-gathering techniques can be used to assess needs. Clients, advocates, administrators, and other appropriate people can be asked to list needs based on their own knowledge and experience. An examination of existing data (client records, administrative reports, and research studies) helps identify gaps in the delivery of direct services, changes in health status, and similar signals of distress. Instrument development (discussed in Chapter 4), sampling (Chapter 3), and data analysis (Chapter 5) are utilized to discover needs specific to a particular population.

Two important assumptions underlie needs assessments: (1) that important information not available elsewhere can be obtained from a needs assessment; and (2) that the information gathered from a needs assessment can and will be used to improve decision-making. Frequently, mandated needs assessments suffer from unrealistic expectations on the part of those who initiate them. If the needs assessment is to be effective, potential utility should be considered:

- Who will use the results of the needs assessment?
- What kind of information will be needed?
- How will needs assessment data be interpreted?
- What practical applications are expected to result?

These considerations will enable the researcher to make appropriate decisions on the needs assessment regarding:

- types of survey instruments or other information-gathering tools
- types of reporting categories, such as age, socioeconomic status, sex, educational attainment, and so forth
- the population of interest
- whether to sample from the population of interest or to use the entire population
- data collection methodology
- data analysis strategy
- general reporting policies
- a time schedule for completion

Potential problems should not deter the researcher from undertaking a needs assessment, but certainly negative outcomes must be considered. One possible outcome of a needs assessment is adverse publicity. Needs assessment results can be misunderstood and misinterpreted. Thus, the researcher should make every effort to do more than merely present tables and figures; instead, results should be developed in clear language and presented in the context in which they are most fairly interpreted.

There are several limitations to needs assessment. It is a very costly and time-consuming exercise, and without proper resources and technical assistance it can generate much more heat than light. Bias can enter into any needs assessment approach; for example, it is easy to miss those most in need since they are also the most difficult to locate. A very infirm older person will not be likely to show up at a hearing or even respond to a mailed questionnaire. Needs assessments give an indication of the magnitude of needs but not who needs assistance and where they may be found. If gaps in service are discovered, the analyst will have difficulty ranking needs unless the survey was constructed to do so. There may also be confusion between needs and wants—the latter being less urgent but nonetheless desirable. A needs assessment can be a useful planning device, but only if its limits are recognized and appropriate action taken.

The major use of a needs assessment is to find out what benefits or services clients or potential clients need. The results of a well-done and carefully analyzed assessment allow decision-makers to redirect resources to areas of greatest need. Needs assessments also give the administrator and practitioner guidance on how best to plan their activities in order to serve those most in need. A needs assessment provides clients and their advocates with a way of quantifying their claims. In general, a needs assessment is similar to the marketing surveys used by some businesses—it allows service providers to know their market and make adjustments to better serve their clients. If the same assessment instrument is used over and over again, it may serve as a useful benchmark and indicator of progress made in serving older clients. The following example illustrates the technical and political problems that can occur during a needs assessment.

Example 5: A needs assessment gone awry
The Legal Service Office in a Texas town was beginning its operations and wanted to meet the needs of its older clients rather than set its own goals for service. To this end, potential clients were asked to rank their most pressing legal problems. The expressed needs were weighed, and Legal Services announced that its first priority, as determined by the needs assessment, was to initiate a class action suit to obtain equitable city services for its clients. Immediate outcries were heard. The city (and state) complained that outsiders at Legal Services were agitating the local population instead of meeting more basic needs and suggested that Legal Services be abolished. The group of potential clients whose hopes had been raised by the survey but whose needs were not given first priority complained that Legal Services was not doing enough for them. Local lawyers complained that Legal Services was planning on doing mainly cases leading to exciting arguments before the Supreme Court, thereby reducing the number of such cases available to private attorneys.
Moral: Before a needs survey begins, it is important to consider as

thoroughly as possible the multiple effects of a wide range of possible responses to the survey results.

Policy Analysis

Policy analysis incorporates elements of evaluation and state-of-the-art research to judge the impact of a public policy. Public policies provide guiding principles for governmental response to social problems like aging and are affected by demography, historical trends, and social values and ideologies. Public policies can be general, applying to all members of society, or they can be specific, applying to segments within society.

Public policy may (1) provide a solution to a problem, (2) attempt to address needs before they become problems, or (3) attempt to maximize the quality of life for individuals. All levels and functions of policy are appropriate to the aging.

Because policy analysis requires critical assessment of alternatives, quantifiable results are usually reviewed in an effort to determine what has been successful and what has failed. Alternative policies are usually checked against criteria, such as cost-effectiveness, and the selected policy must provide the best results for the least costs. Findings from policy analysis may be used to develop new policies that alleviate identified gaps or inequities. The analytical tools most often used are evaluation and critical state-of-the-art review. Unfortunately there is no uniform approach to policy analysis and, as a result, little comparability among results.

An important consideration in analysis of policy with regard to the aging is the cohort effect. *Cohort* refers to individuals born within a certain time span and subject to specific social and historical pressures and events that may be unique. Cohort effect is particularly important when comparisons are made of like-aged adults at different points in time (50-year-olds in 1960 and 50-year-olds in 1980) or of differently aged adults at the same point in time (40- and 60-year-olds in 1980). Public policy based on the needs of 65-year-olds in 1980 (cohort 1915) may not be appropriate for the needs of 65-year-olds in 2000 (cohort 1935) or 2020 (cohort 1955), since attitudes toward receipt of services may change in that forty-year period.

Example 6: An implementation analysis of a public policy
What factors must be considered in introducing training of adult children to care for aging parents?

An implementation analysis first sketches out the basic components of such a program. The analyst then searches for similar programs and studies their history. What resources did previous programs require, what obstacles did they overcome, and how long did it take to set them up? After answering these questions, the analyst can lay out a timetable for introduction of the program. Implementation analysis can help set a realistic time frame for the introduction and establishment of a new service.

Next, the question of resources is addressed. What are the skills required to run such a program? Are the persons with such skills available? Then there are questions concerning potential obstacles. What difficulties are anticipated in finding suitable locations for the program, what regulations exist which may inhibit program development, and what barriers may prevent potential clients from using the services of the new program?

The last set of questions concerns the politics of the program. What programs already exist which may oppose the new approach? What distinguishes the program from existing programs? What, if any, political and community support may be found for the program as it is introduced?

In our research we find several universities already training adult children, that some nursing organizations have reservations about the planned approach, and that there are legal complications involved in teaching people how to care for an impaired person—even a family member. It is now necessary to review these potential obstacles and devise a strategy for overcoming them. Possibly the planned program must be modified to meet contingencies which were not anticipated when the enabling legislation was drafted. In extreme cases, an amendment to some legislation may be required before the program can be introduced. But these modifications will increase the possibility that the program's intent will be realized.

Future Projections

Future projections extrapolate current trends into the future for the purpose of improved planning. Policy analysis often involves future projections since policies are generally developed with a long-range view and thus will affect future as well as current cohorts of elderly. Past changes, current trends, and emerging technologies can be used to project into the future. Although an exercise in imagination, future projection is based on current realities.

The benefit of future projection is its ability to test various trends, assumptions, and interventions against their anticipated consequences. Several types of projections made by a variety of professionals and derived from the same data base allow a comparison of alternatives based on different assumptions about the future.

The major difficulty in predicting for the elderly involves changing characteristics among cohorts. The needs of future elderly may not be the same as those of current elderly. And policies that have impact for all those over the age of 65 may not take into account the differing needs of 65- and 85-year-olds. Related to this issue is the difficulty in predicting morbidity (illness) and mortality (death) rates. The health status of the elderly appears to be changing at such a rapid rate that care must be taken to make reasonable estimates which are neither too optimistic nor too pessimistic. Similarly, changing labor force and retirement patterns suggest caution in predicting future economic needs of the elderly.

Simulation is a technique commonly employed in future projections. The basis of simulation is the devising of formulas which relate various factors to one another. For example, the change in birth rate will affect the number of future older persons. In a simulation, the birth rate is adjusted in a variety of ways to see how the manipulated adjustments affect the future. Other factors affecting longevity, such as sanitation, nutrition, and environmental pollutants, are considered also. Simulations are often known as future games or gaming and are most often computer-based programs. They are used to show planners and practitioners how various interventions in a simulated world will affect the shape of a simulated future.

Example 7: A future projection
    The amount of money available to pay Medicare benefits in the year 2000 is unknown but depends on several factors. One of those factors is the number of workers paying taxes; another is the number of older adults who need constant nursing home care because of conditions like organic brain syndrome. Twenty percent of elders over age 90 need such care now; we might assume that this proportion will stay the same, that the absolute number of elders will rise, and that the absolute number of workers will not rise. This scenario leads to a prediction that funds available for Medicare benefits will be insufficient in 2000. If we change the assumptions and assume that research will find a way to reduce the number of cases of organic brain syndrome, we might then predict that money may be sufficient in the year 2000.

References

Carney, Thomas F. *Content Analysis*. Winnipeg: University of Manitoba Press, 1972.

Garson, D. G. *Handbook of Political Science Methods*. Boston, Ma.: Holbrook Press, 1976.

Hyman, H. H. *Secondary Analysis of Sample Surveys*. New York: Wiley, 1972.

Lowy, L. Introduction. In E. W. Markson, and G. R. Batra (eds.), *Public Policies for an Aging Population*. Lexington, Ma.: Lexington Books, 1980.

Morris, R. *Social Policy of the American Welfare State*. New York: Harper and Row, 1979.

Perkins, H. *Human Development and Learning.* Belmont, Ca.: Wadsworth, 1969.

Quade, Edward S. *Analysis for Public Decisions.* New York: Elsevier, 1975.

Schatzman, L., and Strauss, A. L. *Field Research.* Englewood Cliffs, N.J.: Prentice-Hall, 1973.

Suchman, E. A. *Evaluative Research.* New York: Russell Sage, 1967.

Williams, W., and Elmore, Richard F. (eds.). *Social Program Implementation.* New York: Academic Press, 1976.

Chapter

3

Data Collection: Sampling

Data collection requires choosing a sampling technique and a measurement instrument. The choices are partly determined by the previous decisions made about methods and designs and partly determined by the analyses to be performed. If no choice of samples or measures is available, be certain that the data that will be obtained are appropriate to the research question, the method, the design, and the analysis. If there *is* a choice about sample and measures, verify that the choices made meet the constraints of question, method, design, and analysis.

This chapter presents important information about selecting a study sample. Chapter 4 identifies the advantages and disadvantages of different types of measurement instruments.

Sampling means treating some number of subjects from a population as representative of that population. There is no guarantee that the sample is representative; rather, it is assumed to be representative. Samples are usually thought of as people, but not all populations

---

Decision-Making Process for Sampling

1. Do I need a probability sample?	Table 3.1
2. Would a stratified sample or an intact-group be better?	Figure 3.2
3. How large should my sample be?	Table 3.3
4. Does the analysis planned affect the choice of samples?	Table 3.4
5. Are there special aging issues to be considered before sampling?	Page 62 *ff.*

---

or samples are made up of people. Some populations are composed of articles, programs, dwelling units, or visits. For example, a colleague recently obtained a sample of texts on aging from the population of textbooks on aging published over the past ten years in order to do a content analysis of texts.

Types of Samples

Common question: How do I find a nice random sample?

Better question: What type of sample is most efficient for my purposes?

Not every study requires a sample that represents the characteristics of the entire population. Using the wrong type of sampling strategy wastes effort, at best. At worst, the wrong sampling strategy invalidates the findings of the study. Generalizing from a nonrepresentative sample (for example, elders who work as volunteers) to the entire elder population is meaningless. On the other hand, wasting money and time to obtain a large, representative sample to make a generalization about one subgroup (for example, rural elder black women) is almost as misguided because of the huge amounts of time and effort spent on tasks that do not answer the question.

In Table 3.1, several types of samples are described. If investigators cannot work with a whole population of people, events, or programs, as is usually the case in research on aging, they need to decide whether the results of the study should reflect, or be generalizable to, that whole population. If results need to be generalizable, the investigator can try one of two approaches:

1. If the characteristics of the general population are known, the investigator can choose a sample that matches those characteristics (stratified or purposive sample). If, for example, a researcher is interested in the leisure activities of female retirees, the sample should reflect the prior labor force participation patterns of retired women. The prior occupation of 32 percent of the retirees would be clerical, 21 percent would be service-related, and so forth. A sample composed of retired university professors would be inappropriate since most older retired women are not college-educated and did not hold professional positions.
2. If the characteristics of the general population are unknown, or if known characteristics are irrelevant, the investigator can make a random choice of respondents on the assumption that all characteristics will be present in the sample (cluster or systematic sample).

Table 3.1
Types of Samples

Sample	Example
Probability Samples (use some form of random sampling in one or more of their stages)	
Random Sampling—drawing a sample in such a way that each member of the population has an equal chance of being selected	Households are chosen by means of a random number table.
Systematic Sampling—randomly choosing the first subject from numbers 1–n, and subsequent subjects at every nth interval	If $n = 10$, some number between 1 and 10 is randomly selected, e.g., 3. From a list of retirees, the 3rd, 13th, 23rd, and so on are selected in order to assess retirement satisfaction.
Stratified Sampling—dividing the population into strata (male/female, black/white) from which random samples are drawn	Retirees are divided on the basis of blue- and white-collar occupations and on the basis of sex to assess retirement satisfaction.
Cluster Sampling—successive random sampling of sets and subsets	Within a state, cities are randomly selected; then companies within the cities, then retired employees of the companies, in order to assess retirement satisfaction.
Nonprobability Samples (do not use random sampling)	
Quota Sampling—using knowledge of strata of the population (sex, race, etc.) to select sample members in numbers proportionate to their distribution in the population	Labor force participation rates are 60% male and 40% female, so a sample to assess retirement satisfaction would have 60% men and 40% women.
Purposive Sampling—making a deliberate effort to obtain representative samples by including presumably typical subjects in the sample	Only men and women who name paid work as their primary role are included in a study of retirement satisfaction, since others are presumed not to have adjustment problems.
Intact-Group Sampling—using available samples at hand	An investigator studies retirement satisfaction of all the members of a country club to which he or she has access.
Matched Sampling—selecting two groups with like characteristics and then manipulating variables in some way in the experimental group only	Two groups of retirees are matched in terms of age, sex, years on job, and one group receives counseling.

Source of definitions: Kerlinger, F. N. *Foundations of Behavioral Research,* 2nd ed. New York: Holt, Rinehart and Winston, Inc., 1973.

If results need not be generalizable to all, the study results can be cautiously applied to individuals fitting the characteristics of the sample (quota, purposive, or intact-group sample).

The sample design process is illustrated in Figure 3.1.

The most common sample types are stratified (probability) samples and intact-group (nonprobability) samples. Table 3.2 compares some of the characteristics of the two sample types. Informational situations that can be explored differ for the two samples. Anything can be explored in a stratified sample, but only certain issues relevant to the particular sample can be explored in an intact-group sample. If a researcher is checking the need for wheelchairs, for example, that information can be validly obtained both in the stratified sample of elders and in the intact-group sample of nursing home patients. If the investigator is assessing the frequency of purchase of two types of aspirin, the stratified sample is suitable. An intact-group sample of nursing home patients would be inappropriate, but an intact-group sample of drugstore shoppers would be suitable.

Determination of causes and outcomes is limited for the intact-group sample because the range of behaviors and events has been restricted. When analyses are performed for data collected from a stratified sample, it is possible to talk about causes and effects if a causality-testing design has been employed. With an intact-group sample, what seems to be an effect might very well be an artifact of the special sample characteristics, and it is only safe to talk about two events occurring together without assigning causality to one event. For these reasons a stratified sample permits a higher level of explanation; an intact-group sample demands a lower level of explanation which may, however, be more than adequate for the goals of the project.

Sample Size

Common question: How big must the sample be?

Better question: What size sample is necessary to reach my research objectives?

Sample size is influenced by the type of sample used in a study, the data collection methods to be employed (see Chapter 4), the kinds of analyses that will be performed (see Chapter 5), and the cost. If a probability sample is drawn, there are advantages to using a large number of respondents. The possibility of sampling error (i.e., effects due to unique qualities of the sample) is reduced, the data offer greater reliability, and the power of the statistical tests applied

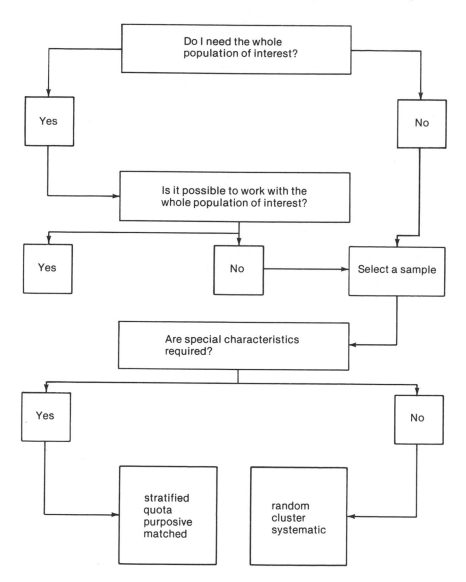

Figure 3.1   Sampling Decisions

Table 3.2
Features of Stratified and Intact-Group Samples

	Stratified sample	Intact-group sample
Subjects	Obtained by stratifying on the basis of population characteristics, randomly sampling within strata, so that sample shares key characteristics of whole population	Obtained by targeting an intact-group of interest and using the entire group as the sample, or by choosing a subsample group that represents the group of interest
Costs	Higher because two stages and more subjects involved	Lower because one stage and fewer subjects involved
Causes	Entire range of relationships can be examined for possible cause and effect	Selected relationships are examined without attributing cause and effect
Analysis	Can analyze cause–effect relationships	Can only look for co-occurrence
Level of explanation	High level (explains many factors under a variety of circumstances)	Low level (explains only some factors under selected circumstances)

to the data is increased. The advantages of small samples are economy and greater depth of data if the time saved tackling many cases is used to work more intensively with fewer cases (see Table 3.3).

Because of the problems of sampling error and attrition, larger samples are preferable wherever practical. Sampling error is a statistical term in probability sampling that refers to the degree to which the sample deviates from the characteristics of the population from which it is randomly selected. The larger the sample, the greater the likelihood that it will embody all characteristics of the total population. Attrition refers to loss of subjects from a sample. Social/psychological attrition is generally caused by lack of interest, active refusal, or change of residence on the part of subjects. Biological attrition is generally caused by physical illness or death. Social/psychological attrition is a problem in all kinds of social science research. Where the aged comprise a sample, biological attrition is a real concern as well. A sample should be large enough to render data generalizable even where attrition occurs.

Large samples should not be used just because large numbers are good in and of themselves. Samples that are too large can be as dangerous as samples that are too small. The larger the sample, the

Table 3.3
Characteristics of Large and Small Samples

	Large sample	Small sample
Strengths	smaller sampling error greater reliability statistical power* generalizability no attrition problem data-extensive	economy convenience data-intensive
Weaknesses	more costly more time-consuming depth study too expensive	larger sampling error less reliability attrition problem
Applications	interaction of large num- ber of uncontrolled variables total sample divided into subsamples population containing a wide range of variables and characteristics group differences ex- pected to be small but meaningful	in-depth case studies complex techniques of evaluating behavior, i.e., interviewing proce- dures, projective in- struments

*Ability of the test to find a significant relation that is present in the data.

stronger the possibility that scope of information will be emphasized at the expense of depth, since there will be no time to follow up questions to each respondent. If a sample is too large, even very weak associations may become statistically significant (Table 3.4).

A simple formula allows quick calculation of appropriate sample size (Burstein, 1971). First, the level of significance must be determined (customarily a level of $p \leq .05$ is acceptable). Second, the prevalence of the variable of interest must be estimated, based on prior studies. If a random sample of 300 elderly indicates that 60 require special transportation services, the sample proportion, c/n, equals 60/300, or 20 percent. A researcher who wants to determine whether special transportation services are required in another community would *estimate* the need at 20 percent and calculate a sample size accordingly. Often, however, prior studies which could help in making this estimate are unavailable. When this is so, an extremely conservative estimate, 50 percent, is used.

The calculation of an appropriate sample size for a study of special transportation requirements is as follows:

Table 3.4
General Guide to Sample Size Effects on Statistics

Statistic	N considerations
Descriptive	Any size N is usable
Inferential	
Correlation (e.g., relate age and frequency of sexual relations)	Large N (100+): very small correlations may turn out to be significant but may not explain much of the relationship
	Small (10 or less): usable, but not likely to be statistically significant
Causation (e.g., compare group getting a drug with group not getting drug to see effect on weight loss)	Large N (100+) in each treatment group: usable
	Small N (5 or less): cannot use this design with some statistics; not likely to get a significant difference between groups
Multiple regression (e.g., many interrelationships among 10 demographic variables)	Must have 10+ cases for each of the variables, i.e., 100 cases in the study example cited
Multifactorial (e.g., many treatment groups that differ on several dimensions; for instance, comparing weight loss for women getting drug, women not getting drug, men getting drug, men not getting drug)	Small N in each treatment group (5 or less): cannot use this design with some statistics; not likely to get a significant difference between groups

1. Calculate

$$\hat{\hat{p}} = \hat{p} + \hat{e}$$

where $\hat{p}$ = estimated sample proportion
  $\hat{e}$ = level of significance

For our example,

$$\hat{\hat{p}} = .20 + .05$$
$$= .25$$

2. Calculate

$$\hat{Q} = \frac{\hat{\hat{p}}}{\hat{p}} \times \frac{2 - \hat{p}}{2 - \hat{\hat{p}}}$$

where Q = upper confidence limit divided by number of items in sample
      $\hat{Q}$ = estimated Q

For example,

$$\hat{Q} = \frac{.25}{.20} \times \frac{2 - .20}{2 - .25}$$
$$= 1.25 \times \frac{1.80}{1.75}$$
$$= 1.25 \times 1.029$$
$$= 1.324$$

3. Turn to Table 3.5. Look across the row, β, until the desired level of significance is found. For our example, $p = .05$ so the fourth column is used. Look down the column, $\beta = 5$ percent, until the value of $\hat{Q}$, calculated previously, is found. For our example, $\hat{Q} = 1.324$. The closest value on the column is 1.326, so this is what we will use.
4. Look across the row. For $Q = 1.326$, the c value is 35.
5. Calculate

$$n = \frac{c}{\hat{p}}$$

where n = sample size
      c = 35 (from Table 3.5)
      $\hat{p}$ = estimated sample proportion (.20 in this example)

Thus,

$$n = \frac{35}{.20}$$
$$= 175$$

The sample should be 175 subjects.

Suppose, however, that the estimated sample proportion (.20 in our example) is unknown. Calculating the sample size conservatively with an estimated sample proportion of .50, we find:

1. $\hat{\hat{p}} = \hat{p} + \hat{e}$
   $= .50 + .05$
   $= .55$

2. $\hat{Q} = \frac{\hat{\hat{p}}}{\hat{p}} \times \frac{2 - \hat{p}}{2 - \hat{\hat{p}}}$
   $= \frac{.55}{.50} \times \frac{2 - .50}{2 - .55}$
   $= 1.1 \times \frac{1.50}{1.45}$
   $= 1.1 \times 1.034$
   $= 1.137$

Table 3.5
Values of Q and c for Determining Sample Size by the Poisson
Procedure; $p \le .25$ (but not 0)

γ or β

c	γ_1: 99.5% γ_2: 99% β: 0.5%	99% 98% 1%	97.5% 95% 2.5%	95% 90% 5%	90% 80% 10%	80% 60% 20%
			Q			
1	7.430	6.638	5.572	4.744	3.890	2.994
2	4.637	4.203	3.612	3.148	2.661	2.140
3	3.659	3.348	2.922	2.585	2.227	1.838
4	3.149	2.901	2.560	2.288	1.998	1.680
5	2.830	2.622	2.334	2.103	1.855	1.581
6	2.610	2.428	2.177	1.974	1.755	1.513
7	2.448	2.286	2.060	1.878	1.682	1.462
8	2.322	2.175	1.970	1.804	1.624	1.422
9	2.222	2.087	1.898	1.745	1.578	1.391
10	2.140	2.014	1.839	1.696	1.541	1.365
11	2.071	1.954	1.789	1.655	1.509	1.343
12	2.012	1.902	1.747	1.620	1.482	1.325
13	1.961	1.857	1.710	1.590	1.458	1.309
14	1.917	1.818	1.678	1.563	1.438	1.295
15	1.878	1.783	1.649	1.540	1.419	1.282
16	1.843	1.752	1.624	1.519	1.403	1.271
17	1.811	1.724	1.601	1.500	1.389	1.261
18	1.783	1.699	1.580	1.483	1.375	1.252
19	1.757	1.676	1.562	1.467	1.363	1.244
20	1.733	1.655	1.544	1.453	1.352	1.236
21	1.712	1.636	1.529	1.440	1.342	1.229
22	1.692	1.618	1.514	1.428	1.333	1.223
23	1.673	1.602	1.500	1.417	1.324	1.217
24	1.656	1.587	1.488	1.406	1.316	1.212
25	1.640	1.572	1.476	1.397	1.308	1.207
26	1.625	1.559	1.465	1.388	1.301	1.202
27	1.611	1.547	1.455	1.379	1.295	1.197
28	1.598	1.535	1.445	1.371	1.289	1.193
29	1.585	1.524	1.436	1.363	1.283	1.189
30	1.574	1.513	1.428	1.356	1.277	1.185
31	1.563	1.503	1.419	1.350	1.272	1.182
32	1.552	1.494	1.412	1.343	1.267	1.179
33	1.542	1.485	1.404	1.337	1.262	1.175
34	1.533	1.477	1.397	1.331	1.258	1.172
35	1.524	1.469	1.391	1.326	1.253	1.169

γ or β

	γ_1: 99.5%	99%	97.5%	95%	90%	80%
	γ_2: 99%	98%	95%	90%	80%	60%
	β: 0.5%	1%	2.5%	5%	10%	20%
c			Q			
36	1.515	1.461	1.384	1.321	1.249	1.167
37	1.507	1.454	1.378	1.316	1.245	1.164
38	1.499	1.447	1.373	1.311	1.242	1.161
39	1.491	1.440	1.367	1.306	1.238	1.159
40	1.484	1.434	1.362	1.302	1.235	1.157
41	1.477	1.428	1.357	1.298	1.231	1.155
42	1.470	1.422	1.352	1.293	1.228	1.152
43	1.464	1.416	1.347	1.290	1.225	1.150
44	1.458	1.410	1.342	1.286	1.222	1.148
45	1.452	1.405	1.338	1.282	1.220	1.146
46	1.446	1.400	1.334	1.279	1.217	1.145
47	1.441	1.395	1.330	1.275	1.214	1.143
48	1.435	1.390	1.326	1.272	1.212	1.141
49	1.430	1.386	1.322	1.269	1.209	1.139
50	1.425	1.381	1.318	1.266	1.207	1.138
55	1.403	1.361	1.302	1.252	1.196	1.131
60	1.383	1.344	1.287	1.240	1.187	1.124
65	1.366	1.329	1.275	1.229	1.178	1.119
70	1.351	1.315	1.263	1.220	1.171	1.114
75	1.338	1.303	1.254	1.212	1.165	1.110
80	1.326	1.292	1.245	1.204	1.159	1.106
90	1.305	1.274	1.229	1.192	1.149	1.0991
100	1.288	1.258	1.216	1.181	1.141	1.0935
110	1.273	1.246	1.205	1.172	1.134	1.0887
120	1.260	1.234	1.196	1.164	1.127	1.0846
130	1.249	1.224	1.187	1.157	1.122	1.0809
150	1.230	1.207	1.173	1.145	1.113	1.0749
170	1.215	1.193	1.162	1.136	1.106	1.0700
200	1.197	1.177	1.149	1.124	1.0969	1.0642
250	1.175	1.157	1.132	1.111	1.0861	1.0569
300	1.159	1.143	1.120	1.100	1.0782	1.0517
350	1.146	1.132	1.110	1.0925	1.0721	1.0476
400	1.136	1.123	1.103	1.0863	1.0672	1.0444
450	1.128	1.115	1.0968	1.0811	1.0632	1.0417
500	1.121	1.109	1.0916	1.0768	1.0598	1.0395

Table 3.5
(*continued*)

γ or β

c	γ_1: 99.5% γ_2: 99% β: 0.5%	99% 98% 1%	97.5% 95% 2.5%	95% 90% 5%	90% 80% 10%	80% 60% 20%
			Q			
600	1.110	1.0992	1.0833	1.0698	1.0544	1.0359
700	1.102	1.0915	1.0769	1.0645	1.0502	1.0331
800	1.0947	1.0854	1.0718	1.0602	1.0469	1.0309
900	1.0891	1.0803	1.0675	1.0566	1.0441	1.0291
1000	1.0844	1.0761	1.0640	1.0536	1.0418	1.0275
1100	1.0803	1.0724	1.0609	1.0510	1.0398	1.0262
1200	1.0768	1.0692	1.0582	1.0488	1.0380	1.0251
1500	1.0684	1.0617	1.0519	1.0435	1.0339	1.0223
2000	1.0591	1.0533	1.0448	1.0376	1.0293	1.0193
2500	1.0527	1.0475	1.0400	1.0335	1.0261	1.0172
3000	1.0480	1.0433	1.0364	1.0306	1.0238	1.0157
3500	1.0444	1.0400	1.0337	1.0283	1.0220	1.0145
4000	1.0415	1.0374	1.0315	1.0264	1.0206	1.0135
4500	1.0390	1.0352	1.0297	1.0249	1.0194	1.0127
5000	1.0370	1.0334	1.0281	1.0236	1.0184	1.0121
6000	1.0337	1.0304	1.0256	1.0215	1.0167	1.0110
7000	1.0312	1.0282	1.0237	1.0199	1.0155	1.0102
8000	1.0292	1.0263	1.0222	1.0186	1.0145	1.00952
9000	1.0275	1.0248	1.0209	1.0175	1.0136	1.00897
10000	1.0260	1.0235	1.0198	1.0166	1.0129	1.00851
11000	1.0248	1.0224	1.0189	1.0158	1.0123	1.00811
12000	1.0238	1.0214	1.0181	1.0151	1.0118	1.00776
15000	1.0212	1.0192	1.0161	1.0135	1.0105	1.00693
20000	1.0184	1.0166	1.0140	1.0117	1.00912	1.00600
25000	1.0164	1.0148	1.0125	1.0105	1.00815	1.00536
30000	1.0150	1.0135	1.0114	1.00955	1.00744	1.00489
35000	1.0139	1.0125	1.0105	1.00884	1.00689	1.00452
40000	1.0130	1.0117	1.00985	1.00826	1.00644	1.00423
45000	1.0122	1.0110	1.00928	1.00779	1.00607	1.00399
50000	1.0116	1.0105	1.00880	1.00739	1.00576	1.00378
60000	1.0106	1.00954	1.00803	1.00674	1.00525	1.00345
70000	1.00978	1.00883	1.00744	1.00624	1.00486	1.00319
80000	1.00914	1.00826	1.00695	1.00584	1.00455	1.00299
90000	1.00862	1.00778	1.00656	1.00550	1.00429	1.00282
100000	1.00817	1.00738	1.00622	1.00522	1.00406	1.00267

$$\gamma \text{ or } \beta$$

c	γ_1: 99.5% γ_2: 99% β: 0.5%	99% 98% 1%	97.5% 95% 2.5%	95% 90% 5%	90% 80% 10%	80% 60% 20%
			Q			
110000	1.00779	1.00704	1.00593	1.00497	1.00388	1.00255
120000	1.00746	1.00674	1.00567	1.00476	1.00371	1.00244
150000	1.00667	1.00602	1.00507	1.00426	1.00332	1.00218
200000	1.00577	1.00521	1.00439	1.00369	1.00287	1.00189
250000	1.00516	1.00466	1.00393	1.00330	1.00257	1.00169
300000	1.00471	1.00426	1.00358	1.00301	1.00234	1.00154
350000	1.00436	1.00394	1.00332	1.00278	1.00217	1.00143
400000	1.00408	1.00368	1.00310	1.00260	1.00203	1.00133
450000	1.00385	1.00347	1.00293	1.00246	1.00191	1.00126
500000	1.00365	1.00329	1.00278	1.00233	1.00181	1.00119
600000	1.00333	1.00301	1.00253	1.00213	1.00166	1.00109
700000	1.00308	1.00278	1.00235	1.00197	1.00153	1.00101
800000	1.00288	1.00260	1.00219	1.00184	1.00143	1.000942
900000	1.00272	1.00245	1.00207	1.00174	1.00135	1.000888
1000000	1.00258	1.00233	1.00196	1.00165	1.00128	1.000843

Source: Herman Burstein. *Attribute Sampling* (New York: McGraw-Hill Book Co., 1971), pp. 369–371. Used by permission.

3. The Q value on Table 3.5 closest to $\hat{Q}$ is 1.136.

4. $c = 170$

5. $n = \dfrac{c}{\hat{p}}$

   $= \dfrac{170}{.50}$

   $= 340$

It quickly becomes apparent that a conservative estimate of sample proportion requires a substantially larger sample size. Level of significance also affects sample size. In our first example, $\hat{p} = .20$, a .05 level of significance resulted in a sample size of 175. If a more conservative level of significance (for example, $p < .01$) is employed, sample size increases to 325. Conversely, a more liberal significance level reduces the sample size (i.e., when $p < .10$, sample size = 115).

Rule of thumb 3.1: When choosing your sample, keep in mind the nature of the population to which results should generalize.

Rule of thumb 3.2: Choose the smallest, cheapest sample that will allow you to answer your research objectives.

Special Aging-Related Sampling Problems in Studies of Change over Time

Once the sampling questions concerning size and type have been answered, the researcher must consider a third sampling issue that is unique to research on change over time: How can the effects of generational differences and culture at the time of testing be separated from changes due to aging or change over time? In other words, how can we be sure that results associated with aging are due to aging itself?

Separating those behaviors that are attributable to generational influences from those caused by the biological effects of aging is not easy. Usually, researchers examine a group of older persons and a group of younger persons and conclude that differences between the two groups are due to aging without considering the effects of cultural differences between generations. When the younger group gets different scores than the older group, does that reflect the consequences of getting older or the fact that those born in 1900 (who happen to be older today) and those born in 1960 (who happen to be younger today) lived through very different times?

Depending on the research question, research results may be invalid if your sampling confuses or combines these separate factors. For some questions, combining all factors (aging, generation differences, cultural differences at the time of testing) is fine (e.g., "How many prescription drugs do elders take in 1982?"); in this case the investigator doesn't care why they take the number they take (i.e., whether it's due to age or generational effects) so combining is permitted. For other questions, mixing factors is not permitted (e.g., "Do individual elders drop in IQ over a 10-year period?"); in this question *only* changes-over-time data are useful.

Addressing this issue may mean a change in sampling. Examine the three types of studies described below to see how the sampling and design of each affect the researcher's ability to separate age from generation and time-of-testing influences in the results. After three designs are described, we will present a sampling strategy for distinguishing the effects of the three factors. Even if you cannot take advantage of the better strategy due to other constraints, you should be aware of the limitations on interpreting results that derive from the combination of these factors.

Cross-Sectional Studies

The confusing of cohort and age is most apparent in cross-sectional studies in which two or more generational groups are compared at one point in time. There is no problem making comparisons if the comparisons are kept on a descriptive level; the problem with cross-sectional research lies in attempting to explain the causes of differences between groups.

Example 1: Cross-sectional study of cognitive behavior
In 1968 two researchers decided to do a cross-sectional study of cognitive behavior. Their sample was composed of 25 males and 25 females, ages 25–70, chosen randomly from a community organization of 500 adults. After administering the various measures of mental ability, they found significant differences between groups. See Figure 3.2.

You might examine these data and conclude that people lose cognitive capacity as they grow older. Is this a valid conclusion?

No, because the study has confused generation differences with age differences. Let's pull out three generations and see why this is so (Table 3.6).

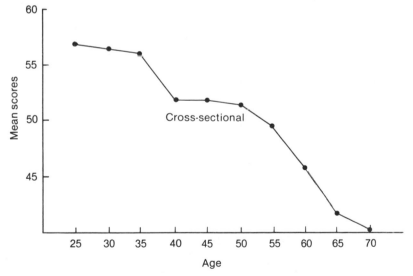

Figure 3.2   Cross-Sectional Results. (Source: K. W. Schaie and C. R. Strother, "A Cross-Sequential Study of Age Changes in Cognitive Behavior," *Psychological Bulletin,* 70, pp. 671–680. Copyright 1968 by the American Psychological Association. Reprinted by permission of the publisher and author.)

Table 3.6

Age	Year of birth	Year of high school graduation
65	1903	1921
45	1923	1941
25	1943	1961

Experience of generational groups:

65-year-old—went to work at age 16 (1919)
> Great Depression, age 26–30 (1929–1933); if married, survival is key issue
> World War II, age 38–42 (1941–1945)—probably desk job if involved at all

45-year-old—more likely to have finished high school
> drafted or enlisted World War II, age 18 (1941)
> goes to college on GI Bill, or to work, age 22 (1945)

25-year-old—high school graduate, high probability of college (class of 1965), just prior to days of political activism; studied, didn't liberate campuses
> better job maybe, because of education
> 1960s huge scientific expansion in response to Sputnik (1957)

The more probable conclusion is that each succeeding cohort had a better primary and secondary education and that members of later cohorts were more likely to go to college. Poor test performance may indicate that older cohorts have had less practice in taking tests; if it was a timed test, they may not have finished.

Much of the variance attributed to age differences in cross-sectional studies must properly be assigned to differences between successive generations.

Longitudinal Studies

A longitudinal study samples once and then retests the same people at several times, usually with a number of years between examinations. Where the cross-sectional study combines the effects of generation and age, the longitudinal study confuses time of testing and age.

Example 2: Longitudinal study of cognitive behavior
Let's use the same test of cognitive behavior, only this time we test a group of people from a single cohort at five-year intervals.

This procedure gives very different results (see Figure 3.3). One

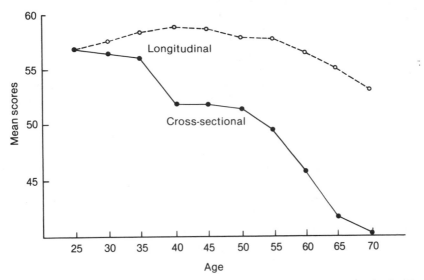

Figure 3.3   Longitudinal Results. (Source: K. W. Schaie and C. R. Strother, "A Cross-Sequential Study of Age Changes in Cognitive Behavior," *Psychological Bulletin,* 70, pp. 671–680. Copyright 1968 by the American Psychological Association. Reprinted by permission of the publisher and author.)

might conclude that people get smarter as they age, with a slight decline after age 55. Is this conclusion more valid than the one drawn from the cross-sectional study?

No, because each time the individual retakes the test (the same test must be administered each time in order to compare changes over time), the repetition results in an improvement in test score. Furthermore, results are affected by cultural trends (like familiarity with tests) at the time of testing.

Let's assume we gave a test on political attitudes and noticed a trend toward liberalism over the course of the study. This would not necessarily mean that people become more liberal as they age; it could simply be a reflection of culture change—i.e., the country may have become more liberal each year. Everyone in the country, if tested, might be categorized as liberal, whereas everyone thirty years ago was conservative, regardless of age. Cultural changes influenced all scores.

Time-Lag Studies

A third type of sampling approach involves sampling several generations of people of a given age (see Table 3.7). This type of study mixes generation and time-of-testing effects, but age is held constant.

Table 3.7

Year Born	Year Tested	Age at Test
1900	1950	50 (group 1)
1910	1960	50 (group 2)
1920	1970	50 (group 3)

Source: Adapted from Jack Botwinick, *Aging and Behavior,* 2nd edition, Table 19.1, page 371. Copyright © 1978 by Springer Publishing Company, Inc. Used by permission.

If the research question of interest involves whether some quality is constant in all generations of 50-year-olds, this design is appropriate. Results showing that succeeding generations of 50-year-olds are not alike may be due to either different life experiences such as education differences or different testing-time experiences such as generational changes in test anxiety.

Keeping the Factors Separated

A complete analysis of age-related change must take into account all three factors: maturation or age effects, generation effects, and time-of-testing effects. Each of the three types of studies described above combines two of these variables, but since one variable in each type of study is common to one other type of study it is possible to determine the relative contribution of each effect.

The simplest sampling situation permitting differentiation among age, cohort, and time utilizes the format of Table 3.8. (Each letter designates a different sampling group.)

Other comparisons are possible.

1. A + C versus B + D is an *age comparison* (50-year-olds versus

Table 3.8

Time of Measurement

Year of Birth		1950	1960	1970
	1910		C 50	D 60
	1900	A 50	B 60	

Note: Age in years is indicated in each cell.
    Vertical cells = cross-sectional comparison.
    Horizontal cells = longitudinal comparison.
    Diagonal cells = time-lag comparison.

Source: Adapted from Jack Botwinick, *Aging and Behavior,* 2nd edition, Table 19.1, page 371. Copyright © 1978 by Springer Publishing Company, Inc. Used by permission.

60-year-olds), which holds cohort constant and varies time of measurement.
2. A + B versus C + D is a *cohort comparison* (1900 versus 1910), which holds age constant and varies the same times of measurement.

With this design it is possible to compare the relative contribution of age and generation effects, each in interaction with two times of measurement.

A more complex example, using three cohorts and three times of measurement, is shown in Table 3.9.

This table allows the following comparisons:

1. Cohort sequential solution = B, C, D, E; we examine two different cohorts at the same age.
2. Time sequential solution = B, D, E, G; we examine two different ages at the same points in time.
3. Cross-sequential solution = A, B, D, E; we examine two different cohorts at the same points in time.

A statistician or a text on developmental research can help with the statistical analysis involved here. The most important thing to remember is that in every project related to aging it should be clear to the researcher and the reader which of the three factors are being controlled and which are not.

Rule of thumb 3.3: Always consider which of the three effects—age, time of measurement, generation of birth—you may be combining in your project results, and make sampling changes as needed.

Table 3.9

Time of Measurement

		1950	1960	1970
	1920	A 30	B 40	C 50
Year of Birth	1910	D 40	E 50	F 60
	1900	G 50	H 60	I 70

Note: Age in years is indicated in each cell.

Unequal Probabilities of Selection (Weighting)

It is not uncommon for a researcher to employ a random selection procedure for a specific study while at the same time purposely undersampling or oversampling the population according to some characteristic. It is very common in aging-related research to oversample the elderly. Such oversampling enables the researcher to work with a larger N with respect to the characteristics in question and hence enables him or her to lower the standard error of the estimate. Undersampling is often employed in the interests of economy. Many national probability samples using personal interviews routinely undersample rural or nonmetropolitan areas because of the higher costs associated with hard-to-reach locations.

When unequal probabilities of selection (UPS) is a factor, a researcher may conduct analysis as usual as long as he or she is looking only at that group upon which the UPS was based. That is, in the case of oversampling the elderly, no special considerations are necessary if the researcher is only looking at the attitudes of the elderly. Similarly, if only rural attitudes are considered in a study that underselected that group, analysis may continue as usual. If, however, the researcher wants to look at results based on a sample of the entire population, the distorting effect of UPS must be accounted for. In the case of the elderly, this would mean weighting *down* the responses of that group, while in the second example it would mean weighting *up* the responses of rural people.

> *Rule of thumb 3.4:* The weight assigned a respondent is always the inverse of that respondent's probability of selection into the sample (e.g., if the proportion of elderly people in the sample is twice their proportion in the general population, their responses each count one-half in an analysis based on the entire population).

A good example of oversampling in gerontological research occurred in the 1981 survey *Aging in America: 1981.* The survey oversampled people between the ages 55 to 64, those 65 and over, blacks, and Hispanics. (For a fuller description of this survey see page 118.) This oversampling enabled researchers to carry out in-depth analysis with these population segments while maintaining high levels of reliability. To facilitate analysis of the entire population, each of these groups was then weighted back to its actual proportion in the overall national results. The existing data set gave the researchers the choice of using either the disproportionate sample sizes or the weighted sample. In this case, the weights can easily be applied using one of the many conventional statistical software packages.

Weights can be assigned and controlled by hand if the researcher is willing to do the necessary work. But the widespread existence of easy-to-use, low-cost software packages has virtually eliminated the need for calculating the appropriate statistics.

Summary

Rule 3.1: When choosing your sample, keep in mind the nature of the population to which results should generalize.

Rule 3.2: Choose the smallest, cheapest sample that will allow you to meet your research objectives.

Rule 3.3: Always consider which of the three effects—age, time of measurement, generation of birth—you may be combining in your project results, and make sampling changes as needed.

Rule 3.4: The weight assigned a respondent is always the *inverse* of that respondent's probability of selection into the sample (e.g., if the proportion of elderly people in the sample is twice their proportion in the general population, their responses each count one-half in an analysis based on the entire population).

References

Baltes, P., et al. *Life-Span Developmental Psychology: Introduction to Research Methods.* Monterey, Calif.: Brooks-Cole, 1977.

Burstein, Herman. *Attribute Sampling.* New York: McGraw-Hill Book Co., 1971.

Duke University Center for the Study of Aging. *Multidimensional Functional Assessment: The OARS Methodology* (2nd Edition). Durham, N.C.: Duke University, 1978.

Miller, D. C. *Handbook of Research Design and Social Measurement.* New York: David McKay Co., 1980.

Webb, E. J., D. Campbell, R. Schwartz, and L. Sechrest. *Unobtrusive Measures: Nonreactive Research in the Social Sciences.* Chicago: Rand McNally, 1966.

Chapter

4

Data Collection: Measurement Tools

After choosing research and sampling techniques, the researcher turns attention to the data collection vehicle, the measurement instrument. The data collection instrument may be an interview, a questionnaire, a standardized measure, or some type of form. Data gathering is done with one of these standard formats to ensure that the same data elements will be obtained for all cases.

Several factors need to be considered in deciding which data collection method to employ (see Table 4.1). The most obvious practical consideration concerning the interview or personal contact approach is cost. Personal testing or conducting an interview-based data collection effort, whether by telephone or face to face, is hard work. The time required to obtain a very large number of cases is another consideration. If immediate results are desired, a special staff of interviewers must be trained. This poses problems in itself, because it is very easy to lose most of the advantages of interview procedure if the interviewers are not highly trained, consistent, and motivated.

One of the advantages of personal contact over the paper-and-

---

Decision-Making Process for Measurement Tools

Table 4.1
Types of Measurement Devices

1. Open-ended	One structured stimulus question, no structured response.	
2. Structured	One structured stimulus question, structured response possibilities.	
3. Scale	Several structured items which purport to measure the same construct and can be added together.	
4. Test	Several structured items which reliably and validly measure the same construct and have been item-analyzed to guarantee their homogeneity. May be standardized and normed for a specific group.	

Note: All may be included in one administration or just one may be used.

pencil approach is that the literacy and eyesight of respondents is not an obstacle. Lack of motivation to respond is also less of a problem because the direct contact with an interviewer produces both pressure to respond and rewards for responding. Personal contact permits administration of complex tests and measurements.

There are many ways to administer measures:

1. examination of content on records
2. group paper-and-pencil
3. individual paper-and-pencil
4. individual interview/test (in person)
5. individual test/interview (telephone)

The personal approach can be much more flexible than paper and pencil, depending on the skill of the interviewer/tester. An interviewer has the opportunity to explain to the respondent any ambiguities that emerge. Furthermore, the interviewer may be able to explore a given area of the study in depth. He or she may leave the interview with important ideas that could lead to improvements in the study design.

Personal Contact Approach

The face-to-face or telephone interview is a fundamental form of collecting information from subjects; the investigator elicits information directly from respondents by asking them a series of questions and records their responses on a questionnaire.

There are three broad classifications of interviews: the standardized or closed-ended, the unstandardized or open-ended, and the semistandardized interview. In the first case the interviewer is held to the specific wording of the interview question schedule or the standardized tests being used. In the second case the interviewer is free to develop each situation in whatever way he or she deems most appropriate for the study's purpose. In the third case the researcher may have to ask a number of specific key questions, but is also free to probe beyond the answers to these questions.

Each of these types has its advantages and shortcomings. The standardized interview encourages uniformity in the behavior of the interviewer and makes it easier for other investigators to duplicate the interview situation. The unstandardized interview has the advantages of discovery: a skilled interviewer familiar with the study's goals may be stimulated by a respondent's answers to develop new ideas about the topic under study. Unconfined by the limits of a standardized interview, the investigator is free to explore such ideas and go beyond the original formulation of the problem. He or she has the flexibility to adapt the measurement instrument to whatever is most fruitful for a given respondent. The semistandardized interview seeks to combine the advantages of each of the other types.

Conducting the Interview

Regardless of which approach is used, an interview requires certain basic steps. Introduce yourself and explain why you are doing the research. Assure the respondent of his or her anonymity. Allow the respondent the right to terminate the interview at any time. Tell the respondent how long the interview will take and keep within that limit. Obtain the respondent's informed consent.

A good interviewer really listens to the respondent, remaining nonjudgmental or neutral regarding beliefs, attitudes, or views the respondent expresses. Do not inhibit responses or create hostility in the respondent by betraying your own attitudes. Try to record, in his or her own words, the respondent's answers to open-ended questions; summarizing what has been said may distort the respondent's meaning. Inform the respondent that you are taking the time to record the answers accurately and fairly. After completing the interview, quickly review the answers and ask for clarification from the respondent on any items that remain unclear.

Refusals

Despite the best efforts of the researcher, not all potential respondents will agree to be interviewed. While interview refusals are not generally considered to be sources of significant bias in social research, for the gerontologist the case may be quite different, as high rates of interview refusals have been reported in studies with older populations (Atchley, 1969). In investigating the characteristics of a sample of retired women who refused to be interviewed, Atchley found that they tend to be in poor health, see themselves as lacking sufficient income, have fewer social contacts, and prefer to be alone. Keep in mind that high rates of refusal may mean that a bias has been introduced into a sample.

Paper-and-Pencil Approaches

The mail questionnaire has long been a popular type of survey instrument. At one time, because of such drawbacks as the possible lack of response and the inability of the researcher to check the responses given, the mailed questionnaire was viewed as an economical but less desirable alternative to face-to-face interviewing. Recently, however, some questions have been raised regarding the supposed superiority of face-to-face interviewing as a data collection technique (Dillman, 1978; Leinbach, 1982).

The mail questionnaire provides easier contact with persons living in remote areas. Further, it often elicits responses from people who might refuse a personal interview. Finally, interviewer bias, a potential problem in a personal interview situation, is virtually eliminated.

Transmittal Letter

"Covering letters prove to be one of the few direct opportunities for influencing respondents and motivating them to reply" (Linsky, 1975, p. 92). Therefore the impact of the transmittal letter used by a researcher must be carefully evaluated. Investigating the different effects on response rates of a form letter and a computer-generated personal letter, Matteson (1974) discovered that the computer-generated letter elicited a significantly higher response rate than the form letter.

Color of Questionnaire

Questionnaire color appears to have a limited impact on response rates. Matteson (1974) found that response rates for individuals receiving a computer-generated cover letter were not affected by questionnaire color. On the other hand, when a form letter accompanied the questionnaire, the colored form elicited a 23 percent greater response rate than the white.

Use of Deadlines

A study on the effects of a deadline on mail survey responses (Nevin and Ford, 1976) found that deadline dates did not stimulate a more immediate response, but did seem to decrease the rate of returns following the deadline date. A longer deadline date had a significantly favorable influence on overall response rates. Since the deadlines specified in the cover letters were five days, seven days, and nine days, these findings are obviously limited.

Postcard Enclosure

Enclosing a postcard with the questionnaire increases response rates. Respondents are asked to sign the card and to return it when they return the questionnaire. This ensures anonymity of the individual responses, yet allows the researcher to identify and follow up nonrespondents. Linsky (1975), reporting on two descriptive studies utilizing this technique, indicates that both attributed their response rates of 82 percent and 89 percent to the inclusion of postcards.

Follow-up

Follow-up letters or postcards sent to those who initially fail to respond result in additional responses.

Linsky (1975) found: "In a careful study based on a large sample, 58 percent of those who received a postcard follow-up reminder eventually responded, compared to only 37 percent of a matched sample who received only the original communication and questionnaire" (Linsky, 1975, p. 85). Since postcard follow-ups appear to be effective in stimulating response, their low cost recommends their use. Although more expensive, some studies use a telephone or personal follow-up, especially if postcards have produced only limited response.

Response Rates

Despite the fact that the mail questionnaire generally elicits low initial response rates, it appears to be an effective device where the older population is concerned. Cottrell and Atchley (1969) report that when questionnaires were mailed to women who had been interviewed in a previous study and to women who had refused an interview, virtually all of the respondents who had agreed to be interviewed returned the mail questionnaire. Furthermore, *half of the women who had refused to be interviewed also returned the mail questionnaire.* Cottrell and Atchley suggest that older people are unusual in their willingness to complete and return a mail questionnaire. Factors that lead older respondents to refuse interviews—feeling threatened by an interviewer, uncertainty regarding the focus of an interview, lack of time to devote to an interview—are circumvented through use of a mail questionnaire.

Sample Size Based on Estimated Response

The usual response rate for the initial mailing of a questionnaire is about 50 percent, sometimes less. The response rate goes to above 70 percent if there is a follow-up campaign. The usual follow-up is to send a postcard or letter asking the respondent to fill in the questionnaire and mail it as soon as possible. If there is still no response, a second copy of the questionnaire is sometimes sent. In some cases, a follow-up is done by telephone in which the respondent is interviewed and the questionnaire is filled out by the researcher. The response rate for face-to-face or telephone surveys is closer to 80 percent.

The acceptable response rate for a survey varies, but as a rule a response rate of over 70 percent of the sample is adequate. The usual practice for ensuring an acceptable response is to oversample. For a sample of 100 people from a pool of 2,000, send questionnaires to 150 people. A response rate of 70 percent will yield 105 responses. Since some of the questionnaires are incomplete or recorded in error, and since some of the respondents fail to qualify, this leaves a sample of close to the desired 100. A special interest in including a certain type of individual in the sample, such as elderly rural persons, requires oversampling persons in that category to ensure sufficient numbers in the final sample.

The Mailed Questionnaire

Because the respondent to a questionnaire can judge the study only by what he or she sees, the questionnaire design must be as impressive and attractive as possible to produce adequate returns.

Here are several concrete suggestions for designing a questionnaire package:

1. *Keep the questionnaire brief.* Rarely are very extensive bodies of data secured through the use of a questionnaire. Questionnaires that require more than 15 to 25 minutes to complete do not elicit many returns, particularly among older respondents with physical or mental handicaps.

2. *Not all respondents can be reached by questionnaires.* While questionnaires have been used for a range of populations, not all respond equally well. Persons with low levels of literacy, who are socially or economically disadvantaged, or who have physical or mental handicaps often exhibit poor response rates. Age *per se,* however, *does not seem to affect response rates.*

3. *Identify the auspices.* Indicate who is sponsoring or sanctioning the study. The cover letter which accompanies the questionnaire should explain the nature of the organization sanctioning the study as well as the one carrying it out. Nothing should appear to be hidden or suspicious. Include the name and telephone number of a contact person.

4. *Explain why the study is being done.* The cover letter should explain why the information requested is needed. The information need not be elaborate, but should be sufficient to explain the purpose of the questions.

5. *Urge the respondent to answer.* Beyond mentioning the groups authorizing and carrying out the study and the need for the research, the cover letter must encourage the respondent to participate. An array of appeals have been used by social researchers. Some have included payment for completing the questionnaire. Others have promised to provide services such as reports. In general, an altruistic appeal appears to be the most effective. A statement that "this information is needed to improve the status of older Americans" is likely to have more appeal than a token payment for completing an instrument.

6. *Include clear directions.* Beginning users of questionnaires tend to overrate the care with which respondents fill them out. The researcher should seek to remove as many blocks to completion of the instrument as possible. Demands on respondents' time and attention should be minimal and directions should be few and simple in both the cover letter and the questionnaire. Pay special attention to layout. Make sure the questionnaire is easy to read and answer. Make instructions clear and concise.

7. *Emphasize the guarantee of anonymity.* While few questionnaires ask for information that is very private, respondents ordinarily will not answer if they have any reason to suspect that information about them will be made public. The cover letter and any other

descriptive information therefore should include a guarantee of the respondents' anonymity. There should be no requests for names nor any questions that are so detailed as to make identification easy, such as street addresses. Make it clear that respondents can refuse to answer any question.

> *Rule of thumb 4.1:* Recognize the advantages and shortcomings of the paper-and-pencil and the personal contact interview approaches to data collection and choose accordingly.

Instruments

Let's move from administrative considerations to considerations of measurement. As Table 4.1 shows, instruments can vary in complexity and structure. Problems of test construction, reliability, and validity intrude here. When we speak of instruments, we also usually picture people answering the questions. *Instrument* here will refer to measures of either people or other kinds of cases. The measure may be a checklist or a formatted form used to analyze a meeting or to content-analyze textbooks.

Instruments can include both open or open-ended questions and closed or fixed-alternative questions. The open or open-ended question does not provide a list of alternative answers; for example,

What are the best years of a person's life? _____

Why do you feel this way?_____

Any other reasons?_____

The closed or fixed-alternative question, on the other hand, limits the respondent to a choice among specific alternatives; for example,

> If you had to choose, what would you say are the best years of a person's life?

Teens _____

20's _____

30's _____

40's _____

50's _____

60's	_____
70's	_____
Other (specify)	_____
Not sure	_____

Each type of question has its advantages. The open question, because it puts very few words in the mouth of the respondent, more effectively reveals the respondent's own definition of the situation, whatever it is. If the respondent does not understand the question or grossly misunderstands, this will be revealed in answers to open questions. In addition, the phrasing of the open question is closer to that used in ordinary conversation and as a result may encourage spontaneity on the part of the respondent as well as reinforce motivation to communicate effectively and thoroughly.

The closed question is analogous to the leading questions that are not permissible in most aspects of courtroom procedure. The elderly respondent especially may react negatively to fixed-alternative questions because they preclude highly individualized answers. The respondent may even feel that such procedures are inaccurate and thus the value of the interview is questionable. On the other hand, the fixed-alternative or closed question produces greater uniformity among respondents along the specific dimensions in which the investigator is interested. The investigator is assured that he or she will be able to obtain relatively complete information from the entire sample about the specific phenomena with which he or she is concerned. Many answers to open questions are not useful in testing specific hypotheses because they constitute responses along many different dimensions, a problem the fixed-alternative format avoids.

There is also a practical consideration related to the use of closed questions; it is considerably less expensive and time-consuming to process answers to closed rather than open questions. As a researcher investigating topics concerned with aging, you need to create the best instrument for data collection that takes time and resource limitations into account.

The "Why" Question

The "Why?" question, a type of open question, has been the subject of particular attention from some social scientists; one procedure for asking and analyzing such questions is called reason analysis. The approach involves a careful assessment, through pretesting or preliminary interviews, of the range of possible reasons that might be given in response to a particular "Why?" question.

Through pretesting, for example, the interviewer might identify four reasons why an older person would want to work, e.g., for income, for status, to pass the time, to boost his self worth. During the actual interviewing, he or she might follow the general "Why?" question with a series of questions designed to explore whichever of these four are omitted by the respondent. In addition, the interviewer might attempt to describe the choices through time and differentiate specific decisions from more general ones. Finally, he or she would attempt to put together all the pieces of information in an outline of the dynamic relationships among all these factors.

Reason analysis provides an illustration of what is known as the funnel technique in questionnaire- and interview-schedule design. Many studies include a range of questions, some open and some closed, and the investigator must put them in order. In the funnel technique initial questions are open and subsequent questions are more specific and generally closed. Reason analysis may begin with the general "Why?" question and then proceed to the specifics of the choosing process. This technique permits an analysis of the respondent's spontaneous frame of reference while assuring that data will be collected from each respondent on each of the desired topics.

Wording and Question Order

Phrase questions in a clear and neutral way when constructing an instrument. This is of special importance when an interview deals with sensitive topics in which an answer might have a very high or very low degree of social desirability. Among the guidelines developed for wording questions are the following:

1. Indicate that other people have what might ordinarily be considered a socially undesirable attitude or characteristic (for example, "Most people have thought about suicide at one time or another.").
2. Attempt to achieve some balance of social desirability among choices (for example, "Some political leaders believe . . . while other political leaders believe . . .").
3. Structure the question in such a way that the respondent is assumed to possess the socially undesirable characteristic, thus placing on him or her the burden of denial (for example, "How much are your monthly payments?" might be preferable to "Have you purchased anything on the installment plan during the last two years?").
4. Substitute euphemisms for more value-loaded language (for example, *training methods* might be superior to *methods of discipline* in discussing child-rearing). And, in general, try to avoid words

that convey a high degree of social desirability or undesirability. At the same time, take care not to be vague.

5. Before asking the respondent to express criticism of something, provide an opportunity for voicing praise.

6. Structure the question in such a way that the respondent will be able to admit a lack of knowledge gracefully (for example, "Do you have any feelings about how X should behave?" might be preferable to "How do you feel that X should behave?"). The funnel technique also provides a mechanism for achieving this effect.

Some special considerations must be taken into account when surveying the elderly. Many older persons have limited English-speaking ability. If you are preparing face-to-face or paper-and-pencil questionnaires, you may want to prepare them in the native language of your respondents. The usual technique is to translate your questionnaire from English into the primary language of your respondents, say Vietnamese. To check the accuracy of the translation, have a third party, not the original translator, translate the Vietnamese version back into English. The two English versions should be quite close. Any wide variances should be corrected by new translations.

In interviews, using interviewers fluent in the language of the group members is often desirable. In some cases, family members may be used as translators, but some precision is lost and the respondent will probably be less candid in giving answers to a family member. In working with ethnic elderly, use interviewers from the same ethnic group or with an affinity to members of the group.

When dealing with the ethnic elderly, an ethnographic technique may be used to produce questions that reflect the everyday language of the respondent. Rural elderly who have lived their lives as mountain-folk use different terms than their peers in the valley or flatlands. The gerontologist, the sociologist, and the transportation expert all use different definitions of the term *mobility*.

To find out the meaning of everyday terms used to describe activities, the researcher asks a respondent to describe a behavior in his or her own language—as if the researcher had no knowledge of the respondent's way of life. In mountain areas, for example, *goin' to a holler* means making a visit to a family living in a clearing or holler. The meaning of the word *friend* will differ among ethnic groups. By probing the meaning of words used in everyday speech, the researcher gains the information needed to construct a set of questions that reflect the actual language of respondents from different ethnic groups. When several ethnic or regional groups are included in the same survey, terms that might be ambiguous to one or more of these groups can be explained by a clarifying clause or phrase.

The criteria used for determining question order are based on the possible effects a given question might have on subsequent ones. Some of the rules of thumb in general use are the following:

1. On a given topic, general questions should usually precede specific ones. This advice is in accord with the funnel technique in which initial questions are open and subsequent questions are closed. If, for example, respondents are asked if the party leader's age is one of the reasons for political party preference before they are asked what the reasons for preference are, they might be tempted to include the leader's age among the reasons in answering the more general question.

2. The entire sequence of questions should follow some logical order, so that the respondent is not called upon to make abrupt transitions and so that the sequence aids the respondent in answering the questions. One common logical order is the time sequence, in which the respondent is asked about the past, the present, and the future in that order. Other possibilities are to move from the specific to the abstract or from the familiar to the unfamiliar.

3. Some questions are such that they might exert an important effect on all subsequent questions. For a given study, questions about income or religion might so antagonize a respondent that the remainder of his or her responses would be greatly affected. Such questions, if asked at all, should be included as late as possible in the instrument.

> *Rule of thumb 4.2:* Regardless of which format is selected, rules of clarity, question order, and respondent motivation must be followed.

Original Versus Preconstructed Measures

At some point in the process of conducting a primary research study the investigator must ask a hard question: Should I develop my own scales or indices to measure my key variables, or should I use previously constructed ones? Inexperienced and even veteran researchers tend to prefer constructing all elements of their questionnaire or interview schedule from scratch. After all, they reason, if this is an original investigation, then all data-gathering tools should be original; isn't that what primary research is all about? No, it is not. Primary research means collecting and analyzing original *data* using the most powerful and appropriate data collection instruments; considerable time and expense can be saved by using already validated and standardized scales.

An investigator can pick and choose from the literally thousands of existing scales and indices for measuring social variables. Avoiding these options may mean unnecessary expenditure of limited time and resources. Furthermore, creating an original scale works against the replication and accumulation of research findings.

Standard Tests and Scales

Tests have several characteristics that set them apart from other measures. These characteristics may be useful if the test measures a concept of interest. Tests are designed to be

1. reliable, i.e., to give the same results each time a subject is tested in a short interval
2. valid, i.e., to measure what they say they are measuring and nothing else
3. scaled, i.e., to have *total* scores that make conceptual sense
4. normed (sometimes), i.e., to have a built-in means of comparing one respondent with everyone else in his or her group
5. item-analyzed (sometimes), i.e., checked for range of difficulty and homogeneity

While all measures should have the first two qualities, few are checked systematically. The norms are handy, especially if they permit comparison with older respondents. Not all groups of answers can be added together; tests are structured so that several items can be combined in a total score.

> *Rule of thumb 4.3:* Before choosing the scales or indices to incorporate into your data collection instrument, conduct a state-of-the-art review.[1]

> *Rule of thumb 4.4:* Where feasible, previously constructed and tested scales and indices are preferred to investigator-constructed ones. If no appropriate measures are available, construct your own, applying the same guidelines employed in the rest of the instrument and referring to test-construction manuals as needed.

---

[1] For an excellent inventory of commonly used scales and indices see Delbert C. Miller, *Handbook of Research Design and Social Measurement* (New York: David McKay, latest edition). Tests usable with elders can be found by references in journals reporting research done with the elderly.

Summary

The data collection instrument is the main vehicle for obtaining information in a primary research study. In developing the instrument the investigator should keep the following precepts in mind:

Rule 4.1: Recognize the advantages and shortcomings of the questionnaire and the interview approaches to data collection, and choose accordingly.

Rule 4.2: Regardless of which form is selected, rules of clarity, question order, and respondent motivation must be followed.

Rule 4.3: Before choosing the scale or indices to incorporate into your data collection instrument, conduct a state-of-the-art review.

Rule 4.4: Where feasible, previously constructed and tested scales and indices are preferred to investigator-constructed ones. If no appropriate measures are available, construct your own, applying the same guidelines employed in the rest of the instrument and referring to test-construction manuals as needed.

References

Atchley, R. C. Respondents vs. Refusers in an Interview Study of Women: Analysis of Selected Characteristics. *Journal of Gerontology,* 1969, *24,* 42–47.

Cottrell, F., and Atchley, R. C. *Women in Retirement: A Preliminary Report.* Oxford, Ohio: Scripps Foundation for Research in Population Problems, 1969.

Deutscher, I. *What We Say/What We Do.* Glenview, Ill: Scott, Foresman, 1973.

Dillman, D. A. *Mail and Telephone Surveys.* New York: John Wiley and Sons, 1978.

Dohrenwendt, B. S. Sources of Refusals in Surveys. *Public Opinion Quarterly,* 1968, *32,* 81.

George, L. K., and Bearon, B. *Quality of Life in Older Persons: Meaning and Measurement.* New York: Human Sciences Press, 1978.

Groves, R. M., and Kahn, R. L. *Surveys by Telephone.* New York: Academic Press, 1978.

Haperman, P., and Sheinberg, J. Education Reported in Interviews. *Public Opinion Quarterly,* 1966, *30,* 299.

Leinbach, R. M. Alternatives to the Face-to-Face Interview for Collecting Gerontological Needs Assessment Data. *The Gerontologist,* 1982, *22*(1), 78–82.

Linsky, A. S. Stimulating Responses to Mailed Questionnaires: A Review. *Public Opinion Quarterly,* 1975, *39*(1), 82–101.

Mangen, D., and Peterson, D. *Research Instruments in Social Gerontology.* (Vol. 1). Minneapolis: University of Minnesota Press, 1982.

Matteson, M. T. Type of Transmittal Letter and Questionnaire Color as Two Variables Influencing Response Rates in a Mail Survey. *Journal of Applied Psychology,* 1974, 59(4), 535–536.

Nevin, J. R., and Ford, N. M. Effects of a Deadline and a Veiled Threat on Mail Survey Responses. *Journal of Applied Psychology,* 1976, 61(1), 116–118.

RMC Research Corporation. *The Older American Status and Needs Assessment Questionnaire.* Contract No. HEW-OS-74-15. Bethesda, Md., 1975.

Chapter

5

Data
Analysis

Research has been defined as a systematic collection of information leading to meaningful, replicable results. Data are elements of information. The researcher must analyze data to interpret research findings and attach meaning to them. Data analysis might consist of summarizing research results or discerning complex patterns of causal relationships. In either case, the goal is to impose meaning on raw information and to predict future events based on discovered patterns of causality or association.

The interpretive biases of the investigator necessarily limit the meanings that can be found. In a field such as gerontology where the state of the art often prohibits the theory-based generation of data,

Decision-Making Process for Reduction and Analysis of Data

1. Which style of analysis is demanded by my design choice?	Table 1.2
2. Which style of analysis is demanded by my sampling choice?	Figure 3.1
3. Which style of analysis is demanded by my measure choice (my type of data)?	Table 5.4
4. Is my purpose to statistically summarize descriptive data?	Page 88 *ff.*
5. Is my purpose to statistically test interrelationships or commonalities?	Page 96 *ff.*
6. Is my purpose to statistically test causes or group differences?	Page 103 *ff.*
7. How can I get more information from these data using statistics?	Page 105 *ff.*

the researcher's choice of analytic method becomes extremely important; the future course of research on aging in a particular area might be governed by first interpretations. The choice of analytic method is based on many factors: the nature of the research question, the system chosen to number or scale the data, whether causal or associational information is needed, the number of variables included in any one analysis. Unless research is confined to a one-case study or state-of-the-art review, one analysis is seldom sufficient to derive all possible meaning from a data set; some quantitative description complements the qualitative description of results.

In this chapter some very basic steps in analysis are outlined. Several sophisticated analytic approaches are also suggested (but not described in detail) so that the reader might explore some newer approaches which are especially useful in handling data from gerontological studies. If the reader is already familiar with basic analytic procedures he or she might go directly to the subsection on "Non-ratio Data."

Basic Analytic Methods

Common question: What do I do with all this information I've gathered?

Better question: How can I summarize trends and variations in my data in the most meaningful way given a particular scaling or number system?

Once the design and data-gathering steps detailed in the previous chapters have been completed, the researcher will have a large quantity of data or items of information. Since numerical data by themselves are meaningless and since large amounts of qualitative or numerical data are unwieldy, the information must be (1) reduced, (2) manipulated or transformed, and (3) interpreted. Data recording the number of years of school completed for every person 65 years of age and over in a particular state, for example, constitute an enormous amount of information incomprehensible in raw form. Such data are more useful when the average educational level has been calculated or when relevant categories provide some structure (e.g., 0–6 years of school, 7–12 years, 13–17 years, over 17 years).

Reduction

Data reduction consists of clustering information into categories or of computing statistics. Statistics, generally categorized as either descriptive or inferential, are used to evaluate and communicate the results of the study. *Descriptive statistics* describe information the researcher has gathered. They can be numbers, percentages, averages, measures of dispersion or of relationships between numbers. *Inferential statistics* go beyond the data to describe the universe from which they were gathered; i.e., they proceed from the sample to the population and can be used to describe relationships within the data set. If a sample of older persons in upstate New York report visiting their physician an average of twice during the last year, the problem is to estimate the corresponding mean number of visits for the total population of older persons in that region. Since relations between the sample and the population are known, the researcher can judge the importance of effects found in the data. Looking at other scores, he or she can infer relationships which provide reasons for the number of visits.

Manipulation

To understand the ways in which data can be manipulated or transformed, we first need to recognize that data are expressed with focus on either qualitative or quantitative characteristics. Qualitative analyses distinguish one class of items from another, such as men from women, blue-eyed persons from brown-eyed persons, or Protestants from Catholics, by differentiating quality or kind. Quantitative measures (such as age, health status, educational attainment, or income) vary in magnitude. Quantitative measurement is obtained by (1) direct enumeration, (2) use of a standard unit by which items are measured (e.g., years, dollars, feet), (3) use of an index or behavioral equivalent measure (e.g., the Bradburn Affect Scale), and (4) ranking, in situations where classes can be distinguished from one another as greater or lesser but the amount of difference between ranks is not known or not standardized (e.g., subjective measures of social class membership).

Four fundamentally different but equally important ways of analyzing qualitative or quantitative data are through (1) frequency distributions, (2) central tendency, (3) dispersion, and (4) relationship.

Frequency Distributions

Determining frequency distributions entails separating variables into mutually exclusive classes and counting the number in each class. Classes may be based on qualities or on scores of some kind. The technique summarizes a number of observations and provides orderly statements about the data. Table 5.1 shows a hypothetical distribution of the religious affiliations of older persons. It shows that the overwhelming majority (36 out of 37) report some religious affiliation and that the Protestant church is the most frequently reported category. This example illustrates a univariable or single variable frequency distribution. Like any research field, gerontology is primarily concerned with bivariate (two variable) and multivariate distributions and relationships. Like the univariate cases, multivariate distributions serve to reduce data and suggest relations between variables. See how concisely Table 5.2 summarizes a reasonably large amount of data.

If adequately labeled and properly presented, a bivariate or multivariate distribution chart is easily read and interpreted. First check the table heading, the row and column captions, and any footnotes. Include important information such as the nature of the sample, the location and time of sampling, and the name of the sampler, if different from the investigator. The reader should note the row and column totals as well as the individual cell frequencies so that patterns can be discerned. Table 5.2 relies on a combination of raw numbers and percentages to present information, since using percentages and ratios simplifies comparisons.

Percentages must be used properly. Two cautions are in order: (1) percentages can make qualitative data appear to be quantitative, and (2), percentages are susceptible to misuse if important facts are eliminated. One never presents a table of percentages without also showing the actual numbers they represent. The fact that three out of a total of only four people interviewed favored more financial assistance to low income elderly becomes very misleading when stated as "three out of every four" or "75 percent" because the reader might assume the base was 10,000 respondents rather than four.

Analyzing Ratio and Nonratio Data: Overview

Studies of the aging can have two kinds of results: those based on ratio-scale data and those based on nonratio-scale data. Ratio-scale data are expressed in numbers that have equal intervals and a true

Table 5.1
Frequency Distribution of Religious Affiliation

Religious affiliation	Frequency
Protestant	20
Catholic	10
Jewish	4
Other	2
None	1

Table 5.2
Average Duration of Unemployment for Men and Women 45 and Over, 1975
(in thousands)

Sex and age variables	Total		Less than 5 weeks		5–14 weeks		15–26 weeks		27 weeks and over		Average (mean duration in weeks)
	No.	%	No.	%	No.	%	No.	%	No.	%	
Male											
Total, 16–44	4,385	100	1,459	33.3	1,399	31.9	776	17.1	750	17.1	15.3
45–54	501	100	138	27.5	154	30.7	93	18.6	116	23.2	18.9
55–64	300	100	79	26.3	90	30.0	52	17.3	78	26.0	20.1
65 years and over	103	100	27	26.2	23	22.3	20	19.4	32	21.1	24.2
Female											
Total, 16–44	3,445	100	1,435	41.7	1,053	30.6	513	14.9	443	12.9	12.6
45–54	394	100	132	33.5	118	30.0	68	17.3	76	19.3	16.4
55–64	216	100	74	34.3	57	26.4	35	16.2	51	23.6	18.1
65 years and over	52	100	12	23.1	14	26.9	8	15.4	18	34.6	25.1

Source: U.S. Department of Labor, Bureau of Labor Statistics, *Employment and Earnings*, Vol. 22, No. 7, January 1976, Table 15 (modified), p. 144.

zero reference point. Nonratio-scale data are expressed in numbers that lack a zero point (see Table 5.3). For example, elders may be categorized as *retired, other unemployed,* and *employed*; this is a nominal (nonratio) scale. They rank living alone first, living with a friend second, and living in a home third, which gives an ordinal (nonratio) scale. They visit a senior center five times per month, on the average (ratio-scale datum). Few types of relational analysis commonly taught apply to the nominal and ordinal data described above. Texts often spend time only on T-tests, ANOVAs, and other techniques suitable for ratio-scale data.

The best designed studies on aging include results based on both ratio-scale and nonratio-scale data. Table 5.4 outlines statistical tests usable with nominal (category), ordinal (rank), and ratio-scale data tests. The tests usually can be performed in fifteen minutes using hand calculations. Different tests apply in each situation depending on data type, number of groups responding, similarities and differ-

Table 5.3
Data Types

Type of data	Expressed in	Example	Meaning of numbers
Nominal	Categories	Married = 1 Single = 2 Divorced = 3	Numbers are only names; there is no true zero; 3 is not more than 1; 3 is not ranked higher than 1.
Ordinal	Ranks	1st choice = 1 2nd choice = 2 3rd choice = 3	Numbers represent order; no true zero; interval between 1 and 2 need not be equal to interval between 2 and 3.
Interval	Ranks with equal intervals	Five-point scale, ranging from *satisfied* to *dissatisfied*	Numbers represent order and equal intervals and ranks; no true zero.
Ratio	Ranks with equal separations, equal intervals and zero	Cost of an item or number of doctor visits	Numbers represent orderly ranks with equal intervals and a true zero.

Note: Data type restricts choice of statistics for analysis. See Table 4.2 for statistics usable with each data type for each analytic purpose.

Table 5.4
Appropriate Inferential Statistical Tests[1]

| Data type | 1 group | Contrasting group results | | | | Relating two measures for the same group |
| | | 2 groups | | Many groups | | |
		Related*	Independent**	Related*	Independent**	
Nominal	Binomial or two Chi-square single group	McNemar test	Fisher exact probability Chi-square	Cochran test	Chi-square	Contingency coefficient Typal analysis
Ordinal	Kolmogorov-Smirnov One sample runs test	Sign Wilcoxin	Median test Mann-Whitney U Kolmogorov-Smirnov Wald-Wolfowitz Moses	Friedman two-way ANOVA	Extension of median Kruskel-Wallis one-way ANOVA	Spearman rho Kendal tau Kendal partial Kendal concordance coefficient
Ratio (or interval[2])		T-test for related groups	T-test for independent samples	Analysis of covariance	Analysis of variance	Pearson correlation coefficient Multiple regression Factor analyses Discriminant function analysis Path analysis Canonical correlation

*Related: same subjects (or cases appear in more than one group).   **Independent: each group has different subjects (or cases).
[1] Each type of data may be analyzed using tests in its own row or in any row above it.
[2] Although in theory only ratio data can be analyzed with the tests listed, in practice interval data are also used with no apparent effect on results.

Source: S. Siegel, *Nonparametric Statistics for the Behavioral Sciences* (New York: McGraw-Hill, 1956). Used by permission.

ences between groups (independence), and the research objective, which can be to test either (1) differences between groups or (2) the degree of similar response patterns on two measures for the same group.

To use Table 5.4, determine whether the data are nominal, ordinal, interval, or ratio. A given study may have several measures, each with a different type of data requiring different handling. Next, determine whether the goal is to (1) contrast different groups or (2) compare two different measures administered to the same group. If you are examining contrasts or differences, choose techniques for two-group or multigroup analysis and utilize a contrast statistical test to see if the obtained difference could have happened by chance. In the case of a single group, look for score patterns not likely to occur by chance alone. If you are looking for the degree of similarity, use a statistic describing degree of association to determine whether results could have occurred by chance. If results are not due to chance, interpretation that an orderly pattern exists in the data is appropriate.

> *Rule of thumb 5.1:* Don't discard difficult data until you have explored analytic methods specifically designed for nonratio-scale data.

Central Tendency

A second important descriptor of data sets is central tendency, the typical score of a variable. The mode, median, and arithmetic mean are the three central tendency measures used in gerontological research. The mode (usable with all types of data) is the mutually exclusive category occurring with greatest frequency. In Table 5.5 the mode average is "one visit to a physician in the last year." The median average, usable with any type of data except the nominal, is the category or point above or below which half of the total frequency lies ("two visits in the last year"). The mean or arithmetic average, usable with interval or ratio data, is the sum of all the scores divided by the total number of scores (52 ÷ 28, or 1.9 visits to a physician in the last year).

Each measure has its own advantages and disadvantages. The median average is not affected by extreme scores and can be used to measure both numbered and rank-ordered variables. The main advantages of the mode average are the ease with which it can be computed and its applicability to nonratio data. The mean average has wider statistical application and can be manipulated in more ways than can the mode or median. The mean is also the most stable of the three measures in a sampling sense; means from two samples of the same population are more likely to be closer in value than are their corresponding modes or medians. On the other hand, the mean's

Table 5.5
Number of Visits to a Physician in the Past Year

Physician visits in last year (x)	Frequency (f)	Frequency of visits (fx)
5	1	5
4	3	12
3	6	18
2	5	10
1	7	7
0	6	0
	28	52

applicability is limited to quantitative interval or ratio-scale variables and it is unduly affected by extreme scores.

Dispersion

Averages describe typical values in an array, but dispersion more completely describes a distribution. There is an obvious difference between a 65-year-old male whose resting pulse rate measures 68, 66, and 70 at three different times and his contemporary whose resting pulse rate is 58, 68, and 78 at three different times. The average scores are identical, but the spread of scores differs dramatically. Average deviation and standard deviation are two commonly used statistics which measure dispersion. The range of scores in a distribution (percentile range, interquartile range) and variance (derived by squaring the standard deviation) are also used. Generally the standard deviation and the variance are the preferred measures, since they are the basis for a number of statistical procedures and are readily manipulated; however, they can only be used with ratio-type data. The source books listed at the end of this chapter contain procedures for calculating measures of dispersion.

Relationships

Common question: How can I prove that two variables are related?

Better question: What are all the ways in which I can describe the noncausal associations among my variables within the limits of my nominal, ordinal, interval, or ratio-scaling system?

Noncausal Association Among Variables

No study (except the exploratory type) should proceed without a hypothesis or best guess about the possible outcome. If a hypothesis concerning the cause of a phenomenon is not possible, then estimates about which event will vary along with the phenomenon of interest should be proposed.

A number of statistical procedures are available to determine whether two variables covary as hypothesized and whether the association between variables is significant in a data set. If two variables are directly related, then increases or decreases in variable *A* are paralleled in variable *B*. If an increase in variable *A* is associated with a *decrease* in variable *B* or vice versa, the relationship is an inverse one. Association between two variables does not mean that one set causes the other; the two variables have simply been found to vary together systematically, so that known measurements of one help predict measurements of the other.

Every inferential statistical test is designed to evaluate some hypothesis by comparing test or experiment results with outcomes that would be expected by chance. Correlations test hypotheses suggesting that two or more variables change simultaneously. The correlations coefficient (r) for quantitative or ratio variables and the Spearman rho (ρ) for rank order or interval variables are two commonly used measures of association. Other measures of correlation are listed in Table 5.4. All yield a value between -1 and $+1$, with 0 indicating no relations between variables and the two extremes indicating a perfect inverse relation (-1) or a perfect direct relation ($+1$). Correlations of 0.5 (or -0.5) are considered strong and those above 0.75 (or below -0.75) are considered very strong. Squaring the correlation gives an estimate of the proportion of a variable that is explained by a particular association. For example, if a first blood pressure reading (BP #1) and a second blood pressure reading (BP #2) are correlated for twenty individuals, BP #1 and BP #2 may be found to be related with a value of 0.70. Squaring that value gives 0.49, suggesting that about half of the variability in BP #2 can be predicted by knowing BP #1 scores and vice versa. (The remaining variability [i.e., dispersion of scores] may be due to inaccuracy of the instrument reading pressures, to patient nervousness at one reading or the other but not both, to differences in resting or exercise before one reading, etc.).

When all possible correlations are calculated among a number of variables, they are usually presented in a matrix. An example of a correlation matrix, intercorrelations of scores representing problem areas concerning the aged, is presented in Table 5.6.

Once the correlations have been calculated, we can determine the degree to which correlations tend to cluster. This can be done by

Table 5.6
Correlations Among Problems the Elderly Face

	Income	Health	Housing	Transportation	Education	Age discrimination	Employment	Spare time	Crime	Nutrition	Consumer business problems
Income	1.00	.60	.48	.47	.27	.34	.34	.34	.38	.57	.31
Health	.60	1.00	.56	.47	.32	.37	.35	.37	.38	.51	.37
Housing	.48	.56	1.00	.51	.36	.40	.41	.44	.41	.53	.41
Transportation	.47	.47	.51	1.00	.30	.32	.30	.39	.38	.52	.32
Education	.27	.32	.36	.30	1.00	.39	.44	.39	.29	.28	.36
Age discrimination	.34	.37	.40	.32	.39	1.00	.58	.37	.34	.34	.42
Employment	.34	.35	.41	.30	.44	.58	1.00	.44	.34	.35	.42
Spare time	.34	.37	.44	.39	.39	.37	.44	1.00	.39	.40	.37
Crime	.38	.38	.41	.38	.29	.34	.34	.34	1.00	.44	.33
Nutrition	.57	.51	.53	.52	.28	.34	.35	.40	.44	1.00	.43
Consumer business problems	.31	.37	.41	.32	.36	.42	.42	.37	.33	.43	1.00

Note: denotes highest value in column
 denotes highest value in row, if that is different from highest value in column

Source: U.S. Department of Health, Education and Welfare, Administration on Aging, Assessing the Status and Needs of Older Americans: Utilization Manual (Washington, D.C.: G.P.O., 1974), p. 37.

a variety of cluster analysis techniques. The most expeditious and simple technique is typal analysis, which groups variables that are relatively highly correlated into clusters. This process is quite straightforward. The correlation matrix for all variables (in this case problems faced by the elderly) is calculated. The highest absolute value in each column (besides the correlation of the variable to itself) is circled. Then the highest of these circled values is found (0.60). The two variables that account for this correlation (in this matrix, *Income* and *Health*) are the basis for the first cluster. The correlations of each with other variables are examined to determine whether some third variable should be brought into the cluster because it is more highly correlated with either of the first two than with any other variable; in our example, *Nutrition* correlates more highly with *Income* than with any other category. If the third variable is brought in, then its other correlations are similarly examined to see if other variables belong in the cluster. This process continues until all appropriate variables have been brought into the first cluster. Then the procedure is repeated from the beginning, excluding those variables already in the first cluster, until the matrix has been exhausted.

Figure 5.1 shows the general kinds of clusters that can result from typal analysis, with double lines indicating the first pair of variables in the cluster. Type 1 clusters are simple two-variable clusters; depending on the specific problem areas involved, the incidence of problems in both areas may be reduced by treating only one. This strategy is also valid, although perhaps to a lesser extent, for Type 2 clusters. Type 2 clusters may include more than three variables as long as they are all intercorrelated. Type 3 clusters may be thought of as a chain: while variable 1 and variable 3 are both related to variable 2, they are not significantly related to each other (here we begin to get into multiprogram solutions to problems). Type 4 clusters can lead to programmatic changes because one problem area is clearly related to all of the others. Variations and combinations of these general types are common in the application of typal analysis.

Figure 5.2 shows the results of typal analysis applied to the preceding correlation matrix of problems of the elderly (Table 5.6). The double lines designate the variables that initiate the clusters. Two relatively independent clusters are formed; the first focuses on income, health, housing, and nutrition; the second centers around employment and age discrimination. Cluster 1 indicates the very close ties among income, health, housing, and nutrition. The centrality of nutrition in the cluster suggests that persons with nutritional problems have a large variety of other problems and that a multiprogram approach may be required to significantly improve the quality of their lives.

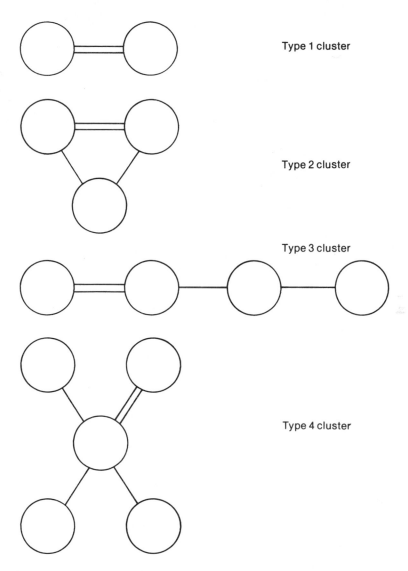

Figure 5.1   Types of Clusters That Will Result from Typal Analysis

Typal analysis does not produce an index of causal relations. Its primary function is to help the analyst understand how the variables relate to one another. The above example demonstrates how responses can be grouped together to better illustrate the various problems of the aged. This particular example also shows the relatively close interrelationships among problems of the elderly in the survey area and suggests that a multiprogram approach is necessary

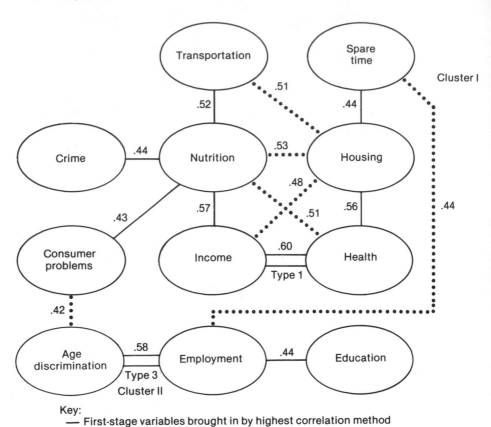

Figure 5.2   Typal Analysis of Correlation Matrix of Problems of the Elderly.

to improve the status of the elderly there. Furthermore, the analysis indicates that employment-related programs should be distinct from other social services.

Cluster analyses have been criticized for forcing some related variables to appear nonrelated. Perhaps more sophisticated techniques are needed for the overall picture of relatedness to emerge. One possibility is to change the rules on cluster inclusion; another is to indicate more links among clusters. A guiding theory helps the investigator make these important but somewhat arbitrary decisions by providing criteria along which to compare the hypotheses suggested by clustering. Absent an overall theory (a frequent situation in gerontology), the results of the initial exploratory sets of clusters must lend themselves to reasonable interpretation and be replicated (if possible) to prove that the entire exercise is not simply a fishing expedition. If several analyses show similar results *and* if replications are found in other samples *and* if interpretations make sense, the clustering will have led to meaningful conclusions.

As can be seen by returning to Table 5.4, there are other ways to describe patterns of association among correlated variables. When many variables are involved, Ns are large, and correlational data are available, several types of computer-assisted multivariate analyses might be performed to answer complex questions. *Factor analysis* answers the question "Can a smaller number of constructs be created from my overly large set of variables?" *Multiple regression analysis* answers the question "Can a differentially weighted combination of predictors (i.e., variable scores that, when known, permit an estimate of some other score or performance) be found which predicts better than any single variable would?" *Canonical correlation* answers the question "How should I best weight (1) variables in a group of predictors and (2) variables in a group of predicted statistically independent variables so that the correlation between the grouped variables is as high as it can be?" *Discriminant function analysis* answers the question "How can I differentially weight several variables to predict membership in a group?" Notice that in every case one differentially weights several variables so that they are better predictors than one variable would be. Notice too that if the investigator identifies the most important predictors (by examining the magnitude of the weightings), he or she will probably be better able to interpret the dynamics behind complex relationships. Each method is described below and a conceptual summary appears in Figure 5.3.

One method of identifying the most important predictor—factor analysis—uses a computer to assess which variables overlap in some higher-order (more inclusive) dimensions. For example, factor analyses of intelligence measure intelligence test scores by loading or clustering first on a general intelligence factor and again on a verbal or a numerical factor. Through examining factor loadings the researcher can interpret one test as really being three tests in one. The reasons why individuals succeed or fail on a test become clearer when underlying factors are known.

Multiple regression, another computer technique, allows the researcher to predict scores on one variable on the basis of scores from several other variables by using a formula that weights them in the set of predictors that works best. Multiple regression and factor analysis are useful when there are many variables in a set.

Through discriminant function analysis the researcher can predict a subject's membership in one of several groups on the basis of computer-weighted scores on other variables. For example, whether an individual belongs in the group of *users of senior centers* or in the group of *nonusers of senior centers* can best be predicted by considering the subject's age, sex, working status, and friends' attendance, with working status scores and friends' attendance scores weighted dou-

Figure 5.3   Complex Multivariate Analyses Reduce Unwieldy Sets of Measures

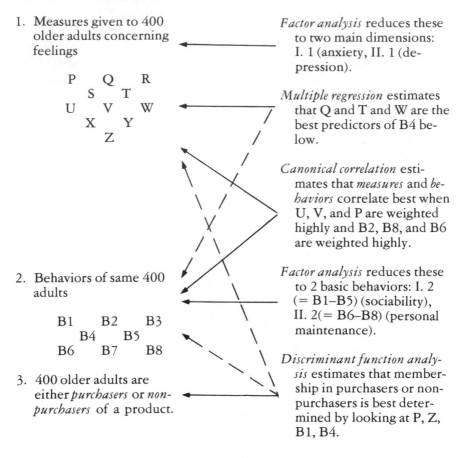

1. Measures given to 400 older adults concerning feelings

     P   Q   R
       S   T
     U   V   W
       X   Y
         Z

Factor analysis reduces these to two main dimensions: I. 1 (anxiety, II. 1 (depression).

Multiple regression estimates that Q and T and W are the best predictors of B4 below.

Canonical correlation estimates that *measures* and *behaviors* correlate best when U, V, and P are weighted highly and B2, B8, and B6 are weighted highly.

2. Behaviors of same 400 adults

     B1   B2   B3
       B4   B5
     B6   B7   B8

Factor analysis reduces these to 2 basic behaviors: I. 2 (= B1–B5) (sociability), II. 2(= B6–B8) (personal maintenance).

3. 400 older adults are either *purchasers* or *non-purchasers* of a product.

Discriminant function analysis estimates that membership in purchasers or non-purchasers is best determined by looking at P, Z, B1, B4.

ble. Prediction on the basis of all four variables is more accurate than prediction on the basis of just one variable.

Path analysis, a special multivariate technique, is also performed by computer using intercorrelated variables. A path analysis proposes a hypothesis of what correlations would look like *if* variable *A* truly caused variable *B* which in turn caused variable *C* and then compares that proposition to the actual correlations. Hypotheses can also be set up for other supposed causal interactions. For example, one might test the hypothesis that variable *A* plus variable *B* causes variable *C*. Notice that path analysis is not a direct manipulation of variables to assess causal effects (which will be discussed in the next section) but is only an attempt to match actual correlations with correlations that would be expected if a causal model were true.

Rule of thumb 5.2: Be ready to handle complex multiple associations among several variables.

Causal Association Among Variables

It is possible to test the hypothesis that one variable causes another or, as is usually found in gerontological studies, that several variables working together cause changes in another variable. The influencing variable is called the independent variable; the influenced variable is called the dependent variable since it is changed or acted upon. The causal effect is not simply assumed but is actually observed when the independent variable is manipulated. This differs from path analysis in which no manipulation is done. For example, while there is some evidence from correlational data that consumption of saturated fat causes hardening of the arteries, only a manipulation in which two equivalent groups are fed high- and low-saturated fat diets (while other factors are held constant) and the groups are then examined for arterial changes can prove that diet is (one) cause of those changes. It is not always possible to test causal hypotheses in human populations, so causality is often inferred from correlational data or statistical manipulation. If possible, causality should be tested directly by experimentation. In gerontological studies with small samples, subjects may be used as their own controls.

Analysis of experimental studies means comparing performance scores of two groups that intentionally or unintentionally were treated in different ways. The hypothesis tested proposes that the differing treatment (independent variable) causes the groups to differ on the variable being tested or measured (dependent variable). The statistical test used to evaluate this hypothesis depends on the scaling of the data (nominal, ordinal, internal, or ratio). If one effect is manipulated, the number of subgroups in which different effects are expected depends on the number of levels of the independent variable. If more than one independent variable is manipulated, the number of subgroups affected depends on the number of levels of each one. All the subgroups must be randomly filled with subjects who receive the manipulations appropriate to the subgroup.

In multifactorial designs (those with several independent variables) causes may interact with one another. Causes may correlate with some other variable, in which case special statistical methods such as analysis of covariance would be needed. Effects of the manipulations are determined by examining central tendency and dispersion in each experimental group and then contrasting the groups.

Statistical methods that test hypotheses of association as well as those that test hypotheses of between-group differences do so by developing information on central tendencies and dispersions. Note that various research approaches require that the researcher select either association tests or between-group difference tests; therefore, before an approach is chosen, the requirements of the test that goes with that approach must be met. A statistics book and Table 5.4 will help.

> *Rule of thumb 5.3:* When choosing a research approach (Chapter 2), be aware that you are choosing a statistical test too (Table 5.4).

Avoiding Lost Findings

Common belief: When I answer my research question, data analysis is over.

Better belief: Much information beyond the answer to my research question can be gleaned from my findings.

The researcher is like a diagnostician who searches for the most fundamental source for a collection of symptoms. When a patient comes in complaining of a pain, a poor diagnostician treats the pain by giving pain killers and never goes beyond that. A better diagnostician goes beyond the descriptive and attempts to infer the cause, let's say an infection causing the pain. The best diagnostician goes two steps beyond description to seek not only the immediate cause, but also the fundamental source of the problem, in this case perhaps a deeply embedded foreign object.

Every research project can yield some higher-order information. A researcher who designs an applied study cheats himself or herself when he or she simply reports percentages or intercorrelations of all the variables in a massive table. Significant findings may be overlooked unless the researcher considers all the deeper levels of analysis presented in Table 5.7. There is always more than one way to look at a data element. There is no need to retain the first number system assigned to a variable or the first hypothesis formulated. Results of the study can be discussed in relation to the findings of others who used similar populations or similar questions. Serendipitous results should always be examined closely and refined with extra analyses if possible. Don't be like the prospectors who tossed lumps of uranium aside as worthless just because they weren't gold.

> *Rule of thumb 5.4:* Dig deeper into the data and follow up interesting leads with additional analyses.

Table 5.7
Getting Depth from Data
(given basic scores on several sociological, psychological, physical measures)

Level of analysis	Type of statistics
First	Describe the data in the aggregate—averages, medians, modes, percentages
Second	Break responses into subgroups based on other factors in your study and describe again—e.g., doctor visits of all elders who responded is further described as doctor visits of healthy, employed elder men; healthy, employed older women; sick, employed older men, etc.
Third	Test for significant relations among the subgroups of variables—e.g., the interaction of health and sex scores. Keep in mind that these significant effects are signs of interactions that can either enrich or ruin later analyses.
Fourth	Examine data for causal relations or correlations; this differs from the third level in that you are now doing more sensitive analyses on ratio-scale data addressing your hypothesis.
Fifth	Examine the relations in the fourth level while controlling for the covariates mentioned in the third. Are the relations still there?
Sixth	Serendipity is responsible for many findings. Keep your eyes open for surprising and unexpected results. A good researcher should expect that he or she will come across an interesting finding that was not anticipated in his or her proposal. Expect the unexpected.

Summary

Rule 5.1: Don't discard difficult data until you have explored analytic methods specifically designed for nonratio-scale data.

Rule 5.2: Be ready to handle complex multiple associations among several variables.

Rule 5.3: When choosing a research approach, be aware that you are choosing a statistical test too.

Rule 5.4: Dig deeper into the data and follow up interesting leads with additional analyses.

References

Barnett, V. (ed.). *Interpreting Multivariate Data.* New York: Wiley, 1981.

Draper, N., and Smith, H., Jr. *Applied Regression Analysis* (2nd ed.). New York: Wiley, 1981.

Guilford, J. P. *Fundamental Statistics in Psychology and Education.* New York: McGraw-Hill, 1971.

Williams, B. *A Sampler on Sampling.* New York: Wiley, 1978.

Chapter

6

Resources for Research on the Aging

During the past thirty years, technological advances have produced dramatic changes in the information sciences. The advent of computers has revolutionized our ability to store, document, manipulate, and gain access to information. Vast quantities of data are now easily accessible. But as our access to information grows, our skills for sifting through the data must become more refined. In this chapter we will look at the different ways in which information is made available to us and discuss some of the often neglected skills that are needed to take advantage of this information.

At the beginning of the research process, the researcher develops a question. Perhaps the intent is to test a hypothesis or to study the works of others who have tested similar issues. As the question develops, more information is needed to answer it and the next logical step is locating that information. The key to doing quality research is collecting relevant data based on relevant information, but it is not a simple task. Information is available in a wide variety of forms. New technologies have enabled us to store and transform information on a vast scale. Unfortunately, our ability to categorize and map this vast sea of information has not always kept pace with our ability to store it. The researcher of today, like his or her counterpart in the past, must be ready and willing to exercise a great deal of patience sorting through much irrelevant data to eventually uncover treasure chests of information. There are, however, some important differences between the tools of the researcher today and those of the researcher of even thirty years ago with respect to collecting information. Computerized data searches, for example, are now common and growing at a spectacular rate. Information specialists are rapidly becoming well-versed in new ways of retrieving information. Centralized storage facilities or archives now provide quick and easy access to primary data sets. The archives can be used to locate pertinent data across a wide range of studies for both simple and elaborate forms of analysis. The researcher must be able to take advantage of new retrieval sources to keep pace with the rapid growth of information.

The Process of Locating Information

Common procedure: (1) Check local library sources; (2) gather new information.

Better procedure: (1) Search literature through print and computerized systems; (2) reanalyze existing data set; (3) gather new information.

Think of information collection as a process made up of three overlapping phases. Taking on these phases in the proper sequence will enhance the researcher's final product and may save a good deal of time and money. This process applies to everyone seeking information, both the novice collecting information for the first time and the experienced researcher exploring new ground.

Searching the Literature

The initial phase of the collection process, commonly referred to as the *literature search,* is one in which the researcher is looking for any information related to the topic at hand. The literature search is the most wide-ranging and usually the least expensive phase of collecting information. For someone unfamiliar with the field of inquiry it means starting at the beginning—defining the problem and determining where to look for relevant information. For the specialist it means reexamining pertinent sources for new leads and being certain nothing new in the field has slipped through. (Some common sources of gerontological information are listed in the Appendix.)

Anyone attempting to search through relevant sources should be aware that many are available through on-line systems. *On-line* simply means that the information (e.g., the listings of a particular index) is stored and accessed through computer-assisted networks. These systems can do quick searches of vast listings, often providing annotations and detailed summaries. On-line systems are now available through most university libraries and the Library of Congress. A more detailed description of specific on-line systems is provided on page 178.

The information in the literature can assist the researcher in a variety of ways. It may serve to refine or fundamentally change the initial question; it may add new questions; it may lead to a new perspective on and a better understanding of the issues; it may even satisfactorily answer the initial query, thereby obviating, at least temporarily, the need to search for additional information. Suppose, for example, that an organization which serves elderly persons in an urban community wants to open a clinic for battered elderly persons but is unsure where it should be located. A literature search turns up a few studies which dealt with such a question in communities that closely parallel the community at hand. The studies conclusively suggest the type of neighborhood which would best house such a facility. Follow-up studies discuss the effectiveness of the sites chosen. This information may be enough for the agency to recommend a site for their facility, thereby saving them the expense of conducting their own surveys.

Many researchers never go beyond the literature search in seeking information on a given subject. Current studies and information provide researchers with virtually unlimited opportunities for refining, reorganizing, and otherwise generating new knowledge. But available studies are not always sufficient. Let's go back to our example of the home for battered elderly. Suppose that after reviewing the literature on the subject the researchers are still not prepared to recommend a site for their home. Even though previous studies of this question exist, they are not conclusive for the current project. Perhaps there are several locations which meet the specifications for viable sites suggested in the earlier studies. Or perhaps the earlier studies included different ethnic or demographic groups than those now under study and the researchers are unwilling to assume that their groups will react in the same way. Or maybe the earlier studies were conducted almost ten years ago, which poses serious questions about how and whether populations and attitudes have changed.

These are just a few examples of the problems faced by researchers as they examine the literature; existing studies seldom answer all of the questions raised by a new study. At this point the researchers must carefully evaluate the trade-offs in accepting or rejecting certain information and must decide what type of information can be relied upon without violating the unique features of the study at hand.

In our example, since the success of the entire project may depend on choosing the right site, the researchers want to be quite certain about their choice. Let us further suppose that our researchers conclude that while the earlier studies are very similar to the current project, they do not report essential information about how neighborhoods of different demographic composition reacted to the prospect of the home. In one earlier study the areas under consideration for placing the home were almost identical to those in the current project, but the literature only reported how one neighborhood (the neighborhood that was actually chosen) reacted to the home. Although the researchers could follow suit and choose the same type of neighborhood for their site, they wonder if one of the other neighborhoods might be an even better location. The suggestion is made that a new survey of attitudes might determine once and for all which neighborhood would be best suited for the home. But before taking this expensive step, the researchers raise another possibility. Perhaps the earlier study did collect information from different neighborhoods but simply did not report it. The literature states that the raw data from the study were deposited with one of the major archives. A telephone call to the center enables a researcher to obtain copies of the questionnaire used in the studies as well as a description of the methodology; this information reveals that information from many different neighborhoods was indeed generated. Another telephone call to the original researcher solves the rest of the puzzle. Although information was collected from all neighborhoods, the findings from only one were fully analyzed. This was because the original researchers knew they could easily obtain a grant for placing the home in this particular community. Once they concluded that this community would be acceptable, they needed to look no further.

Locating Unanalyzed Data

This sequence of events brings us to the second phase of the information-collection process, secondary analysis. Secondary analysis is the phase many researchers skip. In secondary analysis the researcher actually goes over the raw data of a study. Herbert Hyman (1972) describes secondary analysis of survey data as "the extraction of knowledge on topics other than those which were the focus of the original survey" (p. 1). The key to secondary analysis is that although the data have already been collected, they have been categorized or analyzed only according to the needs of the original researcher. Hence another researcher can use his or her skills to generate answers to new questions from old information.

In our example, the researchers can compare and contrast the reactions of all of the neighborhoods to the home. They can do this themselves by obtaining copies of the raw data and code books from the archives, thereby doing their own secondary analysis, or they can have the archives conduct the necessary data manipulations. In either case, the cost is only a fraction of what it would be to conduct a new attitudinal survey. Not only will our researchers answer their questions, but they will do so in less time and for less money.

Of course one does not need to work through data archives to conduct secondary analysis. Past surveys that were never sent to an archive but rather are collecting dust in someone's office are one possible resource. A researcher may find a new use for a survey he or she conducted many years ago. Seldom if ever is any data set analyzed to its fullest capacity. More often only a fraction of the data actually collected are ever used. (See Chapter 5 for suggestions on how to get maximum use from your data.)

Because secondary analysis has been such a neglected phase of the information collection process and because of its growing importance in the research arena today, it is treated in more detail in a separate section on page 30.

Collecting New Information

The third and final phase of the information-collection process is primary analysis, the generating of new information. Again going back to our example, suppose the demographic data needed by the researchers were not collected in the earlier studies. If the researchers decide that this missing information is essential to their final decision, they will have to collect it themselves. (See Chapter 3 for the research steps that are part of generating primary information.)

Each phase of the information-collection process will help the researcher decide whether to go on to the next phase. During the literature search the researcher invests mostly time—the time it takes to search through and sort out all that is available. But the researcher also *saves* time by avoiding duplication and pinpointing the most valuable avenues of pursuit. If money is invested at this stage, for either on-line searches or other access to information, it is usually minimal. At the secondary analysis stage the researcher must invest considerably more money and more time. Usually data sets must be purchased or rented and computer facilities are generally needed to conduct analysis. But these costs are only a fraction of those incurred during the primary research stage. Anyone who has conducted primary research is aware of just how costly and time-consuming it can be.

Of course there will be times when researchers go directly to secondary or primary stages of the information-collection process. For instance, a researcher may have access to a private data set that has been usefully analyzed or the research topic may be so specialized that only primary information can satisfy the researcher's needs. But even in instances such as these, earlier phases of the information-collection process should not be completely ignored. Although perhaps only primary information can answer a specific question, the literature and the secondary sources can still provide valuable assistance in the design and execution of that research. Perhaps there are studies of similar problems which can help the researcher refine his or her questions, or maybe tangential aspects of the study are covered in the literature and may help avoid duplication or raise red flags over potential trouble areas. Similarly, researchers going directly to secondary sources may be well served by consulting any existing literature on the study question as well as related studies. In the long run, the proper sequential treatment of the information-collection phases will prove to be both time- and cost-effective.

Anyone engaging in research quickly becomes aware that the process of collecting and generating information is a never-ending one. When a researcher proceeds through the literature search to secondary analysis and then to primary research, the final results quickly raise many more questions that can be better understood by consulting other aspects of the literature. The literature review may raise new questions that can be answered by going back to the primary research, this time as a secondary source, for new analysis. This new analysis may, in turn, open up new avenues of primary research, and so on. Such is the process of collecting information.

> *Rule of thumb 6.1:* Do not engage in secondary analysis until you have completed the literature search. And primary analysis should wait until both the literature search and secondary sources are exhausted.

Considerations of Secondary Analysis

The secondary analyst must have virtually the same skills as the primary analyst and then some. As with primary surveys, the key to secondary surveys is design. Whereas primary analysts *create* data through new tools, secondary analysts *re-create* data by arranging existing information in new ways, thus producing new research designs. But whether a survey is constructed anew or reanalyzed, the rigors of quality assessment are the same. Both primary and secondary analysts must plan the research in terms of budget and resources. The quantitative techniques for both types of researchers are identical. The only essential difference between the two is that the secondary analyst will have less control than the primary analyst (e.g., he or she cannot change a question wording).

Since the data utilized by the secondary analyst have already been collected, the key considerations with respect to available data are as follows: (1) location, (2) assessment of value, (3) procurement, and (4) analysis.

Location

Ways of locating information are addressed, in part, in the section on data archives and in the listing of archives and information sources at the end of this chapter. As mentioned earlier, other networks such as personal contacts and references that are uncovered during the initial phase of the information-collection process should also be used to obtain relevant data sources. Because of the fragmented nature of current information systems, a researcher must be prepared to do a considerable amount of telephoning, searching, and letter writing. This is especially true with respect to gerontological information, which has been incorporated only slowly into on-line data bases.

Assessment

Assessing the value of available data is probably the most nebulous and clearly one of the most important considerations facing the secondary analyst. Although listed ahead of procurement, assessment generally means obtaining all documentation relating to a survey to see how well it fits current needs. This material is usually obtained through the data center, although pieces of the documentation may exist in the literature. One helpful rule of thumb in doing secondary analysis is to assume as little as possible about the data set to be worked with. The data should be looked at for both what it contains and what it lacks. The researcher must also determine the limitations of the study design.

Some of the more common considerations in determining the value of existing data sets are listed below.

Documentation

Documentation provides background on the method used to collect and analyze the data. The completeness of documentation varies considerably from survey to survey; older surveys are usually in the worst shape. The secondary analyst must determine what is not known about the survey in question, what information has been lost. Perhaps the original researchers used a weighting technique which they did not document and is therefore lost to you. Learning as much as possible about the genesis of the survey is also important. This information is generally the most difficult to obtain but valuable because it can promote understanding of what the original researchers were after, what assumptions they made, and what they perceived to be the shortcomings of the data.

Sample

The sample is a crucial aspect of any survey. The researcher must know to which populations the primary data can and cannot be generalized. All phases of the sampling procedure must be examined closely. To look at general attitudes of the adult American population using one of the many available data bases (e.g., Roper, Harris Surveys, Gallup, Opinion Research Corporation, National Opinion Research Center in Michigan, to name just a few) the analyst needs to know whether an area probability sample or some other method was used (see Chapter 3 for explanations of sampling procedures)—there is a big difference among sampling methods with respect to calculating response error. The secondary analyst will also want to know how many callbacks were used, if any; what types of verification procedures were used; if there were any quotas; if there was any undersampling in particular regions or areas; whether interviews determined routes and respondents; how many primary sampling units (PSUs) were involved; if weights were employed; how subjects were selected in high-rises. A researcher should be aware that most area probability samples of the general population exclude institutionalized people. This means that people in nursing homes, hospitals, and prisons are not represented at all. If telephone samples are used, variables like time of day can influence results. Whatever the sampling technique, it should be closely examined. Special care is needed when comparing different surveys.

Demographic Groups

A researcher interested in examining the attitudes of a particular demographic group, such as those over 65 years old, must first determine if the available information allows identification of the group's responses. Is information available about date of birth or only the general category 65-plus? Did respondents actually give their age, or did interviewers guess at it? Data about the relative size of the cohort of interest is important to allow proper representation in selected analysis. The operationalization for any question of interest must be examined.

Coding

Perhaps a researcher is interested in a particular open-ended question from a survey. Before actually obtaining the results, he or she should determine how responses have been collapsed and categorized. It may be that the important information has not been coded at all.

Question Order and Flow

Questionnaires should be checked to determine the question flow and to determine potential biases deriving from question order.

Interviewers

The qualifications of the interviewers should be sought and noted, as well as all interviewer instructions.

Perhaps the most difficult aspect of assessing the value of data is determining how well it tests the hypotheses currently being researched. Since there is no such thing as a perfect survey, even for the primary analyst, it follows that there also will be limitations the second time around. Trade-offs must always be made. Understanding the limitations of the research and then working around them, however, minimizes the problems created.

Procurement

The problem of procurement is addressed in the section on data archives. Data obtained through resources other than data centers probably will not be subject to very formalized procedures. Since information from archives can be obtained in a variety of forms, a researcher should be certain exactly how much and what type of information he or she actually needs.

Analysis

Analysis of the information is directly related to procurement and how the researcher intends to process the information. Because of many differences in available hardware (computers) and software (statistical packages used to analyze the data), the researcher must ensure that any data received are compatible with his or her system. This is usually a very simple task but can be a serious problem if overlooked. For the archives to analyze the data usefully they must have explicit instructions about the form in which the information should be sent and what analyses they should perform. While the archives vary in their ability to provide data processing, all of the major centers have a good deal of flexibility. If the researcher obtains the raw data, which consists of the data taken directly from the survey instruments, the data should be in the form that can be most effectively processed by his or her facilities.

Some Advantages and Disadvantages
to Secondary Research

The benefits of secondary analysis were organized by Hyman (1972) into three general types: (1) practical benefits, (2) social benefits, and (3) benefits for theory and substantive knowledge.

The most obvious advantage of secondary research over primary studies is a practical one; secondary research costs less. A large and complex secondary study can be completed quickly and cheaply. In what he calls a conservative assessment, Hyman estimates that about 40 percent of a primary research budget is consumed before the data are ready to be analyzed, while only 5 to 10 percent goes into machine work and the production of the report. This breakdown has probably become even more lopsided since Hyman's estimate in 1972. In 1981, the cost of producing new data ready for analysis, based on 55-minute personal interviews with an area probability sample of at least 1,550 people in the continental United States, would be in the neighborhood of $100,000. The raw-data tape from such a survey, along with all documentation, can often be purchased from an archive for less than $100. Generally, a researcher would not need the results from the entire study but only a select portion, thereby reducing his or her costs even further. Archives are able to tell you exactly what type of information is available on a particular subject from a wide variety of surveys.

Another advantage to secondary research is that it often yields better quality surveys than primary research. This is because relatively few researchers have the resources for generating large-scale *quality* surveys. They may therefore take shortcuts in sampling or methodology, using less effective techniques (such as mail questionnaires) or nonrepresentative samples.

If a researcher does ultimately engage in primary research, a review of the secondary sources can help the researcher to design more effective surveys by pointing to serious omissions in the data and by outlining more pertinent questions. Similarly, since in secondary analysis a researcher studies many surveys, there is a rich potential for replication and comparisons not available to the primary analyst.

One other important advantage of secondary analysis is that it allows information to be generated without further intrusion on the public. One of the drawbacks to the recent proliferation of polls and surveys has been the impact on the public. Now more than ever, people are being called on the telephone, approached in their houses, and stopped on street corners and in shops to provide information. At the same time, Americans have become conscious of their privacy. The amount of good will people today can be expected to extend to the many pollsters who want their time and cooperation is limited. In an era when polls and surveys have become a fashionable and lucrative business, secondary analysis can help researchers to avoid abusing the privilege of contacting members of the public.

Of course there are also some important drawbacks to secondary analysis, regarding knowledge of the data and design of the primary research. As mentioned under *Assessment* in the previous section, there is no such thing as a perfect survey. As a rule, the older the survey, the less precise the methods of documentation. Although documentation is becoming better, it can always present a problem. Also, since the researcher was not part of the original study, he or she must usually search hard to understand how the data were generated. The exact data needed may not be available—only variations which will force compromises.

Some Applications of Secondary Studies

Secondary analysis can be used fruitfully to answer a wide range of questions. In the past it has been most commonly associated with academic studies which attempt to test hypotheses or enlarge theory. There are, however, more applied uses for the research that are often neglected. For instance, in our earlier example the researchers used secondary analysis to determine how well suited a home for battered elderly was to a particular neighborhood. The larger questions of ideal types or why one neighborhood may be more amenable than another were not their primary concern. More and more, secondary analysis is being used to address practical questions. The data already available provide an excellent opportunity for applied social scientists to generate much useful information at relatively low cost.

In addition to using secondary studies techniques to answer questions or address theories already formulated, a researcher may wish to use them to examine the holdings of a particular archive in order to uncover potentially fruitful avenues of pursuit. For example, in 1974 the National Council on Aging commissioned Louis Harris and Associates to conduct an extensive survey on the reality of old age in America. Among topics covered in this survey were public attitudes toward old age and expectations about old people, social and economic contributions of older Americans, the self-image of old people and the experience of being old, preparation for old age, the use of community and other facilities by older people, and attitudes toward the media's portrayal of old people.

To extend this impressive data base further, the National Council on Aging commissioned a new survey in 1981. Also conducted by Louis Harris and Associates, this second survey included 3427 personal interviews conducted between June 15 and July 31, 1981. As with the earlier study, the 55-to-64 and the 65-and-over age segments were purposely oversampled disproportionately to their representation in the population and then weighted back to their actual proportions in the overall national results. Blacks and Hispanics were also deliberately oversampled for statistical and analytical purposes and then weighted back to their actual proportion in the national sample.

In addition to providing an update on many of the important issues first explored in 1974, the 1981 study also looked at a variety of new topics. The major topics updated in the report include:

• the myth and reality of aging
• the experience of aging
• social activities and involvement of the elderly
• expectations and attitudes about retirement
• preparation for retirement

The major issues explored in depth for the first time include:

• the economics of aging and retirement
• the changing face of retirement and employment after sixty-five
• social security and the role of government
• health and health care

All or part of the Harris data can be obtained from the Institute for Research in Social Science at the University of North Carolina, which is the primary repository for the Harris Surveys and other archival data. The data provide rich potential for gerontologists eager to discover new patterns, associations, and phenomena.

Secondary analysis can also provide information for the two most basic survey designs—cross-sectional and longitudinal studies (see Chapter 3). Many of the sources listed in this book as well as those identified through the literature search will help pinpoint existing cross-sectional studies of interest to the researcher. Three major types of longitudinal studies bear special consideration from the perspective of the secondary analyst: trend studies, cohort studies, and panel studies.

The proliferation of polls has opened up new opportunities for cohort studies. Cohort studies can now compete with panel studies, described below, for only a fraction of the cost and without the problems inherent in panels. This is not to say that cohort studies are without problems. The different samples upon which the cohorts are based are only representative of those members of the cohort who are alive and available at each stage of the analysis; people will always be entering and leaving the population to which the sample generalizes. There is also the problem of noncomparability in design of the samples and question wordings (e.g., Have the sample selection procedures or the question wordings changed much?). Choosing and tracing the cohort is also a problem (e.g., Is age classified in the same way in each study? What about people who refuse to give their age?). One other problematic factor, and probably the most difficult to assess, is the change caused by factors independent of the questions (e.g., Do the questions that come before the targeted question influence attitudes in any way? Is the questionnaire administered at a particular time of the year which bears directly on the target question?). With careful planning, however, cohort analysis can be a rich avenue of pursuit for gerontologists.

Panel Studies

A panel study is a special type of longitudinal study (see Chapter 3). The difference is that panel studies involve the collection of data over time from the *same* sample of respondents. The sample for such a study is called a *panel*. The advantage of a panel over trend and cohort studies is obvious. By taking the same groups through time the researcher can not only determine how the group has changed, but also which individuals have changed and why. The cohort necessarily compares the aggregate, while the panel has the ability to compare individuals. But despite this strength, panel studies have several serious weaknesses. The first is that they are very expensive and time-consuming. Unlike trend and cohort studies, which can be carried out through secondary analysis, most panels must be conducted as part of a particular research program. And there are other problems unique to the method. One is that the attrition rate is generally high (i.e., people who were part of the original panel refuse or are unavailable for inclusion in later panels). Another difficulty with panel research is that analysis is very complex.

A special note on panel studies with respect to the elderly is in order. There is evidence to suggest that a number of demographic characteristics associated with the elderly are also associated with low levels of involvement in panels. Panel cooperation appears to be especially low in households with fewer than two members, in households with older members, and in households with lower levels of education. This is not to say that panel data on elderly cannot be collected, but researchers should be aware of the problems that may be encountered.

Trend Studies

Trend studies sample populations at different points in time. Although different people are studied each time, direct comparisons can be made by holding the sample methodology constant. Through this technique whole populations can be looked at for changes in attitude and behavior over time. The best known trend studies are those conducted by commercial polling firms such as Harris, Gallup, and Roper. There are also several well-known academically based trend study organizations such as NORC (National Opinion Research Corporation) and the Survey Research Center at The University of Michigan. In addition, there are many lesser known research houses and commercial firms that have collected a great deal of trend data. The American Council of Life Insurance, for instance, a nonprofit trade association for the life insurance industry, has collected attitudinal data on the adult American population annually since 1968. The information, collected through in-depth personal interviews with representative samples, includes attitudes in such areas as Social Security, retirement, retirement finances, the family, sex roles, the responsibility of parents to children and vice versa, death, dying, life extension, government spending for the elderly, and health care. Most of this information is available through the Roper Center.

Cohort Studies

A cohort study is a particular type of trend study. A cohort is simply a group of individuals with a common demographic factor (e.g., age, class membership, number of children). Whereas trend studies are based on a general population (such as the adult American population) over time, a cohort study isolates a particular segment of the larger population and follows this segment across time (e.g., people born between 1940 and 1950). Suppose a researcher wants to examine the way Americans' attitudes toward Social Security change as they get older. A search of secondary sources will uncover many questions with similar or identical wordings on this subject that have been asked in comparable studies over the years. The researcher could determine how 20- to 25-year-olds felt about the system in 1950. Next, the attitudes of 30- to 35-year-olds could be examined in 1960—the same cohort ten years later. The attitudes of this cohort could be looked at again in 1970 when they are 40 to 45 years old and once again in 1980 when they are 50 to 55 years old. In this way the researcher can study the cohort through time.

Data Archives

As indicated earlier, there has been tremendous growth during the past quarter century in the number of machine-readable data files available for secondary analysis. In large part, this growth has been made possible by archival organizations. Archives are multipurpose organizations devoted to the acquisition of data which they process, document, and distribute.

Fortunately for users, the rapid growth in archival development in the United States has been greater with respect to the size of holdings of particular archives than with respect to the number of archives. In fact, a substantial contraction has taken place over the years in the number of institutions anticipating extensive acquisition and dissemination of social science data. The two largest machine-readable data archives in the United States serving the general social science community are the Inter-University Consortium for Political and Social Research (ICPSR) at the University of Michigan and the Roper Center. Most other academic archives generally exist for the purpose of serving the local social science community by providing facilities to order data from these two large repositories and by serving as repositories for data generated locally. (Locally generated data are also held by the larger archives.) For example, about two-thirds of the archival holdings at the University of Iowa have been obtained from ICPSR, Roper, and other archives, while about one-third represent data generated by local researchers.

Considerations in Working with Data Archives

In the section on "Considerations of Secondary Analysis" it was pointed out that the secondary analyst faced four key considerations with respect to his or her data sources:

1. location
2. assessment of value
3. procurement
4. analysis

Since the data sets involved in secondary analysis will typically be provided by archives, two of these considerations, location and procurement, are addressed in more detail below.

Locating Relevant Data

Despite the aforementioned vertical growth in archival holdings over the years, there is no simple method for determining what data are where. Ultimately, success in consulting archival sources depends on the cooperation of the researcher and the archivist. The better prospective users can clearly explain their needs and the more they understand about the manner in which data are stored, the better the results of their search. General descriptions of the holdings of most archives can be found in most libraries in documents provided by the archives. A telephone call or letter to relevant organizations can also provide general information about holdings. A number of archives that gerontologists may find particularly useful are listed at the end of the chapter.

If a researcher simply wants to locate a particular data set, then the search may be easy—depending on how well-known and how up-to-date the survey in question is. For instance, to obtain the raw data from the previously mentioned old age survey conducted by Louis Harris and Associates, the researcher can simply call the Duke University Data Archive for Aging and Adult Development (DAAAD) to work out the details. Generally, however, researchers' needs are not that simple. A researcher is more likely to request *all* information that can be provided on a particular subject rather than one specific study. Keeping the topic specific enough so the quantity of data is not overwhelming while at the same time being flexible enough to accommodate all relevant information is the principal difficulty of locating material. Some guidelines to follow in working with data archives are as follows:

1. Be patient! It is easy to get frustrated by an inability to quickly determine what specific information is available from a given data bank.
2. Bear in mind that each search is unique and that you will have to make decisions as you go along.
3. Be prepared to search the holdings of more than one archive.
4. Be imaginative as to what information might fit your needs.
5. Explain your needs in as much detail as possible to the archivist who is helping you.
6. Be aware that the documentation for holdings varies widely. This is a prime source of frustration, but the reality is that most surveys give low priority to the fact that they may be the source of secondary analysis.
7. Be aware that what looks like a very rich data base from descrip-

tions in the literature might not be as extensive after the coding process reduces data to categories.

8. Understand that you may not find exactly what you are looking for and that a survey you know was conducted may not be documented anywhere.
9. Don't get carried away by only one document; keep searching for other possibilities.
10. Attempt to obtain the most up-to-date studies.
11. Get an estimate of your costs at the outset; this will help you refine the topic as well as save you unpleasant surprises.

Obtaining the Information

The factors to consider when actually obtaining data depend very much on goals. If the goal is to obtain a raw data set from a particular study, the researcher's needs are somewhat different than if he or she is asking an archive to conduct a general search. Some guidelines for obtaining information are as follows:

1. Be sure you know *exactly* what you are getting. If it is a computer printout, get a sample page to check the format. There is generally a good deal of flexibility in how data can be printed, so you can save yourself a lot of trouble by getting the most efficient output for your needs. If you are getting a tape or cards, be certain you understand the format; are the data single punched (i.e., single columns on computer cards are associated with each piece of information, making the data compatible with most software packages)?
2. If more than one archive has the information you want, interrogate each about its ability to match its holdings with your needs.
3. Be sure you know all costs that are involved (e.g., data costs as well as tape, cards, printout, mailing, etc.).
4. Be certain that you receive *all* relevant documentation.
5. When thinking about obtaining data, also think about analysis. That is, what will you do with the data; how will you analyze it?
6. Don't get more information than you actually need; or if you do, know what the relative cost is to you. For example, if you are conducting a secondary analysis of the attitudes of the elderly, do you need information based on other populations that may be part of the data?
7. Be certain that the raw data will be compatible with your hardware and software. Talk to your computer people and determine what tape specifications are best and whether you can apply the software with which you are most familiar.

Government Archives

Like private archives, government archives in recent years have been very active in putting together data files. Unfortunately, unlike the private sector, the government has done very little to coordinate the vast holdings. Obtaining governmental cooperation in the preservation and dissemination of data resources produced with public funds has been a subject of major frustration for archivists and researchers alike.

At present the National Technical Information Service is responsible for combining the many independent data-file directories into one computerized system. But the fact that the agencies involved approach categorizing in a very heterogeneous fashion makes development of such a system particularly difficult. Many of the publications that report on statistics generated by the government are listed in the data references at the end of this section.

1980 Census

For any researcher interested in statistical data, the U.S. Census is a gold mine which provides detailed information on the social, labor force, and income characteristics of the population.

Table 6.1 is a list of all data items collected in the 1980 census. In this list, questions asked about every person and housing unit are called *100 percent of complete-count questions. Sample population items* and *sample housing items* are asked at only one household in every six throughout most of the country.

Census Reports

Tabulations of census data are available in three different formats—in printed reports, on computer tapes, and on microfiche. If information is not required in great detail for a large number of areas, printed reports will probably be the most convenient and readily available source. Data presented in 1980 census reports are and will be similar in kind and quantity to the data contained in reports resulting from the 1970 census. The bureau is considerably behind its initial schedule for making reports available. To find out what is available at a given time, readers are advised to call one of the regional offices listed below.

The Census Bureau issues several guides and other references which should be of substantial help to 1980 census data users.

Table 6.1
1980 Census Data

*100-percent popula-
tion items*
*Household rela-
tionship
Sex
Race
Age
Marital status
*Spanish/Hispanic
origin or descent

*100-percent housing
items*
Number of housing
units at address
*Complete plumbing
facilities
Number of rooms
in unit
Tenure (whether
the unit is owned
or rented)
*Condominium iden-
tification
Value of home (for
owner-occupied
units and con-
dominiums)
Rent (for renter-
occupied units)
Vacant for rent, for
sale, etc.; and pe-
riod of vacancy

*Sample population
items*
School enrollment
Educational attain-
ment
State or foreign
country of birth
Citizenship and year
of immigration

**Current language
and English
proficiency
**Ancestry
Place of residence 5
years ago

Activity 5 years ago
Veteran status and
period of service
*Presence of disabil-
ity or handicap
Children ever born
Marital history
Employment status
last week
Hours worked last
week
Place of work
**Travel time to work
*Means of transpor-
tation to work
**Persons in carpool
Year last worked
Industry
Occupation
Class of worker
*Work in 1979 and
weeks looking
for work in 1979
*Amount of income
by source in 1979
**Total income in
1979

Sample housing items
Number of units in
structure
*Stories in building
and presence of
elevator
Year unit built

*Year moved into
this house
Source of water
Sewage disposal
Heating equipment
Fuels used for
house heating,
water heating,
and cooking
*Costs of utilities and
fuels
Complete kitchen
facilities
Number of bed-
rooms and bath-
rooms
Telephone
Air-conditioning
Number of auto-
mobiles
**Number of light
trucks and vans
**Homeowner shelter
costs for mort-
gage, real estate
taxes, and hazard
insurance

*Derived items (illus-
trative examples)*
Families
Family type, size,
and income
Poverty status
Population density
Persons per room
("overcrowding")
Household size
Institutions and
other group quar-
ters
Gross rent
Farm residence

*Changed relative to 1970
**New items

1980 Census User's Guide—the primary guide for serious users of 1980 census data.

Data Users News—the bureau's monthly newsletter for data users. It reports on new publications and computer tapes, developments in bureau services to users, upcoming conferences and training courses, and related matters. A subscription is $4 per year and includes the quarterly supplement, *1980 Census Update.*

Bureau of the Census Catalog—a comprehensive listing of all new publications, computer tape files, and special tabulations. A subscription is $19 per year; the catalog is issued quarterly with monthly supplements.

1980 Census Indexes—comprehensive subject matter and geographic indexes to data tables for both published and computer tape files from the 1980 census. The indexes may be published in several parts and will probably be available on microfiche and computer tape. The bureau will also prepare on a cost-reimbursable basis special tabulations of data from the 1980 census based on customer specifications. Such tabulations can cover any specific geographic area or subject matter and are subject to confidentiality restrictions. Such tabulations are expensive and may take considerable time to produce.

Data User Services—specialists are available at the bureau's Washington headquarters and twelve regional offices to answer inquiries and provide consultation on data products and services by telephone, correspondence, or personal visit. For further information contact the following offices.

Washington contact:

Data User Services Division
Bureau of the Census
Washington, DC 20233
(301) 763-2400

Regional office contacts:

Data User Services Officer
Bureau of the Census
1365 Peachtree St., N.E.
Room 638
Atlanta, GA 30309
(404) 881-2274

Data User Services Officer
Bureau of the Census
441 Stuart St.
8th Floor
Boston, MA 02116
(617) 223-0668

Data User Services Officer
Bureau of the Census
230 South Tryon St.
Suite 800
Charlotte, NC 28202
(704) 371-6144

Data User Services Officer
Bureau of the Census
55 E. Jackson Blvd.
Suite 1304
Chicago, IL 60604
(312) 353-0980

Data User Services Officer
Bureau of the Census
1100 Commerce St.
Room 3C54
Dallas, TX 75242
(214) 767-0625

Data User Services Officer
Bureau of the Census
575 Union Blvd.
Denver, CO 80225
(303) 234-5825

Data User Services Officer
Bureau of the Census
915 2nd Ave.
Room 312
Seattle, WA 98174
(206) 442-7080

Data User Services Officer
Bureau of the Census
Federal Building and U.S.
  Courthouse
Room 565
231 West Lafayette
Detroit, MI 48226
(313) 226-4675

Data User Services Officer
Bureau of the Census
1 Gateway Center
4th and State Streets
Kansas City, KA 66101
(816) 374-4601

Data User Services Officer
Bureau of the Census
11777 San Vicente Blvd.
8th Floor
Los Angeles, CA 90049
(213) 824-7291

Data User Services Officer
Bureau of the Census
26 Federal Plaza
Federal Office Building
Room 37-130
New York, NY 10007
(212) 264-4730

Data User Services Officer
Bureau of the Census
600 Arch St.
Room 9226
Philadelphia, PA 19106
(215) 507-8314

Social Science Archives of Special Relevance to Gerontologists

The Roper Center

> Box 4   164R
> University of Connecticut
> Storrs, CT 06268
> (203) 486-4440

Description

A nonprofit educational research facility maintained on behalf of the social science community by the University of Connecticut, Yale University, and Williams College, the Roper Center is the oldest and largest archive of sample survey data in the world. It is often described as a data-extensive archive because the holdings cover a very wide range of issues.

The collection includes raw-data files, together with supporting documents, for some nine thousand separate studies conducted in the United States and more than seventy-five foreign countries. The earliest surveys reach back to the mid 1930s; about five hundred surveys are added each year. The materials in the collection represent public opinion research on virtually the entire range of subjects that can be probed through surveys.

Services Offered

1. Copies of raw data sets and documentation in order to permit detailed secondary analysis on outside computer facilities.
2. Searches for items bearing on some policy issue or social question. Once pertinent data have been located, Center staff will further analyze them according to user's interests—providing, for example, the responses of various subgroups within the general population.
3. More elaborate forms of analysis, yielding as the final product a detailed report on the opinions, attitudes or values of the population on some issue.

Selected Data Bases

The Center's collection includes surveys conducted by the Roper Organization, the Gallup Organization, the New York Times Poll, Yankelovich, Skelly and White, Inc., the Los Angeles Times Poll, and National Opinion Research Center (General Social Survey).

Fees

The Center offers two fee schedules: one for members of the International Survey Library Association and one for nonmembers. Library Association member institutions pay an annual fee to provide their faculty and students direct access to Roper Center services at no cost to the individual. Colleges, universities, and other nonprofit organizations not participating in the ISLA program obtain data sets and research services at a rate 50 percent higher than that charged participating members.

The Inter-University Consortium for Political and Social Research

P.O. Box 1248
Ann Arbor, MI 48106
(313) 763-5010

Description

The ICPSR is a nonprofit partnership between the Center for Political Studies and over 220 member universities and colleges. It is located in the Institute for Social Research at The University of Michigan and is described as a data-intensive archive because a narrow range of issues are covered in depth.

The ICPSR receives, processes, and distributes machine-readable data on social phenomena from over 130 countries; there are over 15,000 data files in the archive. Surveys of mass and elite attitudes, census records, election returns, international interactions, and legislative records are maintained in forms easily used for classroom exercises and basic research. The contents of the archive extend across economic, sociological, historical, organizational, social psychological, and political concerns. Of special interest to gerontologists is the National Archive of Computerized Data on Aging (NACDA) at the ICPSR, which provides copies of computer-readable data files related to the study of aging. (See page 131.)

Services Offered

1. Training programs offering a comprehensive, integrated program of studies in research design, statistics, data analysis, and social methodology.
2. Computing assistance for the effective use of local computing facilities. This ranges from advice on the selection and use of computing equipment and programs to providing a powerful software package (OSIRIS) for use on a member's own computer.

3. Copies of raw data sets and documentation in order to permit detailed secondary analysis of these data on outside computer facilities.

Selected Data Bases

Data bases include census enumerations, comparative socioeconomic, public policy, and political data (1900–1960), National Opinion Research Center (General Social Survey), surveys of consumer attitudes and behavior, national longitudinal surveys of labor market experience, and surveys of consumer finance.

Fees

There are several categories of membership in the ICPSR. Each category is based on the size, program, and location of an institution. ICPSR will also provide services for nonmembers on a cost recovery basis.

Duke University Data Archive for Aging and Adult Development (DAAAD)

Duke University Center for the Study of Aging and Human
  Development
Box 3003
Durham, NC 27710
(919) 684-3204

Description

Activities of the Data Archive for Aging and Adult Development (DAAAD) include the identification, cleaning, documentation, storage, and dissemination of large-scale data sources relevant to the study of aging to the social science and gerontological research communities. Important additional archives include the preparation of uniform codebooks, user's manuals, and measurement manuals summarizing information about the validity, reliability, and other properties of commonly used survey instruments. These services are supplemented by periodic workshops and conferences. The emphasis is on the accessibility as well as the availability of survey data.

Services Offered

1. Distribution of data tapes (variable cost). Write, phone, or visit.

2. Technical and substantive assistance (free). Phone.
3. A reference guide of general information.

National Archive of Computerized Data on Aging (NACDA)

c/o ICPSR
Box 1248
Ann Arbor, MI 48106
(313) 763-5010

Description

The Institute of Gerontology and the Institute for Social Research at The University of Michigan have been supported by the Administration on Aging in a collaborative effort to establish a national archive of computer-readable data in the field of aging. The archive will be complemented by training programs for research methodologists and administrative personnel of agencies serving the aged. This project is engaged in three interrelated tasks. The indexing and dissemination of extant computer-readable data available from a variety of sources represents a central project responsibility. There is also a program of training and activities designed for a wide variety of audiences to stimulate and enhance the use of the archival resources. And there is a consultation service which will provide technical and substantive assistance to interested practitioners and policy makers in the use of the data resources. A periodic newsletter, *The NACDA Bulletin,* is published and distributed without charge. Individuals may request their names be added to the mailing list.

Services Offered

1. Copies of computer-readable data files related to the study of aging with appropriate documentation (free). Write or phone.
2. Consultation on design of empirical research (free). Write or phone.
3. Training in quantitative social science methods and techniques (free). Write or phone.

Machine Readable Archives Division
National Archives and Record Service

Reference Section
Washington, DC 20408
(202) 724-1080

Description

The Machine Readable Archives Division is responsible for preserving and making available those machine-readable records which the federal government decides are of permanent value. Currently, the collection contains over a thousand files, including files on income, demography, the aged, education, taxes, poverty, health, employment, and ethnic populations.

Services Offered

The division sells data files (for $65 per reel) and low-cost copies of documentation. Some files can be reformatted upon request. Staff are available for technical assistance.

National Center for Health Statistics

Center Building, Room I-57
3700 East-West Highway
Hyattsville, MD 20782
(301) 436-8500

Description

The National Center for Health Statistics makes available a number of micro-data tapes from the data collection systems. Tapes are available on such subjects as nursing homes and other health facilities, hospital discharges, natality, mortality, marriage, divorce, the health interview survey, and the health examination survey.

Services Offered

Computer standardized micro-data tape transcripts and appropriate documentation are available at $125 for one reel and $60 for each successive reel. Write or call the Scientific and Technical Information branch for a tape catalog and to check on the availability of tapes before ordering. Technical assistance is also available.

Archives Cooperating with the Laboratory for Political Research of the University of Iowa

Project TALENT Data Bank
AMERICAN INSTITUTE FOR RESEARCH
P.O. Box 1113
Palo Alto, California 94302

Alfred J. Tuchfarber, Jr., Director
BEHAVIORAL SCIENCES LABORATORY
University of Cincinnati
Cincinnati, Ohio 45221

Phillippe Laurent
BELGIAN ARCHIVES FOR THE SOCIAL SCIENCES
Place Montesquieu, 1 Boite 18
B-1348 Louvain-la-Neuve, Belgium

CELADE LATIN AMERICAN POPULATION DATA BANK
United Nations Latin American Demographic Center (CELADE)
Casilla 91
Santiago, Chile

Social Science Data Librarian
CENTER FOR SOCIAL ANALYSIS
State University of New York
Binghamton, New York 13901

CENTER FOR QUANTITATIVE STUDIES IN SOCIAL SCIENCES
117 Savery Hall
DK-45
University of Washington
Seattle, Washington 98195

Per Nielsen
DANISH DATA ARCHIVES
Odense University
Niels Bohrs Alie 25
DK-5230 Odense M
Denmark

Alice Robbin
DATA AND PROGRAM LIBRARY SERVICE
4451 Social Science Building
University of Wisconsin
Madison, Wisconsin 53706

Laine Ruus
DATA LIBRARY
6356 Agricultural Road
Room 206
University Campus
Vancouver, British Columbia
Canada V6T 1W5

Data Librarian
DATA LIBRARY
Survey Research Center
University of California
Berkeley, California 94720

DRUG ABUSE EPIDEMIOLOGY DATA CENTER
Institute of Behavioral Research
Texas Christian University
Fort Worth, Texas 76129

Librarian
Information Documentation Center
DUALABS, INC.
1601 N. Kent Street, Suite 900
Arlington, Virginia 22209

EUROPEAN CONSORTIUM FOR
   POLITICAL RESEARCH
Data Information Service
Fantoftvegen 38
N-5036 Fantoft-Bergen
Norway

Thomas Atkinson, Director
Data Bank
INSTITUTE FOR BEHAVIORAL
   RESEARCH
York University
4700 Keele Street
Downsview, Ontario
Canada

Assistant Director for
   Member Services
INTER-UNIVERSITY CONSOR-
   TIUM FOR POLITICAL AND
   SOCIAL RESEARCH
P.O. Box 1248
Ann Arbor, Michigan 48106

E.M. Avedon
LEISURE STUDIES DATA BANK
University of Waterloo
Waterloo, Ontario
Canada N2L 3G1

Reference Service
Machine-Readable Archives
   Division (NNR)
NATIONAL ARCHIVES AND
   RECORDS SERVICE
Washington, D.C. 20408

Patrick Bova
NATIONAL OPINION
   RESEARCH CENTER
University of Chicago
6030 South Ellis Avenue
Chicago, Illinois 60637

Lorraine Borman
NORTHWESTERN UNIVERSITY
   INFORMATION CENTER
Vogelback Computing Center
Northwestern University
Evanston, Illinois 60201

NORWEGIAN SOCIAL SCIENCE
   DATA SERVICES
Universiteet i Bergen
Hans Holmboesgt. 22
N-5014 Bergen-Univ.
Norway

Robert Darcy
OKLAHOMA DATA ARCHIVE
Center for the Application of
   the Social Sciences
Oklahoma State University
Stillwater, Oklahoma 74074

Stuart J. Thorson
POLIMETRICS LABORATORY
Department of Political Sci-
   ence
Ohio State University
Columbus, Ohio 43210

POLITICAL SCIENCE DATA
   ARCHIVE
Department of Political Sci-
   ence
Michigan State University
East Lansing, Michigan 48823

Ronald Weber, Director
POLITICAL SCIENCE LABORA-
   TORY AND DATA ARCHIVE
Department of Political Sci-
   ence
248 Woodburn Hall
Indiana University
Bloomington, Indiana 47401

David K. Miller, Director
PROJECT IMPRESS
Dartmouth College
Hanover, New Hampshire
   03755

Machine-Readable Archives
PUBLIC ARCHIVES CANADA
395 Wellington Street
Ottawa, Ontario
Canada K1A 0N3

ROPER CENTER, INC.
Box U-164R
University of Connecticut
Storrs, Connecticut 06268

SOCIAL DATA EXCHANGE
ASSOCIATION
229 Waterman Street
Providence, Rhode Island
02906

SOCIAL SCIENCE COMPUTER
RESEARCH INSTITUTE
621 Mervis Hall
University of Pittsburgh
Pittsburgh, Pennsylvania
15260

James Grifhorst
SOCIAL SCIENCE DATA
ARCHIVE
Laboratory for Political Re-
search
321A Schaeffer Hall
University of Iowa
Iowa City, Iowa 52242

JoAnn Dionne
SOCIAL SCIENCE DATA
ARCHIVE
Social Science Library
Yale University
Box 1953 Yale Station
New Haven, Connecticut
06520

SOCIAL SCIENCE DATA
ARCHIVES
Department of Sociology and
Anthropology
Carleton University
Colonel By Drive
Ottawa, Ontario
Canada K1S 5B6

Everett C. Ladd, Jr.
SOCIAL SCIENCE DATA
CENTER
University of Connecticut
Storrs, Connecticut 06268

James Pierson
SOCIAL SCIENCE DATA
CENTER
University of Pennsylvania
353 McNeil Bldg. CR
3718 Locust Walk
Philadelphia, Pennsylvania
19104

Sue A. Dodd
SOCIAL SCIENCE DATA
LIBRARY
University of North Carolina
Room 10 Manning Hall
Chapel Hill, North Carolina
27514

Judith S. Rowe
SOCIAL SCIENCE USER
SERVICE
Princeton University Com-
puter Center
87 Prospect Avenue
Princeton, New Jersey 08540

Patricia Meece
SRL DATA ARCHIVE
Survey Research Laboratory
1005 W. Nevada Street
University of Illinois
Urbana, Illinois 61801

Director
SSRC SURVEY ARCHIVE
University of Essex
Wivenhoe Park, Colchester
Essex, England

Jack Citrin, Director
STATE DATA PROGRAM, SUR-
VEY RESEARCH CENTER
2538 Channing Way
University of California
Berkeley, California 94720

Robert M. deVoursney
STATE GOVERNMENT DATA
  BASE
Council of State Governments
Iron Works Pike
Lexington, Kentucky 40578

STEINMETZARCHIEF
Herengracht 410-412
1017 BX Amsterdam
Netherlands

ZENTRAL ARCHIVE FUR
  EMPIRISCHE SOZIAL
  FORSCHUNG
Universitat zu Koln
Bachemer str. 40
D-5000 Koln 41
West Germany

References

Babbie, Earl R. *Survey Research Methods.* Belmont, Ca.: Wadsworth Publishing Company, Inc., 1973.

Barber, Raymond W. (Ed.). Machine Readable Social Science Data. *Drexel Library Quarterly,* January 1977, *13*(1).

Bell, C. G. The Joys and Sorrows of Secondary Data Use. In R. Bisco (Ed.), *Data Bases, Computers and the Social Sciences.* New York: Wiley, 1970.

Bisco, R. L. *Data Bases, Computers and the Social Sciences.* New York: Wiley, 1970.

Cutler, N. E. Political Characteristics of Elderly Cohorts in the Twenty-First Century. In S. B. Kiesler (Ed.), *Aging: Social Change.* New York: Academic Press, 1981.

Cutler, N. E. Generation, Maturation and Party Affiliation: A Cohort Analysis. *Public Opinion Quarterly,* 1969–70, *33,* 583–588.

Deutsch, Karl W. The Impact of Complex Data Bases on the Social Sciences. In R. Bisco (Ed.), *Data Bases, Computers and the Social Sciences.* New York: Wiley, 1970.

Glenn, N. D. The Social Scientific Data Archives: The Problems of Underutilization. *American Sociologist,* February 1973, *8,* 42–45.

Glenn, N. D. Problems of Comparability in Trend Studies with Opinion Poll Data. *Public Opinion Quarterly,* 1970, *34,* 82–91.

Glenn, N. D., and Zody, R. E. Cohort Analysis with National Survey Data. *Gerontologist,* 1970, *10,* 233–240.

Glenn, N. D., and Grimes, M. Aging, Voting and Political Interest. *American Sociological Review,* 1965, *30,* 843–861.

Hastings, P. K., and Southwick, J. C. Survey Data for Trend Analysis: An Index to Repeated Questions in U.S. National Surveys Held by the Roper Opinion Research Center. Williamstown, Mass.: The Roper Opinion Research Center, 1975.

Hyman, H. *Secondary Analysis of Sample Surveys: Principles, Procedures and Potentialities.* New York: Wiley, 1972.

Hyman, H. *Survey Design and Analysis.* Glencoe, Ill.: The Free Press, 1960.

Karlson, G. Age, Cohorts and the Generation of Generations. *American Sociological Review,* 1970, *35,* 710–718.

Miller, D. *Handbook of Research Design and Social Measurement* (3rd ed.). New York: David McKay Company, 1977.

Riley, M., Johnson, M., and Foner, A. (Eds.). *Aging and Society.* New York: Russell Sage Foundation, 1972.

Rowe, J. R., and Smith, K. W. Using Secondary Analysis for Quasi-Experimental Research. *Social Science Information,* 1979, *18*(3), 451–472.

Sessions, V. (Ed.). *Directory of Data Bases in the Social and Behavioral Sciences.* New York: Science Associates/International, Inc., 1974.

Shanas, E., and Binstock, R. H. (Eds.). *Handbook of Aging and the Social Sciences.* New York: Van Nostrand, 1976.

Social Science and Data Archives: Applications and Potentials. *The American Behavioral Scientist,* March-June 1976, *19*(4).

Zody, R. E. Cohort Analysis: Some Applicatory Problems in the Study of Social and Political Behavior. *Social Science Quarterly,* 1969, *50,* 374–380.

Chapter

7

Principles of Conducting Applied Research in Aging

The application of the methods discussed in this book may eventually help older people lead better lives. Applied research can lead to better decision making, improved planning, and more efficient service delivery. It can also lead to disaster. If improperly done, research can mislead decision makers. Even if research is properly done, the resistance of some organizations to unwanted information—especially if it is negative—has to be experienced to be believed.

Those doing applied research are often in an uncomfortable position. On the one hand, they must maintain the integrity, discipline, and thoroughness of the social scientist. On the other, they must respond flexibly to the urgent and immediate needs of the practitioner. To balance these conflicting demands is not easy.

This concluding chapter will provide guidance on the practical aspects of conducting applied research. There are five basic principles of applied research in aging covered in these pages:

1. The research participant must be protected.
2. The research user must be involved.
3. The researcher must balance integrity and responsiveness.
4. The researcher must anticipate and overcome barriers.
5. The research results must be useful.

Along the way to fulfilling these principles, the applied researcher will meet with frustrations and disappointments. In this chapter there will be tips on how to overcome barriers to applied research and produce results that improve the well-being of older people.

Principle One:
Protect the Participant

The U.S. Department of Health and Human Services (HHS) requires that persons involved in research as participants be protected from harm. Institutions or organizations conducting research on specialized populations (such as the aged institutionalized chronically mentally ill patient) must have a human investigations review committee. The human investigations committee has the responsibility of ensuring that research proposals include adequate protections of the rights and welfare of all participants. The committees, which should consist of five or more persons of varied backgrounds, concern themselves with such matters affecting the participant as:

- exposure to stress
- use of deception
- anonymity and confidentiality
- supervision of assistants
- selection of participants
- inducements or payments to participants
- provisions for privacy and consent

The human investigations committees require assurance that participants are adequately protected in the above matters, that informed consent was obtained, and that the risks to the participant are outweighed by potential benefits to him or her or by the potential importance of the knowledge to be gained.

The following categories of educational, behavioral, and social science research are exempt from the HHS regulations:

1. research involving survey or interview procedures, unless *all* of the following conditions exist:
   a. responses are recorded in such a way that participants can be identified directly or indirectly;
   b. responses, if known outside the research, could place the participant at risk of criminal or civil liability, or damage the participant's financial standing or employability;
   c. research deals with sensitive aspects of the participant's own behavior (such as drug use, alcohol use, sexual conduct);
2. research involving the observations of public behavior unless all of the conditions delineated above exist; and
3. research involving the collection or study of existing data, documents, records, pathological specimens, and diagnostic specimens, if these sources are publicly available or if the information is recorded by the investigator in such a manner that participants cannot be identified directly or through identifiers linked to the participants.

Despite these exceptions, it is still incumbent upon the researcher to adhere to the ethical constraints regarding informed consent and confidentiality.

The Importance of Informed Consent

Obtaining informed consent means that the investigator is obligated to inform the participant or a responsible agent of those aspects of the activity that might reasonably be considered important factors in the participant's decision to enter the project. Consent to participate must be in writing. The seriousness of the risk will determine the amount of detail and specificity the form contains. Figure 7.1 presents a typical consent form.

At the very least, the following information should be supplied to potential participants if consent is to be made on an informed basis:

- Who are the participants?
- What precisely will be done to the participants?
- Are there any risks to the participants? If so, what are they?
- What procedure will be used to ensure anonymity?
- Where will the study be conducted?

Two important facts should be borne in mind regarding informed consent:

1. consent by a participant to cooperate with a project in no way relieves the investigator from basic responsibility for safeguarding the rights and welfare of the participant; and
2. every consent form should contain a statement giving the participant the option to withdraw from the project at any time.

The Assurance of Confidentiality

It is incumbent upon the researcher to protect the identity of his or her participants in order to minimize the risk of social injury (e.g., embarrassment, ridicule, or the censure of one's family and friends). Since conducting an interview anonymously is virtually impossible, a simple but effective method for ensuring anonymity involves assigning a case number to each identified respondent. When all data have been collected and coded by assigned case number *only,* the original list of names and addresses is destroyed. A second list of code numbers is developed to replace the original coding, and the first list of assigned case numbers is also destroyed. In this way, each respondent's data become impossible to identify by anything other than a number.

Figure 7.1   Consent Form for Human Participants in Research Studies

Description

Participant's Name (please print) _____

Project Title _____

_____

Project Director/Researcher's Name_____

_____

In this space describe the project in simple language, so that the potential subject can understand it. Be sure to include the following: (1) explain the procedures to be followed, and identify those which are experimental, (2) describe any discomforts or risks, or state that there are none, and (3) describe any expected benefits.

Certification

I fully understand the program or activity in which I am being asked to participate and the procedures which will be performed. I have had an adequate chance to ask questions and understand that I may ask additional questions any time while the study is in progress.

I understand that I am participating in this activity of my own free will and I am free to withdraw my consent and discontinue my participation at any time while the study is in progress.

This is to certify that I agree to participate in this program or activity, under the direction of the researcher named above.

_____   _____

Date   Signature of Participant (or other authorized
                                               person, such as a child's parent or guardian)

                                          _____

                                          Witness (if necessary)

These protections of the participant reinforce the applied re-searcher's commitment to ethical standards. The ultimate users of research in the field of aging are older people. It would be unfortunate if the research process demeaned the very people it intended to benefit. The next section discusses involving the users in the research process; this form of participant representation should add a further measure of protection for the older person who cooperates in the research.

Principle Two: Involve the Users

One reason that research findings are frequently neglected is that the researcher failed to ask questions of interest to the user. Research findings should answer questions that are vital to *both* practitioner and researcher. Users of research should be directly involved in every stage of the research process. This means involving the users in the decisions concerning the research questions, the hypotheses, the research technique and timing, and the data collection and analysis. By involving primary users in these critical decisions, researchers force themselves to explain clearly how the research may be applied. In discussing a research approach, decision makers and clients gain new insights into study techniques and alternative methods of phrasing research questions. They also become acquainted with procedural matters which may save time during the data-collection phase of the research project.

The research user should also be involved in the analysis of the data collected. After the analysis has been completed is too late to ask users what they want to know—unless the researcher is willing to do parts of the analysis again. Inviting a panel of potential users to review the collected but unanalyzed data and to discuss analytical techniques with the researcher is much better. This will assist the researcher in finding additional ways to use the collected data. It will also force the practitioner and other users to struggle a bit with the raw data and become familiar with the data set.

The user also has a role in interpretation of the study findings. There can be many reasons for rejecting applied research findings. For example, if the research indicates that a program is ineffective, it is commonplace to blame the researcher for (1) missing the point of the program, (2) looking at the wrong program elements, (3) ignoring the important, but difficult to measure, psychic benefits of the program, or (4) all of the above. The research user who participates in interpretation of the data cannot so easily blame the researcher.

More importantly, the interpretation of the findings will reflect the interests of the users and is therefore more likely to be immediately useful than research done in relative isolation.

Principle Three: Balance Integrity and Responsiveness

The researcher is responsible for maintaining quality control over the research process and for protecting the integrity of the research approach. In applied research, the researcher is not aloof from political and practical pressures. He or she cannot fall behind a shield of research purity or an attitude of "science above all else" and expect to survive very long in the field of applied research. The researcher must engage in a give-and-take with the users and sponsors of the research. While meeting the needs of others, he or she must somehow satisfy the demands of good research. This is usually most effectively accomplished by open and frequent communication with, and participation of, those most affected by the research project.

The researcher must work effectively within time and budgetary constraints. In order to maximize effectiveness, the researcher should get as much depth from the data collected as possible (see Chapter 5). The researcher sometimes will work with colleagues from other disciplines. This may require some compromise, as differences in approach and language are worked out. The researcher is usually under pressure to produce results. His or her natural prudence may result in cautions and qualifications long before any findings are produced. What may be considered an urgent need to know by the research sponsor or user may not seem important to the researcher. Yet the applied researcher has the burden of responding to requests for information from both users and sponsors. Such responsiveness is a distinguishing characteristic of applied research.

Using Colleagues to Maintain a Balance

Maintaining a balance between integrity and responsiveness is difficult because many applied researchers work in field settings isolated from other researchers. Unless located in a university or a large firm, the researcher may find few persons interested in the research process. After all, most persons are attracted to the human services for the opportunity to serve their fellows; they may have neither the time nor the motivation to engage in the detailed discussions of methodology that delight researchers. One antidote is to collaborate with research colleagues engaged in studying similar problems.

There are several ways to find out who is currently working on research projects similar to yours. All federally sponsored research is listed by the granting agency shortly after the award. But the most effective method is to call up colleagues and experts in the field and ask them who is currently doing work. A few calls or letters—plus a review of recent conference abstracts published by professional societies in the field—will generate a list of those doing similar work at the present time.

What can be gained by contacting colleagues doing similar research? First, one has the satisfaction of sharing ideas, approaches, and enthusiasms with others. Next, many materials may be shared to mutual benefit: literature citations and annotations, research instruments, and questionnaire items that can be replicated or corroborated. Third, under certain circumstances two or more applied researchers may use the same participants or study site. This is possible when the researchers can coordinate their data-gathering schedule to avoid duplication. Fourth, sharing raw data means each data set can be manipulated by more than one researcher, thereby increasing the possibility that interesting findings will be made. Finally, collaborators can share their results for both criticism and stimulation.

There are pitfalls to collaboration, however. Collaboration requires that participants coordinate their activities. If any colleague is reluctant to cooperate, the venture is likely to fail. A collaboration is most effective when all participants pull their weight equally. If deadlines are set and constantly broken, if understandings are reached and constantly misinterpreted, if quarrels occur and are never settled, if products due are only infrequently delivered, then it is unlikely that a collaboration can be successful. It is probably better to pull out of a collaborative effort that is going bad than to spend time and energy trying to correct repeated deficiencies in the cooperative spirit.

Collaborations take time, effort, and expense. Sometimes the aggravation is tremendous, but the results of a successful collaboration are worth the headaches: shared data, enhanced insights, corroborated findings, and a series of lively debates along the way. Most important, there will be colleagues available to help balance the integrity needed by the pure researcher with the responsiveness required of an investigator working in applied research.

Involving the Sponsor
in Applied Research

Those who pay for research do not own the research—they only think they do. In reality, research is jointly owned by the researcher, the sponsor, and the user. Since the sponsor pays for the research, however, both the user and the researcher recognize that the sponsor has something important to say during the process. Usually, the sponsor will set the general framework for the research—the major questions to be asked, the acceptable approaches which may be used, and the timeframe for producing the research. In the happiest circumstance the sponsor and researcher work along with the user representatives to turn out a product that is beneficial to all parties. In some cases the sponsor all but ignores the researcher until the final report has been received.

Occasionally the sponsor will attempt to interfere directly in the conduct of the study, especially to forestall findings that are against the sponsor's interest. This places the researcher in the dilemma of having to choose between accuracy and acceptability. Usually a compromise can be worked out which violates neither the ethics of the researcher nor the political realities of the sponsor. In the final analysis the researcher's responsibility is to understand the political constraints placed on applied research and to deal with them in a way that best serves the interests of all parties in the research process. If the researcher cannot accommodate himself or herself to these limitations, any differences should be settled as soon as they are recognized.

The sponsor is responsible for making the political constraints as clear as possible at the start of the research. The sponsor should inform the researcher of any potential political conflict in time to avoid an unnecessary flare-up. The sponsor is also responsible for accepting or rejecting the final report and should have several checkpoints set up for evaluating the research project as it progresses. If deadlines are constantly missed or if intermediate products are poorly done, the sponsor should seek improvements. If the research continues to be below standard, the sponsor should then cut the funds.

The relationship between the sponsor and the researcher should be creative and productive. A balance must be struck between the urgent needs of the sponsor and the responsibility of the researcher to remain careful and objective. This balancing act is one of the most important aspects of applied research.

Principle Four:
Persevere

The applied researcher in an organization serving the aging will be faced with several problems. There may be resistance by staff to in-house research; "We do not have enough time to do our work, let alone dabble in research" is a common complaint. The applied researcher must convince his or her co-workers that questions they consider important will be answered by the study. In many cases the in-house researcher will have other work responsibilities in addition to research; switching from a practice to a research frame of mind is hard, so block out time for each activity. And in nearly all cases funds will be limited and time will be short.

The applied researcher must plan carefully. Collecting data "because it is there" results in tedious hours of trying to figure out what to do with it all. When working on in-house research have a clear statement of the questions to be answered during the data-analysis phase from the very beginning. Not only will the research be more efficient, but co-workers may look forward to the answer and reduce the barrier of staff resistance to research.

Another possible barrier pertains to sponsored research. If the sponsor is vague about expectations, the applied researcher may find it difficult to produce clear findings. The best solution is to do an assignment analysis which clearly specifies the purposes, terms, and expected findings of the study. During any in-house research the applied researcher is likely to meet resistance from participants—"What, another study?!?!"—and may also suffer from shortages of time and resources. Here again, careful planning and involvement of the users in the research process help to overcome these resistances.

A further barrier to applied research is a psychological one. The researcher is a systematic, linear thinker; the world is sometimes chaotic and erratic. The researcher can get frustrated. What seemed crystal clear during a brainstorm may turn all fuzzy when explained to a busy executive. The tendency to move in and out of a conceptual fog and up and down the emotional ladder is a trademark of researchers. During letdowns and disappointments, the researcher has two choices: either exercise vigorously or overeat. Sometimes taking a break from the effort will restore one's sense of clarity. Certainly talking to colleagues helps. But the best comfort comes in knowing that, if the researcher is well trained, the mood will pass. It is very easy to feel depressed at the end of a research project. Perhaps too little time was available to complete the analysis or to polish the findings. But more likely, the response to the research report may be far from overwhelming. It is easy to be discouraged if the result of many hours of research and analysis is acknowledged by a mere verbal or written grunt.

This lack of appreciation and failure to provide the researcher with immediate gratification has several causes. Most research reports must be carefully read and digested before they are applied. Decision makers seldom rely solely on a report, but rather add the findings to other information gathered by talking to their spouses, reading the trade journals, and listening to their intuition. Also, for most reports there is a sleeper effect. The report is scanned and filed away for future reference. When it appears applicable, it is taken off the shelf and put to use. Meanwhile, several people have read it and a consensus has developed. The report is approved by certain key figures, and soon "everyone" is citing and using the report. Unfortunately, the report's author is probably on another assignment by this time and finds the belated appreciation gratifying—at last—but also distracting. A way to short-circuit this process, of course, is to work closely with the report's users during the final stages of the research process on applying the findings immediately.

The many challenges made to applied research findings may test the patience and sense of integrity of the researcher. The vagueness of some programs makes evaluation findings easy to challenge. Even if a program has clear objectives, negative findings are often rejected because supporters feel the long-range effects of the program will be positive. The usual tactic is to attack the research method as inappropriate, inadequate, or biased. A frequent point of attack is the sample—"Sure the results are negative; the researchers did not visit states such as (name any states not in random sample) in which the program is a great success."

The applied researcher should never underestimate the sensitivity of vested interests. If a finding casts doubt on a favored program or policy position, interest groups may attack the research. Of course, if the suggestions in this book are followed, the findings will withstand the assault. But there are a few additional protections. The involvement of users will sensitize the researcher to those areas which may be extremely controversial. In such cases the researcher should exercise caution in phrasing the findings. There is no sense in generalizing too broadly or overstating a situation, thereby prompting vested interests to become defensive. On the other hand, the researcher has the responsibility to tell the truth. A finding can be sanitized to the point of meaninglessness. A valid finding should be stated clearly, along with its limitations. The researcher must have the fortitude to answer criticism, some of it unfair, about the study. Sad to say, researchers themselves are not above attempting to discredit colleagues' studies which go against the established wisdom of the day. It takes diplomacy, courage, and tenacity to present a finding that challenges current conventions, but it is through such actions that real change occurs.

Principle Five: Be Useful

Of what use is applied research in the field of aging? It provides the factual knowledge needed to solve a practical problem. If the findings are valid, they can be used to improve the well-being of older people. There are several tests of utility:

- Does the research attempt to answer clearly stated questions?
- Are there users waiting to apply the answers to the questions?
- Have users been involved in the design, data-collection, and analysis phases of the research?
- Are there concrete plans to disseminate the findings to appropriate users?
- Has the research altered policy or practice in a manner which improves the quality of life for older people?

Many applied research methods are described in this book. The application of findings from these methods may be useful when a program is being designed, introduced into the field, managed, or considered for renewal. An applied research method is effective if it meets the following criteria:

1. The method is appropriate for answering the research questions. For instance, a case study will answer exploratory questions, while a quasi-experimental design is needed to test the effectiveness of a clinical intervention.
2. The method is acceptable to users of the research. For example, a project management analysis may be acceptable to managers, while a summative evaluation may be of more interest to policy makers.
3. The method is the most efficient available. For instance, a review of existing case records may be as effective for less cost and effort as a mailed survey in answering certain questions.
4. The use of the findings is determined in advance and actions are anticipated based on the findings. For example, the results of a survey may be used to design a service program needed by local older persons.

For the findings of well-conducted research to be put to extensive use, the report must be widely disseminated. Although prepared with specific users in mind, the report may be interesting to other users as well. The most common form of dissemination is publication in scholarly and trade journals. Preparing a manuscript that follows the format provided by the editors and being willing to rewrite will improve the chances of having articles published. Another common method of dissemination is printing the report in quantity and mailing it to interested parties; funds for printing should be included in the initial research budget. Reports should also be submitted to such on-line computer document sources as the National Technical Information Service. Doing so assures a wide audience, since the reports are key-worded for retrieval along a variety of dimensions, such as subject matter, location, and methodology.

Presentation at professional meetings is another common method of disseminating findings. Less common is attempting to get the results directly to older people themselves; news releases, public announcement spots on TV and radio, and brochures are three methods for doing so. Presentations at senior centers or housing units give the applied researcher an opportunity to meet the ultimate user of the study. Where possible illustrate how the results add to previous findings. In all cases a detailed dissemination plan which specifies target audiences, information to be delivered, and methods of reaching the audience should be worked out at the start of a research project.

The future of applied research in aging is filled with promise. As the aged increase in both number and proportion of the population, there will be a continuing need for information and facts. Knowing which factors lead to distress among the elderly and which interventions are most successful in reducing the distress will become increasingly important.

The growing availability of computers for the small organization will encourage the trend toward agency-based research. Instead of relying on expensive large-scale research studies, practitioners will increasingly use their computers to do research based on client and service activity data already stored in their computers.

For the first time in history, large numbers of people will live in retirement. Planned social change may be required to assure a quality of life acceptable to all members of the elderly population. Since the elderly themselves represent an enormous resource, the applied researcher can help to enable and empower older people to create their own solutions to any problems they may face. Keeping older people healthy, productive, and self-sufficient should be high on the agenda of any applied researcher.

As new programs are designed and introduced into the field of aging, the applied researcher can perform implementation analyses which improve the chances of ultimate success of a program. As programs are operated, the applied researcher can conduct performance management analyses which improve service delivery. Through continued study of effective clinical and field technique, the applied researcher can aid in the discovery of successful techniques and interventions.

The ultimate test of applied research is the benefit it brings to the older population. Will older people be able to function better as a result of the research? Will older people notice improvements in the quality of their lives? Will the economic status of older persons be enhanced? Will older people benefit through improved health? Will older people be empowered to meet their own goals? The answer to at least one of these questions should be "Yes" for any applied research undertaken in the field of aging. The ultimate gratification for applied researchers is knowing that they have contributed to answering the three questions asked by Immanuel Kant:

What can I know?
What may I hope?
What must I do?

and applying the answers to improve the quality of life for older persons.

References

Monroe, Judson. *Effective Research and Report Writing in Government.* New York: McGraw-Hill, 1980.

O'Brien, John, and Streib, Gordon F. (Eds.). *Evaluative Research on Social Programs for the Elderly.* Washington, D.C.: U.S. Government Printing Office, 1977.

Patton, Michael Q. *Utilization-Focused Evaluation.* Beverly Hills, Ca.: Sage Publications, 1978.

Weiss, Carole H. *Evaluation Research.* Englewood Cliffs, N.J.: Prentice-Hall, 1972.

Williams, Walter. *The Implementation Perspective.* Berkeley: University of California Press, 1981.

Appendix

Resources and Information in Gerontology

This Appendix lists resources for the gerontologist and provides summaries of the types of information currently available. It is divided into three sections.

The first section contains bibliographic references. These are further divided into the following categories: indexes and abstracts, periodicals, bibliographies, handbooks, directories, statistical publications, and on-line searching. A sample search is documented so that readers can get a sense for the basic steps involved in doing an on-line search. The relevant on-line data bases for the gerontologist are broken into specific categories (e.g., general, scientific/technical, health, business, and social sciences).

The second section provides a list of organizations and clearinghouses concerned with the aging; the third and final section lists literature related to funding within gerontology.

Bibliographic Sources

Searching the literature is one of the most difficult tasks a researcher faces. The massive volume of information in the literature and the multidisciplinary nature of gerontology make the literature search a time-consuming and sometimes expensive venture. Fortunately, information managers and librarians organize the literature and its references so that a researcher can examine it in a standardized manner. This section identifies the sources needed to identify existing information and research related to gerontology. The following listings emphasize gerontological sources, but because of the cross-disciplinary character of gerontology and the lack of a comprehensive aged-specific resource, these references include some more general resources, such as the Humanities Index, Psychological Abstracts, and Smithsonian Scientific Information Exchange.

Indexes and Abstract Services

Indexes and abstracts refer the user to periodical and report literature. The references are arranged by subject, with most of the gerontological materials indexed under the terms *aged* or *aging, elderly, geriatrics, middle-aged, older adults, old age,* and *gerontology.* Check the index under the terms related to the literature search. For example, on a topic such as the effects of the retirement decision on health, look at related terms such as *retirement* and *retirement age,* as well as *aged.*

The following indexes are selected for the fields they represent. For a complete listing of all available indexing and abstracting services, consult Ulrich's International Periodical Directory, published annually by Bowker (New York). This directory is available in almost every library.

AMERICAN STATISTICS INDEX. Washington, D.C.: Congressional Information Service, 1973–.

Also available on-line.

ARECO'S QUARTERLY INDEX TO PERIODICAL LITERATURE ON AGING. Detroit, Mich.: ARECO, 1982–.

BIOLOGICAL ABSTRACTS. Philadelphia: BIOSIS, 1927–.

Also available on-line.

BUSINESS PERIODICALS INDEX. New York: H. W. Wilson, 1958–.

Indexes pension, retirement, and older worker literature.

CURRENT INDEX TO JOURNALS IN EDUCATION. Phoenix, Ariz.: Oryx Press, 1969–.

Also available on-line as part of the ERIC data base.

CURRENT LITERATURE ON AGING. Washington, D.C.: National Council on the Aging, 1963–.

DISSERTATION ABSTRACTS INTERNATIONAL. Ann Arbor, Mich.: University Microfilms International, 1938–.

Also available on-line.

HOSPITAL LITERATURE INDEX. Chicago: American Hospital Association, 1945–.

Available on-line as part of the HEALTH PLANNING AND ADMINISTRATION data base of MEDLARS (National Library of Medicine).

HUMAN RESOURCES ABSTRACTS. Beverly Hills: Sage Publications, 1966–.

Formerly POVERTY & HUMAN RESOURCES ABSTRACTS.

INDEX MEDICUS. Washington, D.C: National Library of Medicine, 1960–.

Available on MEDLARS data bases.

KEYWORK INDEX TO TRAINING AND EDUCATIONAL RESOURCES IN AGING. Durham, N.C.: Duke University Center for the Study of Aging and Human Development.

The KWIC Project has located, indexed, and identified thousands of educational and training materials in gerontology. Complete ordering information is provided for accessibility.

MONTHLY CATALOG OF UNITED STATES GOVERNMENT PUBLICATIONS. Washington, D.C.: U.S. Government Printing Office, 1895–.

Also available on-line as GPO MONTHLY CATALOG.

POPULATION INDEX. Princeton, N.J.: Population Association of America, 1935 .

PSYCHOLOGICAL ABSTRACTS. Washington, D.C.: American Psychological Association, 1927–.

Also available on-line as PSYCHINFO.

PUBLIC AFFAIRS INFORMATION SERVICE BULLETIN. New York: PAIS, 1915–.

READERS' GUIDE TO PERIODICAL LITERATURE. New York: H. W. Wilson, 1905–.

RESOURCES IN EDUCATION. Bethesda, Md.: Educational Resources Information Center, 1966–.

Available on-line on the ERIC data base.

SOCIAL SCIENCES CITATION INDEX. Philadelphia: Institute for Scientific Information, 1969–.

Also available on-line.

SOCIAL SCIENCES INDEX. New York: H. W. Wilson, 1907–.

SOCIAL WORK RESEARCH AND ABSTRACTS. New York: National Association of Social Workers, 1965–.

SOCIOLOGICAL ABSTRACTS. San Diego: Sociological Abstracts, 1952–.
Also available on-line.

URBAN AFFAIRS ABSTRACTS. Washington, D.C.: National League of Cities, 1971–.

WOMEN STUDIES ABSTRACTS. Rush, N.Y.: Rush Publishing, 1972–.

Periodicals

Periodicals are essential for the researcher because they provide the latest information in printed format. Most often no book is yet available reporting the information and research available in the periodicals. Periodicals also present current thought on issues and people.

Access to the multitude of articles and reports is through use of indexes and abstracting services, many of which are now available on-line.

The periodicals cited focus on gerontology or geriatrics solely. The many other periodicals which frequently publish articles related to aging or the aged are too numerous to list here. The Social Gerontology Resource Center of SCAN has identified over 250 such journals and newsletters.

ACTIVITIES, ADAPTATION & AGING. Quarterly. 1980–
Haworth Press
149 Fifth Avenue
New York, NY 10010

This new journal attempts to provide a multidisciplinary approach to activities with the aged. The contents include articles on theory, case studies, research, and specific programming.

AGE. Quarterly. 1978–
American Aging Association, Inc.
University of Nebraska
42nd and Dewey
Omaha, NE 68105

AGE reports the research and findings on biomedical aging which includes DNA, RNA, hormones, lysosomes, central nervous system, cardiovascular system, and muscle, to name a few subject areas.

AGE AND AGEING: THE JOURNAL OF THE BRITISH GERIATRICS SOCIETY AND THE BRITISH SOCIETY FOR RESEARCH ON AGEING. Quarterly. 1972–
> Bailliere Tindal
> 35 Red Lion Square
> London, WC1R 4SG

> This journal reports research on aging and the clinical, epidemiological, and psychological aspects of medicine in old age. Features a review of recent literature in the field.

AGED CARE AND SERVICES REVIEW. Quarterly. 1977–
> Haworth Press
> 149 Fifth Avenue
> New York, NY 10010

> Each issue presents a lengthy and in-depth literature review of a specific topic, such as life adjustment techniques for the dysfunctional elderly. The review concludes with an extensive bibliography. The second half of every issue contains a selected bibliography of journal literature related to aging and service delivery to the aged.

AGEING INTERNATIONAL. Quarterly. 1974–
> International Federation on Ageing
> 1909 K Street, NW
> Washington, DC 20049

> This bulletin reports recent research and conference reports which have particular value to an international readership. Each issue has a feature article, business news of the federation, and annotated book reviews of international interest.

AGING. Bimonthly. 1951–
> U.S. Administration on Aging
> Washington, DC 20201

> AGING is the official publication of AoA. It reports on programs in area agencies on aging, states, and foreign countries. Notice of research and contract awards, news from other federal agencies, recent publications, course and conference calendar make this a valuable resource for researchers, practitioners, and program planners.

AGING AND LEISURE LIVING. Monthly. 1978–1981
> Modern Life Systems, Inc.
> Random Lake, WI 53075

As the official journal of the National Geriatrics Society, this publication addressed issues of importance to nursing home staff, such as health care delivery, training, programs, and legislation. It ceased publication in 1981.

AGING AND WORK. Quarterly. 1978–
National Council on the Aging, Inc.
600 Maryland Avenue, SW
Washington, DC 20024

Published as INDUSTRIAL GERONTOLOGY from 1969–78, AGING AND WORK reports recent research on employment and the elderly, as well as descriptions of new and innovative programs. Each issue includes updates and important legislation related to aging and work.

AMERICAN GERIATRICS SOCIETY JOURNAL. Monthly. 1953–
American Geriatrics Society
10 Columbus Circle
New York, NY 10019

The JOURNAL contains original papers on laboratory and clinical aspects of geriatric medicine, such as studies of the causes, prevention, and treatment of disorders of the aging, nutrition, mental health, animal research, and social problems. The Society's members are physicians and interested persons concerned with the health of older people and related research.

AMERICAN HEALTH CARE ASSOCIATION JOURNAL. Bimonthly. 1975–
Modern Healthcare
P.O. Box 665
Hightstown, NJ 08520

Written for the administrators of long-term care facilities, the JOURNAL focuses on personnel matters, the nursing home environment, and payment systems, and includes columns on tax information, legislative updates, and recent publications.

BULLETIN ON AGING. Biannual. 1975–
Social Development Branch
Centre for Social Development and
    Humanitarian Affairs
Department of Economic and Social Affairs
United Nations Secretariat
P.O. Box 500
A-1400 Vienna, Austria

The BULLETIN is a newsletter on activities of the United Nations relating to the elderly, and includes recent tabulations on the older population around the world. Selected issues also contain bibliographies of recent publications.

DEATH EDUCATION. Quarterly. 1977–
Hemisphere Publishing Corp.
1025 Vermont Avenue, NW
Washington, DC 20005

Though not entirely aged-related, DEATH EDUCATION contains numerous articles directly related to the elderly. Its focus is on death and dying education, counseling, and care of the dying.

EDUCATIONAL GERONTOLOGY. Quarterly. 1976–
Hemisphere Publishing Corp.
1025 Vermont Avenue, NW
Washington, DC 20005

The audience for this journal includes adult educators, psychologists, and practitioners as well as gerontologists. It focuses on all aspects of gerontology and education. Each issue contains a topical review of the literature and research.

EXPERIMENTAL AGING RESEARCH. Bimonthly. 1975–
Beech Hill Enterprises, Inc.
Box 29
Mount Desert, ME 04660

EXPERIMENTAL GERONTOLOGY. Bimonthly. 1977–
Pergamon Press, Inc.
Maxwell House
Fairview Park
Elmsford, NY 10523

GENERATIONS. Quarterly. 1975–
Western Gerontological Society
785 Market Street, Suite 1114
San Francisco, CA 94103

Contains usually brief articles on policy or service needs issues. Selected issues are devoted to one topic (for example, the rural elderly).

GERIATRICS. Monthly. 1946–
Harcourt, Brace, Jovanovich, Inc.
757 Third Avenue
New York, NY 10017

Written for office-based primary care physicians, GERIATRICS publishes original clinical papers on the care of middle-aged and elderly patients. Each issue contains a news column, a section on new research, and a column on nonclinical issues important to its readers.

GERIATRIC NURSING: AMERICAN JOURNAL OF CARE FOR THE AG-
ING. Bimonthly: 1980–
    American Journal of Nursing
    555 West 57th Street
    New York, NY 10019

    Written for nurses who provide medical care and services to the
    older population, GERIATRIC NURSING includes legislative,
    psychosocial, and medical information.

GERONTOLOGIST. Bimonthly. 1961–
    Gerontological Society
    1835 K Street, NW
    Washington, DC 20006

    Written for the professional practitioner in gerontology, the
    GERONTOLOGIST reports the results of research and innovative
    practice in social gerontology. The journal includes editorials,
    book reviews, audiovisual reviews, and a conference calendar.

GERONTOLOGY & GERIATRICS EDUCATION. Quarterly. 1980–
    University of Texas Press
    2100 Comal
    Austin, TX 78722

    Designed to serve as a forum for the exchange of curricula, this
    journal is written for educators at the college and graduate levels,
    and for those who teach others to serve the elderly. Regular
    features include book reviews, programs in gerontology, and a
    calendar of events.

HEALTH CARE FINANCING ADMINISTRATION REVIEW. Quarterly.
1979–
    U.S. Health Care Financing Administration
    ORDS Publications
    Room 1E9, Oak Meadows Building
    6340 Security Blvd.
    Baltimore, MD 21235

    HCFA REVIEW presents the result of research, statistical and
    demonstration studies conducted by HCFA staff. Each issue re-
    ports program statistics on Medicare and Medicaid. Selected
    issues report the titles and recipients of Research and Demon-
    stration contracts.

HOME HEALTH CARE SERVICES QUARTERLY. Quarterly. 1980–
    Haworth Press
    149 Fifth Avenue
    New York, NY 10010

    A new journal devoted specifically to administration, research,
    theory, and practice of home health care services.

INTERNATIONAL JOURNAL OF AGING & HUMAN DEVELOPMENT. Quarterly. 1973–
Baywood Publishing Co., Inc.
120 Marine Street
Farmingdale, NY 11735

Formerly AGING & HUMAN DEVELOPMENT, this journal emphasizes the psychological and social studies of aging and the aged.

JOURNAL OF CLINICAL AND EXPERIMENTAL GERONTOLOGY. Quarterly. 1979–
Marcel Dekker, Inc.
270 Madison Avenue
New York, NY 10016

JOURNAL OF GERIATRIC PSYCHIATRY. Semiannually. 1967–
Boston Society for Gerontological Psychiatry, Inc.
International Universities Press, Inc.
315 Fifth Avenue
New York, NY 10016

The JOURNAL serves as the official organ of the Boston Society for Gerontological Psychiatry. An entire issue may be devoted to one topic, such as isolation among the elderly. Regular features include book reviews, president's page, and books received.

JOURNAL OF GERONTOLOGICAL NURSING. Bimonthly. 1975–
Charles B. Slack, Inc.
6900 Grove Street
Thorofare, NJ 08086

The JOURNAL serves as the literature source on gerontological nursing. Some of its goals include becoming a focal point of information; providing literature related to nursing care of the elderly in all settings; reporting the latest developments in geriatrics and gerontology; and exploring problem areas and solutions in gerontological nursing.

JOURNAL OF GERONTOLOGICAL SOCIAL WORK. Quarterly. 1978–
Haworth Press
149 Fifth Avenue
New York, NY 10010

A new quarterly journal, this periodical is devoted to the "study of social work theory and practice in the field of aging." It is written to meet the practice needs of social work administrators and for practitioners in gerontology.

JOURNAL OF GERONTOLOGY. Bimonthly. 1946–
Gerontological Society
1835 K Street, NW
Washington, DC 20006

The JOURNAL publishes contributed manuscripts on the biological, medical, psychological and sociological aspects of aging. From 1950–1980 it also published the Shock bibliography in each issue. The JOURNAL contains theoretical and research papers, as well as review articles.

JOURNAL OF LONG-TERM CARE ADMINISTRATION. Quarterly. 1972–
American College of Nursing
  Home Administrators
4650 East-West Highway
Bethesda, MD 20814

The Society represents administrators of long-term care facilities. Its journal publishes material on nursing home administration and health administration.

JOURNAL OF MINORITY AGING. Irregularly. 1978–
National Council on Black Aging, Inc.
North Carolina Senior Citizens Federation, Inc.
P.O. Box 8513
Durham, NC 27707

Formerly BLACK AGING (1975–1977), this is a refereed publication devoted to the dissemination of research and pertinent information to those interested in minority aging.

JOURNAL OF NUTRITION FOR THE ELDERLY. Quarterly. 1980–
Haworth Press
149 Fifth Avenue
New York, NY 10010

The goals of this new journal are to disseminate information on the care, education, and research needed to prepare for meeting the nutritional needs of the elderly.

LONG TERM CARE. Weekly. 1972–
McGraw-Hill
122 Avenue of the Americas
New York, NY 10020

Formerly WASHINGTON REPORT IN LONG TERM CARE.

LONG TERM CARE AND HEALTH SERVICES ADMINISTRATION. Quarterly. 1976–
Panel Publishers
14 Plaza Road
Greenvale, NY 11548

Formerly JOURNAL OF LONG TERM CARE AND HEALTH SERVICES, ADMINISTRATION.

NURSING HOMES. Bimonthly. 1950–
Heldref Publications
4000 Albemarle Street, NW
Washington, DC 20016

Articles address matters such as social services, medical treatment, housekeeping, dietetics, dentistry, and pharmacy. It is written for the owners, administrators, and personnel of nursing homes.

OMEGA: JOURNAL OF DEATH AND DYING. Quarterly. 1970–
Baywood Publishing Co., Inc.
120 Marine Street
Farmington, NY 11735

Publishes reports of recent research on all aspects of death, with emphasis on the psycho-social perspective.

PENSION WORLD. Monthly. 1964–
Communication Channels, Inc.
6285 Barfield Road
Atlanta, GA 30328

Formerly PENSION & WELFARE NEWS, this is a valuable resource of information on pensions and benefits that affect older workers. Written for pension plan sponsors and investment managers.

PERSPECTIVE ON AGING. Bimonthly. 1972–
National Council on the Aging, Inc.
600 Maryland Avenue, SW
Washington, DC 20024

Serves as the house organ of the Council, and contains substantive articles on policy issues and program needs.

RESEARCH ON AGING. Quarterly. 1979–
Sage Publications, Inc.
275 Beverly Drive
Beverly Hills, CA 90212

A new journal in the field of gerontology, RESEARCH ON AGING presents recent research on a broad range of disciplines, including sociology, geriatrics, history, psychology, anthropology, public health, economics, political science, criminal justice, and social work. Some topics receive systematic attention.

SOCIAL SECURITY BULLETIN. Monthly. 1938–
U.S. Social Security Administration
Superintendent of Documents
U.S. Government Printing Office
Washington, DC 20402

The BULLETIN is the official publication of the SSA, and reports research of the Office of Research and Statistics. Program data are in each issue; the cumulative ANNUAL STATISTICAL SUPPLEMENT is also provided to all subscribers.

Bibliographies

Bibliographies serve as a guide to a body of literature on a specific topic and as a means to contend with the burgeoning number of publications. The major characteristics of bibliographies are that (1) they have a standard format for citing the selected publications; (2) they identify the materials so one can locate and/or acquire a copy; (3) they attempt to be select reference lists for an entire body of literature.

A BIBLIOGRAPHY OF DOCTORAL DISSERTATIONS ON AGING FROM AMERICAN INSTITUTIONS OF HIGHER LEARNING. In *Journal of Gerontology*, 1971–.

Compiled annually, sometimes cumulatively, now by Jean E. Mueller and Margaret L. Kronauer. The dissertation titles are arranged under subheadings of the major headings: biological, behavioral, social, and health services. Each entry contains the author's name, title, university, academic year, and the ordering number.

Conrad, James H. AN ANNOTATED BIBLIOGRAPHY OF THE HISTORY OF OLD AGE IN AMERICA. Denton, Tex.: North Texas State University Center for the Studies in Aging, 1978. 31 pp.

The compiler has drawn upon the disciplines of history, social work, sociology, gerontology, and geriatrics for the history of old age.

Council of Planning Librarians. EXCHANGE BIBLIOGRAPHIES. Monticello, Ill.: Council, various.

The Aged and their Families. Richard Portnoy. No. 914. November, 1975. 13 pp.

Alternatives to Institutionalization for the Aged: An Overview and Bibliography. Liz Karnes. No. 877. September, 1975. 29 pp.

A Bibliography on Transportation for Elderly and Handicapped Persons. James H. Miller and others. No. P-9. June, 1978. 40 pp.

Design and Social Planning in Housing for the Elderly, 1975–1977: An Annotated Bibliography. Rosemary Rengers. No. A-13. September, 1978. 140 pp.

Housing and the Aged: 1974–1975: A Selected Bibliography. Jean Koch. No. 1028. April, 1976. 60 pp.

Housing for the Elderly: A Selected Bibliography. David A. Spaeth. No. A-308. August, 1978. 24 pp.

Housing for the Elderly—Design, Economics, Legislation and Socio-Psychological Aspects. Marilyn Dee Casto and Savannah S. Day. No. 1128. September, 1976. 30 pp.

Minority Group Aged in America: A Comprehensive Bibliography of Recent Publications on Blacks, Mexican-Americans, Native Americans, Chinese, and Japanese. Peter T. Suzuki. No. 816. June, 1975. 25 pp.

Mobile Services and the Elderly: A Bibliography. Victor Regnier and others. No. 1378. October, 1978. 21 pp.

Planning for the Aging: A Selected Bibliography of Planning for the Aging in an Urban and Regional Context. David L. Ames. No. P-272. July, 1979. 29 pp.

Psychosocial Issues Relevant to Creating Environments for the Aging: A Selected Annotated Bibliography, 1955 to Present. Lois Sigel. No. A-31. January, 1979. 35 pp.

Retirement Migration: A Bibliography. Pamela W. Reeves and others. No. 1510. April, 1978. 11 pp.

Social Security in the United States: A Classified Bibliography. Gerald Musgrave. No. P-49. August, 1978. 45 pp.

Sociology of Retirement: A Selected Bibliographic Research Guide (1950–1973). Prakash C. Sharma. No. P-67. September, 1978. 14 pp.

Davis, Lenwood G. THE BLACK AGED IN THE UNITED STATES: AN ANNOTATED BIBLIOGRAPHY. West Port, Conn.: Greenwood Press, 1980. 200 pp.

The compiler introduces the bibliography with references to aged slaves in the literature of slavery in the U.S. The citations are arranged by subject with a major heading for each type of publication: general books, dissertations and theses, government publications, and articles. He concludes with a list of Black Old Folks' Homes, 1860–1980, and an index.

Edwards, Willie M., and Flynn, Frances. GERONTOLOGY: A CORE LIST OF SIGNIFICANT WORKS. Ann Arbor: University of Michigan, Wayne State University Institute of Gerontology, 1978. 158 pp.

With the assistance of nearly thirty noted gerontologists, the compilers have produced a basic or core collection of gerontological literature. This bibliography focuses on social gerontology, but also includes sections on health, biology, and nutrition. Some especially useful sections are abstracts and indexes, journals, and the author and title index. A second edition will be forthcoming.

Employee Benefit Research Institute. A BIBLIOGRAPHY ON RETIREMENT INCOME PROGRAMS. Washington, D.C.: EBRI, 1979. 2 volumes, 338 pp.

Prepared under contract by Mathematica Policy Research, Inc., the bibliography is arranged into seven topical areas: demographics, private pensions, public pensions and Social Security, effect of pensions on capital markets and capital formation, the impacts of inflation, providing income security, and modeling retirement income programs. Volume I arranges the entries by author and lists the journals used as sources. Volume II provides annotations of the same citations.

McIlvaine, B., and Munkur, Mohini. AGING: A GUIDE TO REFERENCE SOURCES, JOURNALS, AND GOVERNMENT PUBLICATIONS. Storrs, Conn.: University of Connecticut, 1978. 162 pp.

Intended for researchers and service providers, the bibliography includes reference sources since 1970; federal, state, foreign, and international publications from 1975 to 1977; and important journals in the field, including popular and research titles.

Moss, Walter C. HUMANISTIC PERSPECTIVE ON AGING. Ann Arbor: University of Michigan, Wayne State University Institute of Gerontology, 1976. 76 pp.

This bibliography is included here because all citations come from the humanities; they provide some insight into aging, old age, or death; and the publications listed are readily available and comprehensible to the lay reader. This annotated bibliography begins with an essay on the evolution of the humanistic study of gerontology. The literature on aging and old age is divided into drama, essays, novels, poetry, and short stories. There are sections on autobiographies, reflections on death, and film resources.

Mubarak, Jill, Sapienza, Diane, and Shimane, Robert. GERONTOLOGY AND THE LAW: A SELECTED BIBLIOGRAPHY. Los Angeles:

University of Southern California Asa V. Call Law Library, 1979. 102 pp.

Intended as an aid to legal research, this bibliography is arranged in the following subject areas: general works about the aged, crime, employment, health, housing, income, legal services, social services, and political activity, and special sections on foreign and comparative literature.

National Gerontology Resource Center. INTRODUCTORY READINGS IN GERONTOLOGY. Washington, D.C.: NRTA-AARP National Gerontology Resource Center, 1981.

Compiled for those new to gerontology, the bibliography includes recent texts in gerontology, popular and easily available titles, and selected classics in the field.

Place, Linna Funk, et al. AGING AND THE AGED: AN ANNOTATED BIBLIOGRAPHY AND LIBRARY RESEARCH GUIDE. Boulder, Col.: Westview Press, 1981. 128 pp.

Written for those new to gerontology, this bibliography introduces the reader to general sources of information through library research. The bibliography provides annotated references to major scholarly publications in gerontology, with emphasis on the physiological, psychological, sociological, and environmental aspects of aging.

Rooke, M. Leigh, and Wingrove, C. Ray. GERONTOLOGY: AN AN-NOTATED BIBLIOGRAPHY. Washington, D.C.: University Press of America, 1977. 262 pp.

This bibliography cites important monographs and reports from the late '60s through 1976. The entries are arranged topically after a 35-page list of more general publications. The bibliography includes an author index.

Seem, Bonnie, and Missinne, Leo. COMPARATIVE GERONTOLOGY: A SELECTED ANNOTATED BIBLIOGRAPHY. Washington, D.C.: International Federation on Aging, 1979. 55 pp.

Arranged by author, this bibliography provides "research materials on comparative gerontology which were published since 1960, and which are available at most college and university libraries in the U.S. or are available on interlibrary loan."

Shock, Nathan W. A CLASSIFIED BIBLIOGRAPHY OF GERONTOLOGY AND GERIATRICS. Supplement One, 1949–1955. Supplement Two, 1956–1961. Stanford, Cal.: Stanford University, 1951, 1957, 1963.

Over 50,000 reports, monographs, and articles are referenced in these three volumes. The Shock Bibliography is *the* bibliography in gerontology. The entries are arranged by subject, and primarily cover biology and medicine, with some social gerontology included. An additional subject index cross-references the entries. Each volume contains a valuable author index. The bibliography was published bimonthly from 1950–1980 in the *Journal of Gerontology*. Publication has now ceased, as computer information systems are expected to fill the void.

TRANSPORTATION AND THE ELDERLY: A SELECTED BIBLIOGRAPHY. Washington, D.C.: U.S. Administration on Aging, 1980. 44 pp.

Prepared under contract by Franklin Research Center, the bibliography brings together relevant literature of approximately 475 citations organized under eleven categories: overview literature, planning, needs assessment, methodology and evaluation coordination, area specific planning, programs and services, financing and costs, equipment and facilities, barrier-free access, and bibliographies and other information sources.

Wharton, George F. A BIBLIOGRAPHY ON SEXUALITY AND AGING. New Brunswick, N.J.: Rutgers University, Intra-University Program in Gerontology, 1978. 82 pp.

This is an extensive bibliography of unannotated references to the physical, social, and psychological aspects of sexuality and aging. Selected subjects are sexual counseling, homosexuality, fertility, and other bibliographies.

Handbooks

Compared to other disciplines the field of gerontology has very few handbooks. They are designed to serve along with manuals as quick sources of information about this field.

Binstock, Robert H., and Shanas, Tehel (Eds.). HANDBOOK OF AGING AND THE SOCIAL SCIENCES. HANDBOOK OF AGING SERIES, VOLUME I, James E. Birren, editor-in-chief. Florence, Ky.: Van Nostrand Reinhold, 1976. 684 pp.

This first volume presents views of leading authorities relating to social aspects of aging. Its five sections deal with the study of age-related changes in a variety of social systems, the ways older people affect and are affected by social phenomena, and how societies attempt to provide resources for helping the aged.

Birren, James E., and Schaie, K. W. HANDBOOK OF THE PSY-CHOLOGY OF AGING. HANDBOOK OF AGING SERIES, VOLUME II, James E. Birren, editor-in-chief. Florence, Ky.: Van Nostrand Reinhold, 1976. 740 pp.

Volume II of the series covers all important approaches to the psychology of aging—from primary sensory phenomena to personality and behavior deviation. Twenty-nine contributors examine changes in behavior and capabilities that occur with advancing age. The volume considers stress, disease, the physical environment, cross-cultural perspectives, and the impact of social structure on the elderly.

Birren, James E., and Sloan, R. Bruce. HANDBOOK OF MENTAL HEALTH AND AGING. Englewood Cliffs, N.J.: Prentice-Hall, 1980. 1604 pp.

By crossing disciplines and integrating professions, the editors have assembled over 40 major subjects relating to mental health and later life. The contributed papers begin with a review of mental health and aging, then proceed to the neurosciences, the behavioral sciences, societal factors, diagnosis and assessment, and treatment and prevention. The book concludes with an author index and a 45-page subject index.

Busse, Ewald W., and Glazer, Dan G. HANDBOOK OF GERIATRIC PSYCHIATRY. New York: Van Nostrand Reinhold, 1980. 542 pp.

The editors have compiled the significant works in mental health and aging to serve as a comprehensive reference source on geriatric psychiatry. Part I presents the biological and psychosocial basis of geriatric psychiatry; Part II concentrates on diagnosis and treatment; and Part III addresses the future directions of geriatric psychiatry and the continuum of care.

Finch, Caleb E., and Hayflick, Leonard. HANDBOOK OF THE BIOL-OGY OF AGING. HANDBOOK OF AGING SERIES, VOLUME III, James E. Birren, editor-in-chief. Florence, Ky.: Van Nostrand Reinhold, 1976. 771 pp.

Exploring the varieties of changes brought on by aging in humans and in other mammals, this volume covers the aging processes from a comparative biological and evolutionary point of view and stresses the relevance of animal models to studies of human aging.

Directories

AAHA DIRECTORY OF MEMBERS. Washington, D.C.: American Association of Homes for the Aging, 1983. 110 pp.

AAHA is composed of over 1600 nonprofit homes and 500 individuals. The directory provides members' names and addresses, arranged geographically, and a listing of associate members—business firms and suppliers, state and local organizations, national organizations, and attorneys. There is a separate listing of AAHA's state associations and multifacility sponsors. The directory contains a personal name index.

ABOUT AGING: A CATALOG OF FILMS. Los Angeles: University of Southern California Andrus Gerontology Center, biannual.

Each edition contains an alphabetical listing of films and filmstrips, a topical index, and a list of distributors. This directory serves as a comprehensive source of audiovisuals in gerontology.

AGING AND LONG-TERM CARE: A DIRECTORY OF SELECTED INFORMATION RESOURCES. Washington, D.C.: U.S. Administration on Aging, 1980. 32 pp.

Prepared under contract by Franklin Research Center, the directory identifies agencies, organizations, and governmental bodies which are involved in long-term care services.

A COMPREHENSIVE INVENTORY AND ANALYSIS OF FEDERALLY SUPPORTED RESEARCH IN AGING, 1966–75. Documentation Associates Information Services, Inc. Washington, D.C.: U.S. Administration on Aging, 1976. 10 vol.

The inventory attempts to identify all federally funded projects concerned with the elderly from 1966 to 1975. The one-page summaries are arranged alphabetically by agency, then by the project director's name. Each summary provides the research project's title, contract number, years, funding, principal investigator, address, purpose, approach, results, publications, and index terms. The index volume includes an author and subject index. The final report presents summary analyses of research in systemic and metabolic biomedicine; psychological aspects of aging including pathology and intervention; environmental influences on attitude and behavior; social and ethnographic patterns; education, employment, income, and retirement; health care systems and delivery of services; public policy and services to the aged; and social psychology.

CUMULATIVE INDEX OF AOA DISCRETIONARY PROJECTS, 1965–1978. Humbaugh, Marcia. Washington, D.C.: U.S. Administration on Aging, 1980. 106 pp.

As a publication of the Service Center of Aging Information, this directory compiles in one index (SCAN) a listing of AoA's grants for model projects, training, and research and demonstration. The entries are arranged by project number, performing organization, project manager, location of project, and subject keywords.

DICTIONNAIRE-MANUEL DE GERONTOLOGIE SOCIALE. Zay, Nicolas. Quebec: Les Presses de l'Université Laval, 1981. 767 pp.

An extensive glossary in French, this directory does contain an English-French guide to the French terms.

DIRECTORY OF GERONTOLOGICAL LIBRARIES AND INFORMATION CENTERS. Owens, H. Jean. Detroit: Wayne State University Institute of Gerontology, 1980. 80 pp.

The directory identifies major collections of gerontological publications across the United States.

DIRECTORY OF ONLINE DATABASES. Santa Monica: Cuadra Associates, 1981. 186 pp.

Over 450 bibliographic and nonbibliographic data bases are described in this directory. It is designed to help information specialists and researchers locate publicly available data bases. Each description includes the subject area, data base producer, and service organization. It is sold on a subscription basis and has regular updates.

A DIRECTORY OF RESOURCES FOR AGING, GERONTOLOGY, AND RETIREMENT. Stuebe, Charles. Mankato, Minn.: Minnesota Scholarly Press, 1979. 222 pp.

Though somewhat out of date, this is the latest directory which profiles the many aging organizations, including federal aging agencies, and universities and colleges which offer programs in gerontology. The appendixes include a listing of acronyms, an index to major aging organizations, and a subject and personal name index. Be careful to double-check address information from the directory.

DIRECTORY OF STATE AND AREA AGENCIES ON AGING. U.S. Congress, House Select Committee on Aging. Washington, D.C.: Government Printing Office, 1981. 134 pp.

This directory is the revised edition of the Committee's earlier directory. It serves as the best source of agency addresses, location maps, agency directors, and telephone numbers.

FACTS AT YOUR FINGERTIPS. Fourth Edition. Washington, D.C.: U.S. National Center for Health Statistics, 1979. 135 pp.

This guide directs the user from a subject area (e.g., aging or diabetes) to the statistical reports of the Center and to other sources of information, such as the National Institutes of Health or the American Medical Association. FACTS AT YOUR FINGER-TIPS serves as an easy-to-use index to health data.

FUNDING IN AGING: PUBLIC, PRIVATE AND VOLUNTARY. Cohen, Lilly, Oppedisano-Reich, Marie, and Gerardi, Kathleen Hamilton. Garden City, N.Y.: Adelphi University Press, 1979. Second edition. 308 pp.

This directory is a valuable source for information on funding sources in gerontology. It serves as a first-step guide to seeking funding from the public and private sectors. The Catalog of Federal Domestic Assistance is the resource for federal funding. The state section reports programs initiated by the states. Corporate, foundation giving, and voluntary sections focus on those institutions whose primary interest is aging.

A GUIDE TO SELECTED INFORMATION RESOURCES IN AGING. Washington, D.C.: U.S. Administration on Aging, 1980. 95 pp.

Prepared under contract by Franklin Research Center, this directory is intended as a ready reference source. It helps one to locate institutional sources of information, including federal agencies, clearinghouses, information centers, and national organizations. It also provides a review of the major periodical indexes.

INFORMATION RESOURCES IN SOCIAL GERONTOLOGY. Syracuse, N.Y.: Syracuse University All-University Gerontology Center, 1979. 134 pp.

The directory identifies national, international, and foreign organizations; congressional committees; state and regional agencies; research centers and universities; audiovisual materials, indexes, abstracts, periodicals, and major trade publishers in gerontology.

INNOVATIVE DEVELOPMENTS IN AGING: AREA AGENCIES ON AGING. Washington, D.C.: U.S. Congress, House Select Committee on Aging, 1979. 571 pp.

This directory helps one to locate programs and services (e.g., day care, employment, nutrition programs). Each entry includes the program's title, description, area served, funding amount, and a contact name. The appendixes include a detailed index, a list of information-sharing resources, and a directory of Area Agency on Aging contact people.

INNOVATIVE DEVELOPMENTS IN AGING: STATE LEVEL. Washington, D.C.: Government Printing Office, 1980. 372 pp.

Issued as a publication of the U.S. Senate Special Committee on Aging, this directory serves as a companion volume to INNOVATIVE DEVELOPMENTS IN AGING: AREA AGENCIES ON AGING. The profiles of the state projects are arranged by major subject and indexed again in the subject index. The appendixes include State Units on Aging Resources, State Legislative Resources, Advisory Body Resources, Additional Contacts, and State Legislative Tracking System.

INVENTORY OF DATA SOURCES ON THE FUNCTIONALLY LIMITED ELDERLY. Washington, D.C.: Office of Management and Budget, 1980. 223 pp.

Compiled by the Interagency Statistical Committee on long-term care for the elderly, the inventory reports person-based data on the long-term care population including formal assistance received, informal assistance received, need for assistance, and outcomes. The inventory provides a listing of data sources (long-term care projects) and project identification numbers, as well as data sources listed by project chief's name, by sponsoring organization, by frequency of data collection, by geographic area covered, by last year of data collection, and by data elements (e.g., costs of assistance, mental health services, etc.).

INVENTORY OF FEDERAL STATISTICAL PROGRAMS. National Clearinghouse on Aging. Washington, D.C.: U.S. Administration on Aging, 1979. 113 pp.

The Task Force on Statistics of the Interdepartmental Working Group on Aging compiled in chart format a directory of statistical programs relating to older persons. The entries, arranged by federal agency, indicate the survey or program title, its purpose, the scope and method of data collection, the limitations and reliability of data, the lowest level of geography, age detail, frequency of data collection, method of data storage, the availability of unpublished data, the time lag of data, the publication program, and the name of the information contact person.

MEMBERSHIP DIRECTORY. Washington, D.C.: Gerontological Society, biannual.

The directory provides the names and addresses of the Society's members. Each entry includes the member's title, telephone number, and section affiliations. It is valuable as a means to contact researchers and planners in gerontology. Also included is a directory of the Society's officers and staff, a geographical listing of members, and a listing of members by section affiliation.

NATIONAL DIRECTORY OF EDUCATIONAL PROGRAMS IN GERONTOLOGY. Washington, D.C.: Association for Gerontology in Higher Education, 1981. Looseleaf.

Intended to provide information on courses, degree programs, financial aid for students, and research activities, this directory reports the research and training programs of 121 of 139 members of AGHE. Each institution's outline provides a list of courses, degrees, and research projects, plus a contact name and phone number.

1982–83 CHARTBOOK OF FEDERAL PROGRAMS ON AGING. Schechter, Irma, and Oriol, William. Bethesda, Md.: Care Reports, 1982. 197 pp.

The Chartbook describes federal programs and block grants related to the elderly or aging. It is arranged by federal agency, with a description of each program, its purpose, authority, contact office, FY '80 funding, and eligibility requirements for application. Also included is a perspective column that provides key program details such as priorities of funding and statistical trends and history. It is a unique guide to potential funding, as well as an omnibus of federal funding on aging.

RESEARCH AND DEVELOPMENT PROJECTS IN AGING, TITLE IV-B OF THE OLDER AMERICANS ACT: NEW GRANTS IN FY 1977 AND 1978. Washington, D.C.: U.S. Administration on Aging, 1979. 59 pp.

AOA's research program awards grants and contracts to support research which identifies and studies patterns and factors that affect the lives of older people, and which develops, demonstrates, and evaluates approaches and methods for improving life for older persons. Each project is annotated and then assigned to one of the following sections: old people, families, and the community; employment; retirement; income; housing and living arrangements; services and service delivery; health services and long-term care; crosscutting studies.

RESEARCH PUBLICATIONS AND MICRODATA FILES. Washington, D.C.: U.S. Social Security Administration, Office of Research and Statistics, 1980. 74 pp.

This publication identifies research reports of the Office of Research and Statistics. The reports are arranged by topical areas (for example, foreign social security, disability, and program data and history). Each publication receives a brief annotation and full ordering information. The micro-data files of research at ORS are arranged under retirement and survivors, economic research, supplemental security income, disability, and OASDI statistics.

Statistical Publications

The publications cited below help to answer the frequently asked questions of "how many?" and "how much?" Quantifying the older population is a popular exercise among researchers, students, and the media. There are several useful compilations of statistical data, mostly demographic. The list below is not comprehensive, but is intended as a start to obtaining relevant data. It is always advisable to contact the issuing agency for updated information.

AGING IN THE EIGHTIES: AMERICA IN TRANSITION. Louis Harris & Associates. Washington, D.C.: National Council on the Aging, 1981. 169 pp.

This survey updates the 1975 Harris survey THE MYTH AND REALITY OF AGING IN AMERICA. The elderly and nonelderly respondents indicate their attitudes about the problems facing the elderly: economic status, retirement, and the roles of government and Social Security in the lives of older people.

CHARTBOOK ON AGING IN AMERICA. Allan, Carole, and Brotman, Herman. Washington, D.C.: 1981 White House Conference on Aging, 1981. 141 pp. and Supplement.

A valuable source of recent data on the older population, the CHARTBOOK illustrates and describes major socio-psychological trends. A number of errors in the printing require use of the supplement.

CURRENT POPULATION REPORTS, P-23, NO. 85. SOCIAL AND ECONOMIC CHARACTERISTICS OF THE OLDER POPULATION: 1978. U.S. Bureau of the Census. Washington, D.C.: Government Printing Office, 1979. 44 pp.

This report is a compilation of selected data by the Census Bureau and National Center for Health Statistics. Its charts and graphs cover the following social and economic topics: population, family and marital status, the institutional population, nativity and parentage, mobility and residence, voting and registration, labor force participation, income and earnings, poverty, housing, health and health services, and crime victimization. Most tables report the data on people 65 years old and over, with some tables covering those 55–64 and 50–59 to present comparative data on the status of people just before reaching old age.

THE ELDERLY POPULATION: ESTIMATES BY COUNTY: 1977. National Clearinghouse on Aging. Washington, D.C.: U.S. Administration on Aging, 1980. 162 pp.

This report provides population estimates for the 60-and-over population and the 65-and-over population by county. It is compiled to provide state and area agencies on aging with estimates of their target populations between the censuses. The data indicate total population and number and percent of total population for those over 60 and 65 for 1977 and 1970, as well as the number and percent of change.

EVERY NINTH AMERICAN. Brotman, Herman. In DEVELOPMENTS IN AGING, 1980. Washington, D.C.: Government Printing Office, 1981. 2 vol.

As part of the annual report of the U.S. Senate Special Committee on Aging, this summary of major demographic data is presented in a brief narrative format with accompanying tables. Its frequency of publication almost always assures the user of its currency.

INCOME OF THE RETIRED: LEVELS AND SOURCES. Meier, Elizabeth L., and Dittmar, Cynthia C. Washington, D.C.: President's Commission on Pension Policy, 1980. 87 pp.

Having assembled and analyzed all the relevant data dealing with income and the elderly, the Commission reviewed the characteristics and levels of income of the retired, the relative roles of retirement programs, the roles of savings and earnings, and retirement income goals for the aged. Most of the data are from 1978.

THE NEED FOR LONG-TERM CARE: INFORMATION AND ISSUES. Washington, D.C.: Federal Council on the Aging, 1981. 90 pp.

The factors which affect long-term care policy development are so diverse that the Council saw the need to develop the chartbook. This is a valuable compilation of the data, presented in graph form with brief narrative review of the issues: demographics, health status, use of health services, informal support, and federal policies.

1980 CENSUS OF POPULATION, PC80-S1-1. AGE, SEX, RACE, AND SPANISH ORIGIN OF THE POPULATION BY REGIONS, DIVISIONS, AND STATES: 1980. U.S. Bureau of the Census. Washington, D.C.: Government Printing Office, 1981. 6 pp.

This is an early publication of the most recent census which provides us with age data by state.

1981 PENSION FACTS. Washington, D.C.: American Council of Life Insurance, 1981. 60 pp.

Published annually, this book is a useful source for difficult-to-find data on pensions, both public and private. It includes narrative explanation of the history of pensions, as well as a review of important issues related to pension benefits.

1982–83 CHARTBOOK OF FEDERAL PROGRAMS ON AGING. Schechter, Irma, and Oriol, William. Bethesda, Md.: Care Reports, 1982. 197 pp.

SOCIAL INDICATORS III. U.S. Bureau of the Census. Washington, D.C.: Government Printing Office, 1980. 585 pp.

Published every three years, SOCIAL INDICATORS presents a variety of statistical tables, charts, and graphs which were selected to show "important aspects of our current social situation, and their underlying historical trends and developments." The broad topical areas include population and family; health and nutrition; housing and the environment; transportation; public safety; education and training; work, Social Security, and welfare; income and productivity; social participation; and culture, leisure, and use of time.

SOCIAL SECURITY BULLETIN ANNUAL STATISTICAL SUPPLEMENT, 1981. Washington, D.C.: Government Printing Office, 1982. 272 pp.

The SUPPLEMENT provides calendar-year and trend data from Social Security program statistics. Each program's benefits are reviewed, followed by detailed tables of benefits and beneficiaries, including some historical data.

SOCIAL SERVICES USA: STATISTICAL TABLES, SUMMARIES, AND ANALYSES OF SERVICES UNDER SOCIAL SECURITY ACT TITLE XX, IV-B, AND IV-C FOR THE 50 STATES AND THE DISTRICT OF COLUMBIA FOR FY '79. Washington, D.C.: U.S. Department of Health and Human Services, Office of Human Development, 1981 (HDS #81-02020). 210 pp.

Nearly 8 million persons benefit from the programs identified in these tables: Social Services Programs for Individuals and Families, Child Welfare Services, and Work Incentive Program for AFDC recipients. The tables include summary data. The statistics show the relationship between the categories of people served, the services they received, and each state's expenditures for those services.

STATISTICAL REPORTS ON OLDER AMERICANS. Washington, D.C.: U.S. Administration on Aging, 1977–81.

This series replaces two former statistical series, STATISTICAL MEMOS and FACTS AND FIGURES ON OLDER AMERICANS. Six reports have been published as of this writing: NO. 1: AMERICAN INDIAN POPULATION 55 YEARS OF AGE AND OLDER: GEO-GRAPHIC DISTRIBUTION, 1970; NO. 2: INCOME AND EMPLOY-MENT AMONG THE ELDERLY: 1975; NO. 3: SOME PROSPECTS FOR THE FUTURE ELDERLY POPULATION; NO. 4: SOCIAL, ECO-NOMIC, AND HEALTH CHARACTERISTICS OF OLDER AMERICAN INDIANS: 1978; NO. 5: CHARACTERISTICS OF THE BLACK EL-DERLY; NO. 6: THE OLDER WORKER.

VARIETIES OF RETIREMENT AGES: STAFF WORKING PAPER. Meier, Elizabeth L., and Dittmar, Cynthia C. Washington, D.C.: Presi-dent's Commission on Pension Policy, 1980. 118 pp.

The Commission has identified and analyzed all available data relevant to age at retirement. The report considers retirement trends, old-age normal and early retirement ages, very early retirement, disability retirement ages, mandatory and age dis-crimination legislation, retirement age in relation to retirement costs, and long-range aspects of the problems. Most of the data are for 1978.

On-Line Searching

The exponential growth of the world's information demands a means to gather and examine data and information quickly and efficiently. Computerized retrieval systems—called on-line sys-tems—respond to this need. Unfortunately to date no centralized or comprehensive bibliographic on-line system in gerontology exists. Yet the pressures of time still require that a literature search be conducted on-line. In the absence of a gerontological system, the researcher must either conduct or request a search across the data bases, called a multiple data base search. There are several major limitations to such a search:

1. Because no publicly available data base emphasizes gerontological literature and research, there is no assurance that key, let alone marginal, materials will be retrievable. Certainly, most of the contents of a journal such as *The Gerontologist* will be entered into a data base, or series of data bases, but there may be no way to locate on-line a major report from a gerontology center.
2. The indexing terms used to retrieve the information needed vary from one data base to the next. One data base may use only *older adult*; another may use *aged* and *elderly*.
3. There is some overlap in data bases. For example, a hypothetical

article in *Psychology Today* on elder abuse may turn up in Psych Info, Sociological Abstracts, Magazine Index, and National Criminal Justice Reference Service (NCJRS), as well as Medline.

There are ways to overcome the difficulties of multiple data base searching. First, the researcher should not limit the review of the literature to on-line searching. He or she should contact major library collections and clearinghouses of aging information to assure the recovery of all possible resources. Second, if at all possible the researcher should be present for the on-line search, having previously considered all the possible and probable subject terms for the search, as well as the subject field that may contain relevant information. Informing the searcher of the concepts and limits of the subject will speed up the inquiry. For example, the researcher may want no literature before 1975 or only English references. The searcher will ask questions during the initial interview to help define the search. Finally, the researcher should review the results of the search, and if necessary renegotiate another search with additional search terms and data bases.

Who is involved in an on-line search, and where can a researcher or student get a search done? The agency, institution, or company which collects, abstracts, and indexes the material and which usually owns the data base is the data base *producer*. Most often, the system which mounts the data base, usually along with many other data bases, and which standardizes the software to make many data bases available is called the *vendor*. In bibliographic on-line systems, the major vendors are BRS, SDC's ORBIT, and Lockheed's DIALOG. The *searcher* serves as the intermediary between the user or requester of the information and the vendor or provider. He or she is familiar with the search strategies needed to access each data base. This person is most often affiliated with a library, clearinghouse, or search service. Finally, the *user* is that person who will use the information retrieved. On-line searching is done by large libraries, library networks, and search services. The researcher should explore the resources available through his or her employer, through a university or college, and through the public library system.

Sample On-Line Search

The sample search in Figure A.1 gives the reader a general sense of how an on-line search is conducted. Each search is of course unique. This one was purposely designed to yield a small number of entries; a realistic search would be more comprehensive.

In this search, we are looking for articles relating to health care for elderly women. The data base being searched is Sociological Abstracts, published by Sociological Abstracts, Inc. of San Diego, California; the vendor is DIALOG.

The first line indicates the data base being searched (SS) and the indexing terms used. In this case, the computer is searching for articles that contain the following terms in their abstracts: *elder* or *old age, woman* or *women,* and *wealth* followed by the word *care* or *health with* (*w*) *care.* Note how much flexibility the connectors *and, or* and *with* (*w*) allow the searcher.

The lines associated with number two indicate the number of articles containing each of the indexing terms, as well as those containing the combined terms. The first column of numbers contains codes assigned by the computer to each indexing term. The second column indicates the number of entries located that contain that particular term. For instance, 445 entries contain the term *elderly,* while 131 contain *old age* and 5086 contain the word *women.* The last line set, number twelve, shows that only two entries contain the indexed words that we grouped together. Notice once again how important it is to choose the proper indexing terms. If we had just chosen *health care* as an index term we would have been confronted with 747 articles, most of which did not deal directly with elderly women. In a related search we used the same terms listed above except that we substituted *aged* for *old age.* This search yielded fifty-two entries rather than two. Many of these entries, however, were not relevant to our study because they focused on the health care of young women (e.g., women *aged* 14–24).

We are now in a position to instruct the computer to print all or part of the entries we are interested in. Since there are only two entries involved, we instruct the computer to print the entire abstract (this is done by the code next to number three). If there had been fifty entries rather than just two, we might have wanted to see just the titles or shortened abstracts first to help determine relevance.

Line number four tells us that for set number twelve the computer will now print the complete abstract (format 5) for the first entry. Line number five is an internal code. Next comes the title, author, and source of the article, followed by the complete abstract.

Aging-Related Data Bases

Selected from over one hundred bibliographic data bases, the systems listed below are important sources for research and literature on the aging. Each entry is available from one or more of these vendors, as indicated to the left of each entry:

BRS   Bibliographic Retrieval Services, Inc.
                       1200 Route 7
                       Latham, NY 12110
                       800/833-4707
                       518/783-1161

```
(1)   ? SS (ELDERLY OR OLD AGE ) AND (WOMAN OR WOMEN) AND HEALTH (W) CARE
             7    445 ELDERLY
             8    131 OLD AGE
(2)          9   3186 WOMAN
            10   5086 WOMEN
            11    747 HEALTH (W) CARE
            12      2 (7 OR 8 ) AND (9 OR 10) AND 11
(3)   ? T S12/5/1±2
(4)   12/5/1
(5)   J5601-0    78J5601-0
```

Title   Migrant Labor and Minority Communities: Class, Ethnicity, Age and Gender
as Social Barriers to Health Care

Author   Robinson, James H.
Empire State Coll State U New York, Saratoga Springs 12866

Source   Journal of Health Politics, Policy and Law, 1977, 1, 4, winter, 514-522.
CODEN: jhpldn
Periodicals Department, Duke University Press, 6697 College Station,
Durham NC 27708
Area/Section: 2000/45

Abstract   Abstract: Three works are presented that deal with migrant labor, the
provision of adequate health services to this population, & the barriers to
effective health care for members of poor communities, ethnic minorities,
women, & the elderly: (1) T. Dunbar & L. Kravitz's work (Hand Travelling:
Migrant Farm Workers in America, Cambridge, Mass: Ballinger Publishing Co,
1976), (2) B. N. Shenkin's book (Health Care for Migrant Workers: Policies
and Politics, Cambridge, Mass: Ballinger Publishing Co, 1974), & (3) J. L.
Weaver's study (National Health Policy and the Underserved: Ethnic
Minorities, Women and the Elderly, St Louis: C. V. Mosby, Co, 1976). Wage
& working condition problems affect the health of migrant workers. Because
of their mobility, no one, including the federal government seems willing
to accept responsibility for lobbying for better health care services for
them.   The failure of the federal government in this respect is a study of
the failure of federalism in the US. Access to health care & proper
utilization of existing facilities are as important to Shenkin as the
quality of the care provided. For Dunbar & Kravitz, improvement in migrant
wages & working conditions are the hinges to improved health care. Four
measures for reform are presented: (A) PO arousal concerning the problem of
low wage workers, (B) enforcement of existing legislation, (C) increased
migrant worker labor organizations, & (D) government restriction on illegal
farm worker immigration.   Weaver raises the problem of forming an MD
awareness of the migrant patient population's culture, but he has a naive
faith in the social sciences' ability to develop the necessary
interpersonal skills required in this vein. He also is flawed in minor
areas of his methodological assumptions. Modified AA
Descriptors: LABOR; INEQUALITY; COMMUNITY SERVICE; MINORITY; MIGRATION;
UNITED STATES
Index Phrase: migrant labor, minority communities, health care barriers;
mobility, federalism failure, wages, working conditions, reform measures;

Figure A.1 Sample Data Search (Reprinted by permission of Sociological
Abstracts. © Sociological Abstracts, Inc., San Diego, California)

DIALOG   DIALOG Information Services, Inc.
Marketing Department
3460 Hillview Ave.
Palo Alto, CA 94304
800/227-1927 (except California)
800/982-5838 (in California)
415/858-3785

SDC   SDC Search Service
2500 Colorado Ave.
Santa Monica, CA 90406
213/820-4111
800/421-7229 (except California)
800/352-6689 (in California)

For convenience the entries are categorized under the following
headings: general, scientific/technical, health, business, and social
sciences.

As of this writing, it is not likely that a computerized gerontological information system will be available to the public in the near future. The National Clearinghouse on Aging is facing budget cuts just after it awarded contracts for the computerization of the SCAN system.

General

DIALOG, SDC

CIS (Congressional Information Service)
1970–
Producer: Congressional Information Service
4520 East-West Highway, Suite 800
Washington, DC 20014

CIS serves as a master index to the publications of Congress, including hearings, reports, documents, prints, and special publications. Corresponds to the printed *CIS/Index.* Valuable for retrieving congressional materials on legislation affecting the older population.

DIALOG, SDC,
BRS

COMPREHENSIVE DISSERTATION INDEX
1961–
Producer: University Microfilms International
300 North Zeeb Rd.
Ann Arbor, MI 48106
800/521-0600 (except Michigan)
313/761-4700 (in Michigan)

Virtually every American dissertation degree is entered into this data base, and is retrievable by subject, title, author, institution, and year. Selected masters theses have been included since 1962, as well as thousands of Canadian dissertations and selected papers at foreign institutions.

DIALOG

ENCYCLOPEDIA OF ASSOCIATIONS
Current year's edition of book
Producer: Gale Research Co.
Book Tower
Detroit, MI

This data base provides access to 14,000 professional societies, trade associations, labor unions, cultural and religious organizations, and other national groups. It is valuable for identifying over 133 national groups which officially state their interest in the elderly or professions in gerontology.

| SDC | FED REG |
| DIALOG | March, 1977– |

Producer: Capitol Services, Inc.
511 Second St., NE
Washington, DC 20002
202/546-5600

This data base provides access to the contents of the Federal Register: rules, proposed rules, public law notices, meetings, hearings, and Presidential proclamations.

DIALOG

FOUNDATION DIRECTORY
Current file, one year's data
Producer: Foundation Center
888 Seventh Ave.
New York, NY 10019

The content of this data base is derived from the voluntary reports made to the Foundation Center and from tax returns filed with the Internal Revenue Service. The data base provides descriptions of more than 2500 foundations with assets of $1 million or grants in excess of $500,000 per annum.

DIALOG

FOUNDATION GRANTS INDEX
1973–
Producer: Foundation Center
888 Seventh Ave.
New York, NY 10019

The data base contains information on grants awarded by more than 400 U.S. philanthropic foundations. The printed counterpart to this file is the Foundation Grants Index section of the *Foundation News*. Almost 10,000 new grant records are added each year.

DIALOG

FEDERAL INDEX
1976–
Producer: Predicasts, Inc.
200 University Circle Research
Center
1101 Cedar Ave.
Cleveland, OH 44106

Federal Index consists of information on the U.S. government, including hearings, speeches, bill introductions, and roll calls, as well as regulations, notices, contract awards and other activities of executive agencies, presidential news, proclamations, and court decisions and judicial activities. It corresponds to the printed Federal Index. It is updated weekly and draws material from the Congressional Record, the Federal Register, the Weekly Compilation of Presidential Documents, and the Washington *Post.*

DIALOG, BRS

GPO Monthly Catalog
1976–
Producer: Superintendent of Documents
U.S. Government Printing Office
Washington, DC 20402

This corresponds to the printed Monthly Catalog of the U.S. Government Printing Office. The file contains citations and abstracts of public documents generated by the federal government, including congressional documents.

BRS

THE INFORMATION BANK II
Producer: Mt. Pleasant Office Park
1719-A Route 10
Parsippany, NJ 07054
201/539-5850

Information Bank II is a bibliographic data base of news and business information. The New York *Times* is the major newspaper indexed and abstracted, along with nine other newspapers; top priority is given to the *Wall Street Journal,* the Washington *Post, Business Week,* and the *Financial Times* (London). Over 45 other journals and magazines are entered into the Info Bank. New software (BRS) is improving access to the data base.

DIALOG

MAGAZINE INDEX
1976–
Producer: Information Access Corp.
885 North San Antonio Road
Los Altos, CA 94022
800/227-8431 (except California)
415/941-1000 (in California)

Over 370 popular American magazines are indexed, with no abstracts. Valuable resource for popular stories on the elderly, and for coverage of the major news magazines.

DIALOG

NATIONAL FOUNDATIONS
Current file, one year's data
Producer: Foundation Center
          888 Seventh Ave.
          New York, NY 10019
          212/975-1120

Obtained from public reports to the Internal Revenue Service, this file provides recent data on those 21,000 foundations which award grants for charitable purposes.

DIALOG

NATIONAL NEWSPAPER INDEX
January 1, 1979–
Producer: Information Access Corp.
          885 North San Antonio Rd.
          Los Altos, CA 94022
          800/227-8431 (except California)
          415/941-1000 (in California)

NNI provides coverage of the *Christian Science Monitor,* the New York *Times,* the *Wall Street Journal,* and other major papers. Helpful in obtaining news reports and reports of research related to the elderly.

DIALOG, SDC,
BRS

SMITHSONIAN SCIENTIFIC INFORMATION EX-
    CHANGE (SSIE)
1978–1981
Producer: Smithsonian Scientific Information
          Exchange
          Room 300
          1730 M Street, NW
          Washington, DC 20036
          202/381-4211

SSIE is a data base of 253,000 reports on government and privately funded research projects in progress or begun in the preceding two years. The projects represent major scientific disciplines including the social sciences and economics, biological and medical sciences, and the behavioral sciences. Project descriptions are received from over 1300 organizations which fund research. Due to federal budget cuts, SSIE has not been updated since October, 1981.

SDC

ASI (American Statistics Index)
1973–
Producer: Congressional Information Service,
Inc.
7101 Wisconsin Ave.
Washington, DC 20014

Over 10,000 records per annum contain citations, abstracts, and analytic records on
government-generated reports, serials, and periodicals on social, economic, and demographic
data.

SDC

CRECORD (pronounced see-record)
1976–
Producer: Capitol Services, Inc.
511 Second St., NE
Washington, DC 20002
202/546-5600

The data base provides index and abstracts of the
Congressional Record. The software allows access to bill status, bill history, witness lists, and
access to hearings, floor actions, schedules of
floor activities, and materials inserted into the
Record by members of Congress.

SDC

USRFP1/USRFP2/USRFP3 (U.S. Requests for Pro-
posals)
Government fiscal year
Producer: Washington Representative Services
4040 North Fairfax Dr.
Suite 110
Arlington, VA 22203
703/243-8912

This system contains complete data on all federal
Requests for Proposal in research and development, consulting, training, evaluation, and professional services. USRFP1 contains information
from Sections A, H, and U of the Commerce
Business Daily; USRFP2 contains entries for all
released RFP documents; and USRFP3 provides
supplemental information on a contract after it is
released.

Scientific/Technical

DIALOG, SDC, BRS	BIOSIS PREVIEWS 1969– Producer: BioSciences Information Service 2100 Arch Street Philadelphia, PA 19103 800/523-4806 (U.S., not Pennsylvania) 215/568-4016 X244 or 241 (in Pennsylvania) This data base contains: (1) biological abstracts that include 165,000 accounts of original research annually from almost 8000 journals and monographs; and (2) biological abstracts/reports, reviews, and meetings that include 125,000 citations annually from report literature. The file contained over 1 million records as of January 1981.
DIALOG, SDC, BRS	NTIS (National Technical Information Service) 1964– Producer: NTIS U.S. Department of Commerce 5285 Port Royal Rd. Springfield, VA 22151 703/557-4642 This system consists of federally sponsored research, development, and engineering reports. It also contains federally generated machine-readable files and software and U.S. government inventions available for licensing.
DIALOG	SCISEARCH 1974– Producer: Institute for Scientific Information 325 Chestnut St. Philadelphia, PA 800/523-1850 (except Pennsylvania) 215/923-3300 X357 (Pennsylvania) SCISEARCH covers 90 percent of the world's scientific and technical literature. The data base includes all significant articles, reports of meetings, letters, and editorials from 2600 major scientific and technical journals.

Health

DIALOG

EXCERPTA MEDICA
1972–
Producer: Excerpta Medica
P.O. Box 1126
1000-BC Amsterdam
The Netherlands
Telephone: Amsterdam 26 44 38
Telex: 14 664 (ELNET NL)

This data base provides a comprehensive index of the world's literature on human medicine and related disciplines, nursing, dentistry, psychology, paramedical professions, drugs, and potential drugs.

NATIONAL
LIBRARY OF
MEDICINE

MEDLINE ON
DIALOG, BRS

MEDLARS
1965–
Producer: Office of Inquiries and Publications
Management
National Library of Medicine
8600 Rockville Pike
Bethesda, MD 20014
301/496-6095

MEDLARS is a computerized system of 4,500,000 references to journal articles and books in the health sciences published since 1965. Index Medicus is the printed index for much of the MEDLARS system. The MEDLARS system includes the medical data base MEDLINE, as well as fourteen other data bases in toxicology, chemistry, cancer, audiovisuals, epilepsy, health planning and administration, bioethics, serials, and cataloging. MEDLINE is available through BRS and DIALOG and in medical schools, hospitals, government agencies, the National Library of Medicine, and universities. Searches are conducted for the public through the regional medical library system at low cost.

Business

DIALOG

ABI/INFORM
1971–
Producer: Data Courier, Inc.
            620 South Fifth St.
            Louisville, KY 40202
            800/626-2823 (except Kentucky)
            502/582-4111 (in Kentucky)

This file contains references for literature on management and administration, including marketing and finance. Useful material on pensions and the older worker is also included.

DIALOG, SDC,
BRS

MANAGEMENT CONTENTS
1974–
Producer: Management Contents, Inc.
            Box 1054
            Skokie, IL 60076
            312/967-1122

This system provides access to 210 U.S. and foreign journals, proceedings, and transactions on business- and management-related topics. It is useful for material on pensions and benefits and the older worker.

Social Sciences

DIALOG, SDC,
BRS

ERIC (Educational   Resources   Information
      Center)
1966–
Producer: National Institute of Education
            ERIC
            Washington, DC 20208

ERIC consists of two files: (1) Resources in Education, which contains research reports, and (2) Current Index to Journals in Education, an index to 700 periodicals related to education. ERIC provides document delivery of the non-copyrighted materials it cites.

BRS

FAMILY RESOURCES DATABASE
1970–
Producer: National Council on Family Relations
1219 University Avenue Southeast
Minneapolis, MN 55414
612/331-2774

This system provides family-related literature references, including historic citations, representing all aspects of the family. It includes The Inventory of Marriage and Family Literature from 1973. Materials include journal articles, books and monographs, documents, reports, instructional and audiovisual materials, organizations, programs, research and resource centers, and related data bases.

DIALOG

LABOR STATISTICS (LABSTAT)
Various starting dates
Producer: U.S. Department of Labor
Bureau of Labor Statistics
Washington, DC 20212
Telephone: Contact DIALOG Information Services
800/227-1927 (except California)
800/352-6689 (in California)

This data base contains time series of numeric data compiled by the U.S. Department of Labor. Among its nine subfiles are included consumer price index; labor force; national employment, hours, and earnings; national labor turnover; and state and area employment, hours, and earnings.

SDC

LABORDOC
1965–
Producer: International Labour Organization
Geneva, Switzerland

The almost 5000 records per year entered in this system cover the world's journal and micrographic literature in the field of economic and social development and industrial relations including international relations, economic conditions and policies, demography, management, education, and law.

DIALOG

NCJRS (National Criminal Justice Reference Service)
1972–
Producer: NCJRS
P.O. Box 6000
Rockville, MD 20850
202/862-2900

NCJRS serves as a national and international clearinghouse on practical theoretical information about criminal justice and law enforcement. The data base contains valuable references on the older population as victims, volunteers, and offenders.

DIALOG

PAIS INTERNATIONAL
1972–   (Foreign Language Index)
1976–   (Bulletin)
Producer: Public Affairs Information Service
11 West 40th St.
New York, NY 10018
212/736-6629

This data base provides broad coverage of the social science literature with emphasis on contemporary public issues and the making of public policy.

DIALOG

POPULATION BIBLIOGRAPHY
1966–
Producer: Carolina Population Center
University of North Carolina
Chapel Hill, NC 27514
919/933-3006 or
919/933-3081

International in scope, this file emphasizes the social science aspects of population, including demography, policy, migration, and methodology.

DIALOG, SDC,
BRS

PSYCH INFO (Psychological Abstracts Information Service)
1967–
Producer: American Psychological Association
1200 17th St., NW
Washington, DC 20036
800/336-4980 (except Virginia)
202/833-5908 (in Virginia)

PSYCH INFO covers the world's literature in psychology and related behavioral and social sciences—psychiatry, sociology, anthropology, education, pharmacology, and linguistics. It includes all material in the printed Psychological Abstracts and selected material from Dissertation Abstracts International.

DIALOG, SDC,
BRS

SOCIAL SCISEARCH
1972–
Producer: Institute for Scientific Information
325 Chestnut St.
Philadelphia, PA 19106
800/523-1850 (except Pennsylvania)
215/923-3300 X357 (in Pennsylvania)

This data base corresponds to the printed Social Science Citation Index. It consists of an index to the literature of the social, behavioral, and related sciences. The journals indexed are carefully selected based on citation analysis and other criteria. The references indexed provide access to newly published articles through the subject relationships established by an author's reference in prior publications.

DIALOG

SOCIOLOGICAL ABSTRACTS
1963–   Abstracts from 1973 forward
Producer: Sociological Abstracts, Inc.
P.O. Box 22206
San Diego, CA 92122

Over 1200 journals are scanned for relevant material in the social and behavioral sciences, primarily sociology. The data base corresponds to the printed index Sociological Abstracts. Coverage is provided of original research, reviews, discussions, monographs, theory, conference reports, panels, and case studies.

DIALOG

TRIS
1968–
Producer: Transportation Research Board
2101 Constitution Ave., NW
Washington, DC 20418
202/389-6782

TRIS is a composite file of document abstracts and data files or resumés of research projects relevant to planning, development, operation, and performance of transportation systems.

DIALOG, SDC   UNITED STATES POLITICAL SCIENCE DOCUMENTS
1975–
Producer: University Center for International Studies
4G30 Forbes Quadrangle
University of Pittsburgh
Pittsburgh, PA 15260

This system covers articles from 150 journals in political science and other social sciences, with particular emphasis on public policy, theory, electoral behavior, and public opinion.

Major Governmental Sources of Aging Information

ACTION
806 Connecticut Ave., NW
Washington, DC 20525
(202) 254-7528

ADMINISTRATION ON AGING (AOA)
330 Independence Ave., SW
Washington, DC 20201
(202) 245-0669

BUREAU OF LABOR STATISTICS
Attn: Publications
441 G Street, NW
Room 1539
Washington, DC 20212
(202) 532-1222

BUREAU OF THE CENSUS
Attn: Data User Services
Customer Services, Room 1121-4
Washington, DC 20233
(301) 763-4100

CENTER FOR STUDIES OF THE MENTAL HEALTH OF THE AGING
National Institutes of Mental Health
5600 Fishers Lane, Room LLC03
Rockville, MD 20857
(301) 443-1185

FEDERAL COUNCIL ON AGING
300 Independence Ave., SW
Room 4620, North Bldg.
Washington, DC 20201
(202) 245-0441

GENERAL ACCOUNTING OFFICE (GAO)
Distribution Center
440 H Street, NW
Washington, DC 20548
(202) 275-6241

NATIONAL CENTER FOR
    HEALTH STATISTICS
3700 East-West Highway
Center Bldg. Room 1-57
Hyattsville, MD 20782
(301) 436-8500

NATIONAL INSTITUTE ON
    AGING (NIA)
National Institute of Health
9000 Rockville Pike,
    Bldg. 31
Bethesda, MD 20014   -
(301) 496-1752

SELECT COMMITTEE ON
    AGING
House Annex #1,
    Room 712
Washington, DC 20515
(202) 226-3375

SPECIAL COMMITTEE ON
    AGING
U.S. Senate
Dirksen Office Bldg.,
    Room G-233
Washington, DC 20510
(202) 224-5364

National Organizations and Clearinghouses

A national organization devoted to the subject in which you are interested is an excellent source of information. These organizations often sponsor research, follow legislative developments in detail, publish state-of-the-art reviews and research findings, and sponsor annual and special conferences. Directing your inquiry to the Research Department or Information Center is usually more productive than asking to speak with the Executive Director. Of course, if the organization is very small, the Executive Director may be the only professional staff person. The *Encyclopedia of Associations,* published annually by Gale Publishing Company, is a comprehensive source of information on associations' current names, addresses, directors' names, telephone numbers, goals, publications, major committees, and dates and locations of national meetings. Each entry also provides information on the size of the membership and number of staff.

The following list was adapted in part from *A Guide to Selected Information Resources* (U.S. Administration on Aging, Washington, D.C., 1980), updated and supplemented. Part I includes major gerontological organizations and Part II major information clearinghouses. The funding of information clearinghouses is always difficult to predict. When requesting information from any source, it is essential to include in the inquiry a date by which the information is needed. Many of the organizations concerned with aging are limited by size and budget, yet they try to respond to public inquiries. A realistic timeframe is recommended. If the response is needed immediately and the organization cannot respond in that time, ask for a referral to an alternative source.

Gerontological Organizations

AMERICAN AGING ASSOCIATION
    c/o Denham Harman, M.D.
    University of Nebraska College of Medicine
    Omaha, NE 68105
    Tel.: 404/541-4416
    Exec. Dir.: Denham Harman, M.D.

Purpose: To promote research and education among health professionals and other health workers in longevity and in the biomedical aspects of the aging process.
Publications: Age, quarterly

AMERICAN ASSOCIATION FOR GERIATRIC PSYCHIATRY
    c/o Sanford I. Finkel, M.D.
    230 N. Michigan Ave.
    Suite 2400
    Chicago, IL 60601
    Tel.: 312/263-2225
    Pres.: Sanford I. Finkel, M.D.

Purpose: To improve mental health care of the elderly (this is a professional organization of psychiatrists).
Publications: Newsletter, quarterly
                Membership Directory

AMERICAN ASSOCIATION OF HOMES FOR THE AGING
    1050 17th St., NW
    Suite 770
    Washington, DC 20036
    Tel.: 202/296-5960
    Pres.: M. Joe Helms

Purpose: To represent all nonprofit homes for the aging as well as to work with administrators and planners of homes to identify problems, develop solutions, and protect the interests of present and future residents of homes for the aged.
Publications: Washington Report, biweekly
                Housing Report, monthly
                Legal Report, monthly
                Association Report, quarterly
                Directory of Consultants—Planning Housing & Services for the Elderly
                Directory of Nonprofit Homes for the Aged— Social Components of Care

AMERICAN ASSOCIATION OF RETIRED PERSONS
1909 K St., NW
Washington, DC 20049
Tel.: 202/872-4700
Exec. Dir.: Cyril F. Brickfield

Purpose: To assist in preretirement planning as well as to provide
a wide variety of educational, consumer, and community service
programs to persons aged 55 years and older, and to improve the
image of older Americans. Contains major library collection.
Affiliated with NRTA.
Publications: News Bulletin, monthly
            Modern Maturity, bimonthly
            various programming guides, brochures

AMERICAN COLLEGE OF NURSING HOME ADMINISTRATORS
4650 East-West Highway
Bethesda, MD 20814
Tel.: 301/652-8384
Exec. V. Pres.: J. Albin Yokie

Purpose: To elevate the national standards of nursing home administration via formal education and training, research, and
certification of administrators of long-term care facilities. Contains major library collection.
Publications: Long-Term Care Administration, biweekly
            Journal of Long-Term Care Administration, quar-
                terly
            Symposia Proceedings, annually
            State Licensure Requirements, monograph
            other education materials

AMERICAN GERIATRICS SOCIETY
10 Columbus Circle
New York, NY 10019
Tel.: 212/582-1333
Exec. Dir.: Kathryn S. Henderson

Purpose: To promote education for physicians in geriatrics and to
encourage research in geriatric medicine.
Publications: Journal of the AGS, monthly
            Newsletter, monthly
            Clinical Aspects of Aging, book

AMERICAN SOCIETY FOR GERIATRIC DENTISTRY
4647 W. 30th St.
Georgetown Square
Indianapolis, IN 46222
Tel.: 317/291-8669

Purpose: To educate practitioners and personnel in related health fields about oral hygiene of the elderly.
Publications: Journal, quarterly

ASSOCIATION FOR GERONTOLOGY IN HIGHER EDUCATION
600 Maryland Ave., SW
Suite 204, West Wing
Washington, DC 20024
Tel.: 202/484-7505
Exec. Sec.: Carolyn H. Graves

Purpose: To promote research in gerontology and education and training for careers in gerontology. Also serves as a focal point for information and referral services and for cooperation between public agencies, organizations, and other professionals interested in aging and education.
Publications: Newsletter, 3–4 times/year
Gerontology in Higher Education, annual
National Directory of Educational Programs in Gerontology, biennial

GERONTOLOGICAL SOCIETY OF AMERICA
1835 K St., NW
Suite 305
Washington, DC 20006
Tel.: 202/466-6750
Exec. Dir.: John M. Cornman

Purpose: To help professionals and other interested groups promote education and scientific study of aging.
Publications: The Gerontologist, bimonthly
Journal of Gerontology, bimonthly
Gerontology News

GRAY PANTHERS
3635 Chestnut St.
Philadelphia, PA 19104
Tel.: 215/382-6644
National Convenor: Margaret Kuhn

Purpose: To promote group consciousness-raising and activism among the aging and young people to combat age discrimination.
Publications: The Network Newspaper, bimonthly
Organizing Manual and other books

INTERNATIONAL ASSOCIATION OF GERONTOLOGY
c/o Tokyo Metropolitan Geriatric Hospital
Itabashiju
Tokyo 173, Japan
Sec.: H. Orimo

Purpose: To promote cooperation in research and training in the field of gerontology between gerontologic societies, associations, and other groups and to protect the interests of these groups in foreign and international affairs.
Publications: IAG News in The Gerontologist (Gerontological Society)

INTERNATIONAL CENTER FOR SOCIAL GERONTOLOGY
425 13th St., NW
Suite 826
Washington, DC 20004
Tel.: 202/479-2642
Exec. Dir.: Tom Bell

Purpose: To encourage training of professionals and others working in the field of gerontology internationally. Conducts research and disseminates information to enhance the well-being of the elderly.
Publications: HTAP (Housing Technical Assistance Program) Newsletter, quarterly
Notes, congregate housing newsletter, irregular

INTERNATIONAL FEDERATION ON AGEING
1909 K St., NW
Washington, DC 20049
Tel.: 202/872-4700
Pres.: Robert Prigent
Gen. Sec.: Richard E. Johnson

Purpose: To serve as an information exchange for 26 countries concerning developments in knowledge about aging and to act as an advocate for the interests of these organizations and the elderly.
Publications: Ageing International, quarterly newsletter
special reports and handbooks

INTERNATIONAL SENIOR CITIZENS ASSOCIATION
11753 Wilshire Blvd. West
Los Angeles, CA 90025
Tel.: 213/479-8420
Pres.: Marjorie Borchardt

Purpose: To promote international cooperation to protect the needs and interests of the elderly and to provide an avenue of communication for the elderly in the areas of cultural and educational advancement.
Publications: Newsletter, quarterly

LEGAL RESEARCH AND SERVICES FOR THE ELDERLY
925 15th St., NW
Washington, DC 20005
Tel.: 202/347-8800
Dir.: David Marlin

Purpose: To conduct research, disseminate information, develop programs, and provide technical assistance in program operations and training of personnel for persons and service organizations working with the elderly in crime prevention.
Publications: Criminal Justice and the Elderly, quarterly
Newsletter
several resource manuals and pamphlets

LEGAL SERVICES FOR THE ELDERLY POOR
2095 Broadway
New York, NY 10023
Tel.: 212/595-1340
Exec. Dir.: Jonathan A. Weiss

Purpose: To provide advice and services to lawyers working with the elderly. Services include library, research, education, and litigation.
Publications: Progress Report, quarterly
occasional papers and reports

NATIONAL ALLIANCE OF SENIOR CITIZENS
101 Park Washington Court
Suite 125
Falls Church, VA 22046
Tel.: 703/241-1533
Nat'l Dir.: C. C. Clinkscales, III

Purpose: To serve as a lobbying organization to the state and federal legislatures as well as to inform the public regarding the needs of seniors and policies and programs to serve them.
Publications: The Senior Guardian, monthly
The Senior Independent, quarterly
Senior Services Manual, annual

NATIONAL ASSOCIATION FOR HUMAN DEVELOPMENT
1750 Pennsylvania Ave., NW
Washington, DC 20006
Tel.: 202/393-1881
Pres.: Jules Evan Baker

Purpose: To promote physical and emotional health among persons aged 60 and over through demonstration projects, education, training programs, and research.
Publications: Digest, quarterly

NATIONAL ASSOCIATION FOR SPANISH SPEAKING ELDERLY
1730 W. Olympic Blvd. #401
Los Angeles, CA 90015
Tel.: 213/487-1922
Exec. Dir.: Carmela Lacayo

Purpose: To present the needs of the Hispanic elderly and to encourage their participation in social programs for the aging. Conducts research and disseminates information to interested persons and organizations.
Publications: Legislative Bulletin, quarterly
Our Heritage, quarterly newsletter

NATIONAL ASSOCIATION OF AREA AGENCIES ON AGING
600 Maryland Avenue, SW
Washington, DC 20024
Tel.: 202/484-7520
Exec. Dir.: Raymond C. Mastalish

Purpose: To promote cooperation and communication within the national network concerned with the aging, federal government, and other interested persons and organizations and to provide technical and administrative assistance to Area Agencies on Aging in response to federal legislation and regulations.
Publications: The Point of Delivery, monthly newsletter

NATIONAL ASSOCIATION OF HOME HEALTH AGENCIES
205 C St., NE
Washington, DC 20002
Tel.: 202/547-1717
Exec. Dir.: Bill Halamandaris

Purpose: To lobby and monitor federal and state legislatures regarding policies affecting home health care and to inform its members, who are direct service home health agencies and other interested associations and individuals, on current issues in the home care field.
Publications: Home Health Highlights, biweekly
Update, monthly
Home Health Review, quarterly

NATIONAL ASSOCIATION OF MATURE PEOPLE
Box 26792
Oklahoma City, OK 73126
Tel.: 405/848-1832
Exec. Sec.: Richard E. Shepherd

Purpose: To provide a wide variety of services to persons aged 40 and over, including educational and recreational programs, group discounts on travel, insurance programs, and other purchase items, financial counseling, and legislative lobbying.

Publications: Best Years, quarterly
Newsletter, quarterly
various pamphlets

NATIONAL ASSOCIATION OF RETIRED FEDERAL EMPLOYEES

1533 New Hampshire Ave., NW
Washington, DC 20036
Tel.: 202/234-0832
Pres.: Michael C. Nave

Purpose: To assist pension-eligible federal civil servants aged 50 and over in preparing for retirement as well as to promote the general welfare of retired federal employees and their families through programs and lobbying.

Publications: Retirement Life, monthly

NATIONAL ASSOCIATION OF STATE UNITS ON AGING

600 Maryland Ave., SW
Suite 208—West Wing
Washington, DC 20024
Tel.: 202/484-7182

Purpose: To serve as coordinating body for state units on aging to collect, analyze, and disseminate information between the different state units, federal agencies, and national organizations, as well as to develop training and program models.

Publications: Bulletin, semiweekly
Memos, semiweekly

NATIONAL CITIZENS COALITION FOR NURSING HOME REFORM

1309 L St., NW
Washington, DC 20005
Tel.: 202/393-7979
Dir.: Elma Griesel

Purpose: To promote the development and implementation of the long-term care system at the national, state, and local levels. NCCNHR is an organization of local consumer and citizen action groups and individuals seeking nursing home reform. The organization monitors current issues and developments in long-term care and conducts seminars and training programs.

Publications: Collation, newsletter

NATIONAL CAUCUS CENTER ON BLACK AGED

1424 K St., NW
Suite 500
Washington, DC 20005
Tel.: 202/637-8400

Purpose: To advocate programs to serve the needs and interests of black elderly and to develop and implement programs benefiting the black elderly in the areas of health, housing, employment, education, and professional training.
Publications: Golden Page, newsletter

NATIONAL COUNCIL OF SENIOR CITIZENS
925 15th St., NW
Washington, DC 20036
Tel.: 202/347-8800
Exec. Dir.: William R. Hutton

Purpose: To work with state and federal legislation to benefit the elderly. Composed of 4,000 clubs. Founded in 1961 in the fight for the passage of Medicare.
Publications: Senior Citizens News, monthly

NATIONAL COUNCIL ON THE AGING, INC.
600 Maryland Avenue, SW
West Wing 100
Washington, DC 20024
Tel.: 202/479-1200
Exec. Dir.: Jack Ossofsky

Purpose: To conduct research and develop programs to serve the needs of the aging and to serve as an information, training, and consultation center for all professions, professionals, and organizations concerned with aging and services to the elderly. Contains major library collection.
Publications: Newsletter, monthly
            Perspective on Aging, bimonthly
            Aging and Work, quarterly
            Current Literature on Aging, quarterly
            various books, brochures, and pamphlets

NATIONAL GERIATRICS SOCIETY
212 W. Wisconsin Ave.
Third Floor
Milwaukee, WI 53203
Tel.: 414/272-4130
Exec. Dir.: Thomas J. Bergen

Purpose: To promote proper care of the aged and chronically ill aged by developing operational, administrative, and training standards for all levels of long-term care facilities.
Publications: Aging & Leisure Living, monthly (ceased publication)
            News, monthly

Nursing Care Requirements in Nursing Homes in
the States of the Union (1979 update)
Geriatric Target—1980, monograph
Nursing Procedures Manual

NATIONAL HOMECARING COUNCIL
67 Irving Place
New York, NY 10003
Tel.: 212/674-4990
Dir.: Florence Moore

Purpose: To encourage the organization of homemaker services,
serve as a central source of information, administer an agency
approval accreditation program. NHC's members include local
agencies providing homemaker/home health aide services and
other interested organizations and individuals.
Publications: educational and promotional materials

NATIONAL HOSPICE ORGANIZATION
301 Maple Ave. West
Tower Suite
Vienna, VA 22180
Tel.: 703/938-4449
Administrator: Claire Shanks

Purpose: To design a national policy with regard to standards of
care in program planning and implementation for adoption by
the federal government. Monitors related legislation.
Publications: President's Letter, monthly
            Newsletter, quarterly
            proceedings and reports

NATIONAL INDIAN COUNCIL ON AGING, INC.
P.O. Box 2088
Albuquerque, NM 87103
Tel.: 505/766-2276
Exec. Dir.: Alfred G. Elgin, Jr.

Purpose: To present the needs and concerns of the Indian and
Alaskan-native elderly to the public and to federal agencies and
to advocate improved comprehensive services for them throughout the United States through information, training, and consultation services.
Publications: NICOA News, quarterly
            The Indian Elderly: A Forgotten American, book
            The Continuum of Life: Health Concerns of the
            Indian Elderly, book

NATIONAL RETIRED TEACHERS ASSOCIATION
   1909 K St., NW
   Washington, DC 20049
   Tel.: 202/872-4700
   Exec. Dir.: Cyril F. Brickfield

Purpose: To provide services including group discount and insurance plans, educational and informational programs, and consulting services to retired teachers. Contains major library collection. Affiliated with American Association of Retired Persons.
Publications: News Bulletin, monthly
              Journal, bimonthly

NATIONAL SENIOR CITIZENS LAW CENTER
   1636 W. 8th Street
   Suite 201
   Los Angeles, CA 90017
   Tel.: 213/388-1381
   Exec. Dir.: Burton Fretz

Purpose: To provide technical, consultative, and other assistance to lawyers serving the poor elderly and to state and area agencies on aging to improve and expand legal service delivery.
Publications: Washington Week, biweekly newsletter
              Nursing Home Law Letter, monthly newsletter
              various books and pamphlets available through National Clearinghouse for Legal Services, 500 N. Michigan Ave., Suite 2220, Chicago, IL 60611

SOUTHERN GERONTOLOGICAL SOCIETY
   Gerontology Center
   Georgia State University
   Atlanta, GA 30303
   Tel.: 404/658-2692
   Pres.: Laurin Baumhover

Purpose: To encourage education, research, communication, and service development and delivery throughout the southern region of the United States as well as nationally; to assist in the design and development of research, training, and model and demonstration projects on behalf of the elderly and all people working with and for the elderly.

U.S. NATIONAL INSTITUTE ON AGING
   9000 Rockville Pike
   Bethesda, MD 20205
   Dir.: Robert N. Butler, MD

Purpose: To conduct and support (through project grants and research contracts) biomedical and behavioral research to increase the knowledge of the aging process and associated physical, psychological, and social phenomena. NIA is a component of the National Institutes of Health.

URBAN ELDERLY COALITION
600 Maryland Ave., SW
Suite 205, West Wing
Washington, DC 20024
Tel.: 202/554-2040
Dir.: Pearl Somani-Dayer

Purpose: To gather and analyze information on the needs and problems of the urban elderly and the legislation affecting them; to help develop and provide technical assistance in programming and planning for the urban elderly.
Publications: Legislative Update, quarterly
Technical Exchange, quarterly
occasional position papers

WESTERN GERONTOLOGICAL SOCIETY
785 Market St.
Suite 1114
San Francisco, CA 94103
Tel.: 415/543-2617
Dir.: Gloria Hather-Cavanaugh

Purpose: To educate and inform professionals, students, and older persons in the western U.S. of the issues and activities affecting the quality of life for older persons.
Publications: Generations, quarterly
WGS Connection, bimonthly newsletter

Clearinghouses

AARP NATIONAL GERONTOLOGY RESOURCE CENTER
1909 K St., NW
Washington, DC 20049
Tel.: 202/728-4700
Dir.: Paula M. Lovas

Serves as an information source for the Association's staff and for the gerontological community. It contains a current collection of 9000 volumes related to gerontology and over 300 journals and newsletters.

ANDRUS GERONTOLOGICAL INFORMATION CENTER
University of Southern California
University Park
Los Angeles, CA 90007
Tel.: 213/743-5990
Dir.: Jeanne Mueller

Serves as a major resource for information on the social and behavioral aspects of aging. Provides reference and referral service, as well as on-line searches of AGEX ($10.00 per search) data base. The data base includes the contents of the library collection and a subfile on the publications of the Andrus Gerontology Center staff.

GRIP—Gerontological Information Program
All University Gerontology Center
Brockway Hall
Syracuse, NY 13210
Tel.: 315/423-2890
Administrator: Dorothea Zito

Aims to enhance communication and create closer ties between academic researchers and those who serve the elderly. Provides reference and referrals; prepares bibliographies and state-of-the-art papers.

NATIONAL PACIFIC-ASIAN RESOURCE CENTER ON AGING
Alaska Bldg. Suite 423
618 2nd Ave.   600 Maryland Ave., SW
Seattle, WA 98104   Washington, DC 20024
Tel.: 206/622-5124   202/484-2234
Dir.: Louise Kamikawa

Serves as a clearinghouse and information resource on the social and health services delivery to Pacific-Asian populations. Publishes UPDATE, newsletter.

SCAN—Service Center for Aging Information
National Clearinghouse on Aging
300 Independence Ave., SW
Washington, DC 20201
Dir.: Eva Nash

Formerly composed of an information center and a central control facility, SCAN has been dissolved. The Social Gerontology Resource Center was an information clearinghouse, serving the network on aging, students, and the gerontological community and public. The central control facility was responsible for mounting and maintaining the on-line data base of gerontological literature, reports, and documents.

Funding

During the past three years the field of gerontology has seen the development of several publications which help to identify funding sources for research and demonstration. They represent a very small piece of the growing resource of general funding literature. Cited below are selected general funding sources, along with the specialized aging funding resources. Note in the "On-Line" section presented previously that there are several on-line data bases of profiles of foundations, what they have funded, and what they are interested in supporting.

AGING RESEARCH AND TRAINING NEWS. Schechter, Irma, editor. Bethesda, Md.: Care Reports, Inc. (4865 Cordell Avenue).

This valuable newsletter devoted to funding of aging research contains legislative reports on federal and agency budgets, as well as congressional actions, lists of the amounts and awardees of grants in aging, and recent publications.

THE ART OF WINNING CORPORATE GRANTS. Hillman, Howard. New York: Vanguard, 1980. 180 pp.

The corporate sector is a growing resource for grant seekers. Hillman devotes most of the book to the how-to's of obtaining corporate money, including guides to writing a winning proposal. The remaining sections have questions evaluators ask, a sample proposal, and an annotated bibliography, as well as a contact list of information sources. The appendixes include a review of the history and trends of corporate giving, a sample corporate contributions policy, student aid, and tax-exempt status information.

CATALOG OF FEDERAL DOMESTIC ASSISTANCE. Washington, D.C.: Government Printing Office, annual.

This publication provides the user with access to all programs of federal departments and agencies. The program information is cross-referenced by agency, functional classification, subject, eligible applicants, popular name, authorizing legislation, and federal circular requirements. Other sections include information on proposal writing and grant application procedures and additional information on federal programs and services.

THE CORPORATE FUND RAISING DIRECTORY. New York: Public Service Materials Center, 1981. 176 pp.

Each entry, verified for currency, contains the contact person for grants, primary and secondary areas of giving, best time to apply for a grant, corporate policy for giving appointments, typical grants, total amounts of grants, geographic limitations, and other relevant information.

DIRECTORY OF RESEARCH GRANTS: 1980. Phoenix, Ariz.: Oryx, 1980. 356 pp.

The art of winning federal funding to support research begins with the knowledge of funding sources. Over 100 geriatrics/ gerontology programs are described, including the amount of the grant and the sponsoring agency. The directory includes a brief introduction to proposal writing and a useful bibliography on funding and research.

FOUNDATION DIRECTORY (Seventh edition). New York: Foundation Center, 1979. 596 pp.

This directory serves as a standard reference work for information on nonfederal sources of grant making. The information in this edition is based on 1977 and 1978 reports. The foundations are listed alphabetically by state. The indexes include a subject guide; foundations arranged by state and city, donors, trustees, and administrators' names; and foundations arranged by name.

FOUNDATION FUNDAMENTALS: A GUIDE FOR GRANTS SEEKERS. Kurzig, Carol M. New York: Foundation Center, 1980. 148 pp.

A vast number of grant proposals are rejected because the applicants do not understand how foundations make awards. This guide is written to provide the reader with a better understanding of the processes of foundation giving, including a step-by-step explanation of the research and tools needed to locate the appropriate foundations. The appendixes include a sample subject search, sample geographic searches, a bibliography of funding materials, and a bibliography of area foundation directories (for example, Guide to California Foundations).

FOUNDATION GRANTS INDEX: 1979. New York: Foundation Center, 1980.

Serves as a cumulative listing of foundation grants.

FOUNDATION NEWS. James H. Mooney, editor. Washington, D.C.: Council on Foundations (1828 L Street, NW). Bimonthly.

The publication provides review articles on giving and how to get grants, legislative updates, recent publications of interest, and an update from the Foundation Center on foundation giving.

FUNDING IN AGING: PUBLIC, PRIVATE, AND VOLUNTARY, 2nd ed. Cohen, Lilly, Oppedisano-Reich, Marie, and Gerardi, Kathleen

Hamilton. Garden City, N.Y.: Adelphi University Press, 1979. 308 pp.

This directory is a valuable source for information on funding. It serves as a first-step guide to seeking funding from public and private sectors. The *Catalog of Federal Domestic Assistance* was the source for the federal funding section. The state section reports programs initiated by states. Corporate, foundation giving, and voluntary chapters focus on those institutions whose primary interest is aging.

GUIDELINES FOR THE PREPARATION OF GRANT APPLICATIONS. Washington, D.C.: U.S. Administration on Aging, variable.

Each grant-making division provides guidelines. Contact AoA for the most recent guidelines.

1981–82 CHARTBOOK OF FEDERAL PROGRAMS ON AGING. Schechter, Irma, and Oriol, William. Bethesda, Md.: Care Reports, 1982. 197 pp.

The CHARTBOOK describes federal programs related to aging or the elderly. It is arranged by federal agency, with a description of each program, its purpose, authority, contact office, FY funding, and eligibility for application, as well as a perspective column which provides key program details such as priorities for funding, and statistical trends and history. This is a unique guide to potential funding on aging.

TAFT CORPORATE DIRECTORY. Washington, D.C.: Taft Corporation, 1981. 436 pp.

This edition provides more detailed information than the Public Service Materials Center directory, and its price reflects that difference. The entries contain the same information as in the PSMC directory, and also include detailed grant information and the names of the officers and directors. Taft also offers two services separate from the directory: Corporate Updates— profiles on corporate giving programs and corporate foundations which are undergoing changes; and Corporate Giving Watch—a news monthly to complement the directory and updates.

Selected
Bibliography

Abbot, J. "Covered Employment and the Age Men Claim Retirement Benefits." *Social Security Bulletin,* 1974, 37(4), 5.

Acker, J. "Women and Social Stratification: A Case of Intellectual Sexism." *American Journal of Sociology,* 1973, 78(4), 936–945.

Almquist, E. M. "Women in the Labor Force." *Signs: A Journal of Women in Culture and Society,* 1977, 2(4), 843–855.

American Medical Association. *Retirement: A Medical Philosophy and Approach.* Chicago: AMA, 1972.

Anderson, J. F., and Berdie, D. R. "Effects on Response Rates of Formal and Informal Questionnaire Follow-Up Techniques." *Journal of Applied Psychology,* 1975, 60(2), 255–257.

Andrisani, P. J. "Job Satisfaction Among Working Women." *Signs: Journal of Women in Culture and Society,* 1978, 3(3), 588–607.

Argyle, M. *The Social Psychology of Work.* Middlesex, England: Penguin Books, 1972.

Atchley, R. C. "Respondents vs. Refusers in an Interview Study of Retired Women." *Journal of Gerontology,* 1969, 24(1), 42–47.

Atchley, R. C. *The Social Forces in Later Life.* Belmont, Ca.: Wadsworth Publishing Co., 1972.

Atchley, R. C. "Adjustment to Loss of Job at Retirement." *International Journal of Aging and Human Development,* 1975, 6(1), 17–27.

Atchley, R. C. "Sex Differences Among Middle Class Retired People." Unpublished paper, 1975.

Atchley, R. C. "Orientation Toward the Job and Retirement Adjustment Among Women." In J. F. Gubrium (ed.), *Time, Roles and Self in Old Age.* New York: Behavioral Publications, 1976.

Atchley, R. C. "Selected Social and Psychological Differences Between Men and Women in Later Life." *Journal of Gerontology,* 1976, 31(2), 204–211.

Atchley, R. C. *The Sociology of Retirement.* New York: John Wiley and Sons, 1976.

Atchley, R. C. "Issues in Retirement Research." *The Gerontologist,* 1979, 19(1), 44–54.

Atchley, R. C., and Corbett, S. L. "Older Women and Jobs." In L. E. Troll, J. Israel, and K. Israel (eds.), *Looking Ahead.* Englewood Cliffs, N.J.: Prentice-Hall, 1977.

Atchley, R. C., Pignatiello, L., and Shaw, E. C. "Interactions with Family and Friends: Marital Status and Occupational Differences Among Older Women." *Research on Aging,* 1979, 1(1), 83–95.

Barb, K. H., Goudy, W. J., and Warren, R. D. *Aging and Changes in the Preferred Age of Retirement.* Paper presented at the meeting of the Gerontological Society, San Francisco, November 1977.

Barfield, R., and Morgan, J. *Early Retirement: The Decision and the Experience.* Ann Arbor: Survey Research Center, University of Michigan, 1969.

Barnett, R. C., and Baruch, G. K. "Women in the Middle Years: A Critique of Research and Theory." *Psychology of Women Quarterly,* 1978, *3*(2), 187–197.

Bell, B. D. *Life Satisfaction and Symbolic Response: Toward a Comprehensive Theory of Retirement.* Paper presented at the meeting of the Gerontological Society, Louisville, Kentucky, November 1975.

Bengtson, V. L., Chiriboga, D. A., and Keller, A. B. "Occupational Differences in Retirement: Patterns of Role Activity and Life Outlook Among Chicago Teachers and Steelworkers." In Havighurst, Munnichs, Neugarten, and Thomae (eds.), *Adjustment to Retirement: A Cross-National Study.* Assen, the Netherlands: Van Gorcum and Comp. N.V., 1970.

Blieszner, R., and Szinovacz, M. E. *Women's Adjustment to Retirement.* Paper presented at the meeting of the Gerontological Society, Washington, D.C., November 1979.

Brotman, H. "Every Tenth American." In Senate Special Committee on Aging, *Developments in Aging: 1974 and January–April 1975.* Washington, D.C.: GPO, 1975.

Bultena, G. L. "Life Continuity and Morale in Old Age." *The Gerontologist,* 1969, *9*(4, Pt. 1), 251–253.

Butler, R. N. "A Life-Cycle Perspective: Public Policies for Later Life." In F. Carp (ed.), *Retirement.* New York: Behavioral Publications, 1972.

Butler, R. N., and Lewis, M. I. *Aging and Mental Health: Positive Psychosocial Approaches.* St. Louis: C. V. Mosby Co., 1973.

Campbell, A., Converse, P. E., and Rodgers, N. L. *The Quality of American Life.* New York: Russell Sage, 1976.

Carp, F. (ed.). *Retirement.* New York: Behavioral Publications, 1972.

Cockburn, D., Gilmour, D., Ginsberg, A., Kiefer, U. E., Kurzynowski, A., Omachi, C., Sachs, B., and Sheppard, H. L. "Employment and Retirement: Roles and Activities." *The Gerontologist,* 1972, *12*(2), 29–35.

Cohn, R. M. "Age and the Satisfactions from Work." *Journal of Gerontology,* 1979, *34*(2), 264–272.

Coser, R. L., and Rokoff, G. "Women in the Occupational World: Social Disruption and Conflict." *Social Problems,* 1971, *18*(4), 535–554.

Cottrell, F., and Atchley, R. C. *Women in Retirement: A Preliminary Report.* Oxford, Ohio: Scripps Foundation for Research in Population Problems, 1969.

Coyle, J. M., and Fuller, M. M. *Women's Work and Retirement Attitudes.* Paper presented at the meeting of the Gerontological Society, San Francisco, November 1977.

Cox, E. P., Anderson, W. T., and Fulcher, D. G. "Reappraising Mail Survey Response Rates." *Journal of Marketing Research,* 1974, *11*(4), 413–417.

Cumming, E., and Henry, W. E. *Growing Old: The Process of Disengagement.* New York: Basic Books, 1961.

Davidson, W. R., and Kunze, K. R. "Psychological, Social, and Economic Meanings of Work in Modern Society: Their Effects on the Worker Facing Retirement." In W. C. Sze (ed.), *Human Life Cycle.* New York: Jason Aronson, Inc., 1975.

DeLury, G. E. (ed.). *The World Almanac and Book of Facts 1978*. New York: Newspaper Enterprise Association, Inc., 1977.

Donahue, W., Orbach, H., and Pollak, O. "Retirement: The Emerging Social Pattern." In C. Tibbits (ed.), *Handbook of Social Gerontology*. Chicago: University of Chicago Press, 1960.

Draper, J. E., Lundgren, E. F., and Strother, G. B. *Work Attitudes and Retirement Adjustment*. Madison: University of Wisconsin, Bureau of Business Research and Service, 1967.

Eisdorfer, C., and Wilkie, F. "Stress, Disease, Aging and Behavior." In J. E. Birren and K. W. Schaie (eds.), *Handbook of the Psychology of Aging*. New York: Van Nostrand Reinhold Co., 1977.

Eteng, W. "Adjustment to Retirement and Aging Transitions in Wisconsin" (doctoral dissertation, University of Wisconsin, 1972). *Dissertation Abstracts International*, 1973, *33*, 3810A. (University Microfilms No. 72-27, 322.)

Fillenbaum, G. "On the Relation Between Attitude to Work and Attitude to Retirement." *Journal of Gerontology*, 1971, *26*(2), 244–248.

Fischer, J. S., Carlton-Ford, S. C., and Briles, B. J. *Life-Cycle Career Patterns: A Typological Approach to Female Status Attainment*. Paper presented at meeting of the Gerontological Society, Dallas, Texas, November 1978.

Fox, J. H. "Effects of Retirement and Former Work Life on Women's Adaptation in Old Age." *Journal of Gerontology*, 1977, *32*(2), 196–202.

Friedmann, E. A., and Havighurst, R. J. *The Meaning of Work and Retirement*. Chicago: University of Chicago Press, 1954.

Friedmann, E. A., and Orbach, H. L. "Adjustment to Retirement." In S. Arieti (ed.), *American Handbook of Psychiatry* (Vol. 1, 2nd ed.). New York: Basic Books, 1974.

Fuchs, R. "Different Meanings of Employment for Women." *Human Relations*, 1971, *24*(6), 495–499.

Fullerton, H. N., Jr., and Byrne, J. J. "Length of Working Life for Men and Women, 1970; Appendix: Two Measures of Working Life." *Monthly Labor Review*, 1976, *99*(2), 31–35.

Geist, H. *The Psychological Aspects of Retirement*. Springfield, Ill.: Charles C Thomas, Publisher, 1968.

Gelfand, D., Olsen, J. K., and Block, M. R. "Two Generations of Elderly in the Changing American Family: Implications for Family Services." *The Family Coordinator*, 1978, *27*(4), 395–403.

Gennep, A. V. *The Rites of Passage*. M. B. Vizedom and G. K. Caffee, trans. Chicago: Phoenix Books, 1960. (Originally published 1909.)

George, L. K., and Maddox, G. L. "Subjective Adaptation to Loss of the Work Role: A Longitudinal Study." *Journal of Gerontology*, 1977, *32*(4), 456–462.

Glamser, F. D. "Determinants of a Positive Attitude Toward Retirement." *Journal of Gerontology*, 1976, *31*(1), 104–108.

Glick, P. C. *Perspectives on the Living Arrangements of the Elderly*. Paper presented at the meeting of the Gerontological Society, San Francisco, November 1977.

Goudy, W. J., Powers, A., and Keith, P. A. "Work and Retirement: A Test of Attitudinal Relationships." *Journal of Gerontology*, 1975, *30*(2), 193–198.

Goudy, W. J., Powers, A., and Keith, P. A. "The Work Satisfaction, Retirement Attitude Typology: Profile Examination." *Experimental Aging Research*, 1975, *1*(2), 267–279.

Gove, W. R., and Geerken, M. R. "The Effect of Children and Employment on the Mental Health of Married Men and Women." *Social Forces,* 1977, 56(1), 66–76.

Gubrium, J. F. (ed.). *Time, Roles and Self in Old Age.* New York: Behavioral Publications, 1976.

Guttman, D., Sinnott, J. D., Carrigan, Z., and Holahan, N. *A Survey of the Impact of Needs, Knowledge, Ability, and Living Arrangements on the Decision Making of the Elderly.* Washington, D.C.: Catholic University Press, 1977.

Hampe, G. D., Blevins, A. L., and Nyhus, S. *The Influence of Rural-Urban Residence and Perceptions of Health on Retirement Satisfaction.* Paper presented at meeting of the Gerontological Society, Washington, D.C., November 1979.

Harris, L., and Associates. *The Myth and Reality of Aging in America.* Washington, D.C.: National Council on the Aging, Inc., 1975.

Heidbreder, E. M. "Factors in Retirement Adjustment: White Collar/Blue Collar Experience." *Industrial Gerontology,* 1972, 12(1), 69–79.

Herman, A. "Women in the Labor Force: Trends and Projections." In U.S. Senate, Committee on Labor and Human Resources, *The Coming Decade: American Women and Human Resources Policies and Programs, 1979 (part 1),* 96th Congress, 1st session. Washington, D.C.: GPO, 1979.

Jacobsen, D. "Rejection of the Retiree Role: A Study of Female Industrial Workers in their 50's." *Human Relations,* 1974, 27(5), 477–492.

Jaslow, P. "Employment, Retirement, and Morale Among Older Women." *Journal of Gerontology,* 1976, 31(2), 212–217.

Johnson, L., and Strother, G. B. "Job Expectations and Retirement Planning." *Journal of Gerontology,* 1962, 17(3), 418–423.

Jones, L. H. "Leisure and the Third Age: Third International Course on Social Gerontology." *Current Medical Dialogue,* 1972, 39(9).

Kerlinger, F. N. *Foundations of Behavioral Research,* 2nd ed. New York: Holt, Rinehart and Winston, 1973.

Kimmel, D. C. *Adulthood and Aging: An Interdisciplinary, Developmental View.* New York: John Wiley and Sons, 1974.

Kimmel, D. C., Price, K. F., and Walker, J. W. "Retirement Choice and Retirement Satisfaction." *Journal of Gerontology,* 1978, 33(4), 575–585.

Kreps, J. M., and Clark, R. *Sex, Age, and Work: The Changing Composition of the Labor Force.* Baltimore: The Johns Hopkins University Press, 1975.

Langner, T. S. "A Twenty-two Item Screening Score of Psychiatric Symptoms Indicating Impairment." *Journal of Health and Human Behavior,* 1962, 3(4), 269–276.

Lehr, U., and Dreher, G. "Determinants of Attitudes Toward Retirement." In Havighurst, Munnichs, Neugarten, and Thomae (eds.), *Adjustment to Retirement: A Cross-National Study.* Assen, the Netherlands: Van Gorcum and Comp. N.V., 1970.

Linsky, A. S. "Stimulating Responses to Mailed Questionnaires: A Review." *Public Opinion Quarterly,* 1975, 39(1), 82–101.

Lopata, H. Z., and Steinhart, F. "Work Histories of American Urban Women." *The Gerontologist,* 1971, 11(4, Pt. 2), 27–36.

Lowenthal, M. F., and Robinson, B. "Social Networks and Isolation." In R. Binstock and E. Shanas (eds.), *Handbook of Aging and the Social Sciences.* New York: Van Nostrand Reinhold Co., 1976.

Maddox, G. L. "Retirement as a Social Event in the U.S." In B. Neugarten (ed.), *Middle Age and Aging.* Chicago: University of Chicago Press, 1968.

Matteson, M. T. "Type of Transmittal Letter and Questionnaire Color as Two Variables Influencing Response Rates in a Mail Survey." *Journal of Applied Psychology,* 1974, *59*(4), 535–536.

McClelland, D. C. *The Achieving Society.* Princeton: D. Van Nostrand Co., 1961.

McLaughlin, S. D. "Sex Differences in the Determinants of Occupational Status." *Sociology of Work and Occupations,* 1978, *5*(1), 5–30.

Mechanic, D. "Socio-Cultural and Social-Psychological Factors Affecting Personal Responses to Psychological Disorder." *Journal of Health and Social Behavior,* 1975, *16*(4), 393–404.

Meier, E. L., and Kerr, E. "Capabilities of Middle-Aged and Older Workers: A Survey of the Literature." *Industrial Gerontology,* 1976, *3*(3), 147–156.

Montagna, P. D. *Occupations and Society: Toward a Sociology of the Labor Market.* New York: John Wiley and Sons, 1977.

Moser, C. H. "Mature Women—The New Labor Force." *Industrial Gerontology,* 1974, *1*(2), 14–25.

Nevin, J. R., and Ford, N. M. "Effects of a Deadline and a Veiled Threat on Mail Survey Responses." *Journal of Applied Psychology,* 1976, *61*(1), 116–118.

Palmore, E. "Differences in the Retirement Patterns of Men and Women." *The Gerontologist,* 1965, *5*(1), 4–8.

Parnes, H. S., Jusenius, C. L., Blau, F., Nestel, G., Shorthlidge, R., Jr., and Sandell, S. *Dual Careers: A Longitudinal Analysis of the Labor Market Experience of Women* (Vol. IV). Columbus: Ohio State University, 1975.

Payne, B. P., and Whittington, F. "Older Women: Examination of Popular Stereotypes and Research Evidence." *Social Problems,* 1976, *23*(4), 488–504.

Quadagno, J. S. "Career Continuity and Retirement Plans of Men and Women Physicians: The Meaning of Disorderly Careers." *Sociology of Work and Occupations,* 1978, *5*(1), 55–74.

Ragan, P. K. *Socialization for the Retirement Role: "Cooling the Mark Out."* Paper presented at the meeting of the American Psychological Association, San Francisco, August 1977.

Reno, V. *Women Newly Entitled to Retired Worker Benefits* (Report #9). Washington, D.C.: U.S. Social Security Administration, Office of Research and Statistics, 1973.

Riley, M. W., and Foner, A. *Aging and Society. Volume One. An Inventory of Research Findings.* New York: Russell Sage Foundation, 1968.

Schneider, C. J. "Adjustment of Employed Women to Retirement" (doctoral dissertation, Cornell University, 1964). *Dissertation Abstracts,* 1965, *25,* 4855. (University Microfilms No. 65-3352.)

Shanas, E. "Adjustment to Retirement: Substitution or Accommodation?" In F. M. Carp (ed.), *Retirement.* New York: Behavioral Publications, 1972.

Sheldon, A., McEwan, P. J. M., and Ryser, C. P. *Retirement: Patterns and Predictions.* Rockville: National Institute of Mental Health, Section on Mental Health of the Aging, 1975.

Sheppard, H. L. "Work and Retirement." In R. Binstock and E. Shanas (eds.), *Handbook of Aging and the Social Sciences.* New York: Van Nostrand Reinhold Co., 1976.

Sheth, J. N., and Roscoe, A. M. "Impact of Questionnaire Length, Follow-Up Methods and Geographical Location on Response Rate to a Mail Survey." *Journal of Applied Psychology,* 1975, *60*(2), 252–254.

Siegel, J. S. "Demographic Aspects of Aging and the Older Population." *Current Population Reports* (Series P-23), No. 59. Washington, D.C.: GPO, 1976.

Simpson, I. H., Back, K. W., and McKinney, J. C. "Orientation Toward Work and Retirement." In I. H. Simpson and J. C. McKinney (eds.), *Social Aspects of Aging*. Durham: Duke University Press, 1966.

Smith, P. C., Kendall, L. M., and Hulin, C. L. *The Measurement of Satisfaction in Work and Retirement: A Strategy for the Study of Attitudes*. Chicago: Rand McNally, 1969.

Sobol, M. G. "Commitment to Work." In L. W. Hoffman and P. I. Nye (eds.), *Working Mothers*. San Francisco: Jossey-Bass, 1974.

Sokolowska, M. "Some Reflections on the Different Attitudes of Men and Women Toward Work." *International Labor Review*, 1965, 92(1), 35–50.

Strauss, H., Aldrich, B. W., and Lipman, A. "Retirement and Perceived Status Loss: An Inquiry into Some Objective and Subjective Problems Produced by Aging." In J. F. Gubrium (ed.), *Time, Roles and Self in Old Age*. New York: Human Sciences Press, 1976.

Streib, G. F., and Schneider, C. J. *Retirement in American Society: Impact and Process*. Ithaca: Cornell University Press, 1971.

Sussman, M. B. "An Analytic Model for the Sociological Study of Retirement." In F. Carp (ed.), *Retirement*. New York: Behavioral Publications, 1972.

Suter, L. E., Waite, L. J., and Stolzenberg, R. M. *Birth Expectations and Working Plans of Young Women: Changes in Role Choices*. Washington, D.C.: U.S. Bureau of the Census, 1976.

Sweet, J. A. *Women in the Labor Force*. New York: Seminar Press, 1973.

Szinovacz, M. E. *Female Retirement: Effects on Spousal Roles and Marital Adjustment*. Paper presented at the meeting of the Society for the Study of Social Problems, San Francisco, 1978.

Taylor, C. "Developmental Conceptions and the Retirement Process." In F. Carp (ed.), *Retirement*. New York: Behavioral Publications, 1972.

Thompson, G. B. "Work versus Leisure Roles: An Investigation of Morale Among Employed and Retired Men." *Journal of Gerontology*, 1973, 28(3), 339–344.

Thompson, G. B. "Work Experience and Income of the Population Aged 60 and Older, 1971." *Social Security Bulletin*, 1974, 37(11), 3–20.

U.S. Bureau of the Census. "A Statistical Portrait of Women in the U.S." *Current Population Reports* (Series P-23), No. 58. Washington, D.C.: GPO, 1976.

U.S. Bureau of the Census. "Demographic Aspects of Aging and the Older Population in the United States." *Current Population Reports* (Series P-23), No. 59. Washington, D.C.: GPO, 1976.

U.S. Bureau of the Census. "Projections of the Population of the United States: 1977 to 2050." *Current Population Reports* (Series P-25), No. 601. Washington, D.C.: GPO, 1977.

U.S. Department of Labor, Employment Standards Administration, Women's Bureau. *1975 Handbook on Women Workers* (Bulletin 297). Washington, D.C.: GPO, 1976.

U.S. Department of Labor, Employment Standards Administration, Women's Bureau. *Mature Women Workers: A Profile*. Washington, D.C.: GPO, 1976.

U.S. Department of Labor, Bureau of Labor Statistics. *U.S. Working Women: A Databook* (Bulletin 1977). Washington, D.C.: GPO, 1977.

Walker, J. W., and Price, K. F. *Retirement Choice and Retirement Satisfaction.* Paper presented at the meeting of the Gerontological Society, Louisville, Kentucky, November 1975.

Index